S●vereign Wealth

The Role of State Capital in the New Financial Order

S⬤vereign
Wealth

The Role of State Capital in the New Financial Order

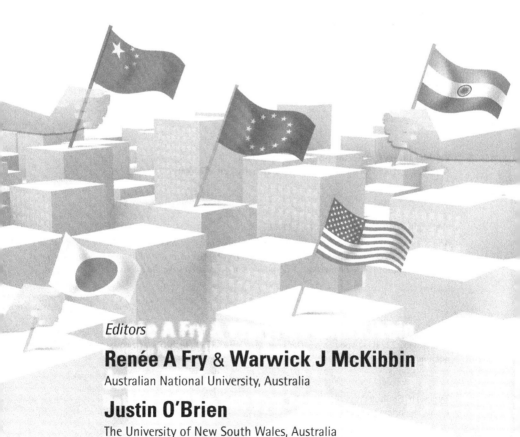

Editors

Renée A Fry & Warwick J McKibbin
Australian National University, Australia

Justin O'Brien
The University of New South Wales, Australia

Imperial College Press
ICP

Published by

Imperial College Press
57 Shelton Street
Covent Garden
London WC2H 9HE

Distributed by

World Scientific Publishing Co. Pte. Ltd.

5 Toh Tuck Link, Singapore 596224

USA office: 27 Warren Street, Suite 401-402, Hackensack, NJ 07601

UK office: 57 Shelton Street, Covent Garden, London WC2H 9HE

Library of Congress Cataloging-in-Publication Data
Sovereign wealth : the role of state capital in the new financial order / edited by Renée A. Fry,
   Warwick J. McKibbin, & Justin O'Brien.
   p. cm.
   Includes bibliographical references and index.
   ISBN-13: 978-1-84816-431-4
   ISBN-10: 1-84816-431-9
   1. Sovereign wealth funds. 2. Investments, Foreign. I. Fry, Renée.
II. McKibbin, Warwick J., 1957–   III. O'Brien, Justin (Peter Justin)
   HJ3801.S69 2011
   332.67'312--dc22

                          2011016219

British Library Cataloguing-in-Publication Data
A catalogue record for this book is available from the British Library.

Typeset by Stallion Press
Email: enquiries@stallionpress.com

Printed in Singapore.

Contents

Preface

This volume arose out of a conference held in Sydney on *Sovereign Wealth Funds in an Evolving Global Financial System* hosted by the Centre for Applied Macroeconomics at the Australian National University and the Lowy Institute for International Policy on September 24–25, 2008. In preparing for this conference we noted that there was a lack of rigorous research that has been done on the topic of sovereign wealth funds. Hence this volume was created to fill this gap, partly reflecting the content of that conference, along with some additional material. The timing of this conference was apt given that it corresponded with one of the worst weeks of financial market crisis that the world has experienced. The view of and the potential role for sovereign wealth funds in the global economy quickly changed in the resulting financial market turmoil. This volume also tries to reflect some of this more current debate. We are grateful to the authors of the papers in the volume who were able to provide us with a balanced and thoughtful analysis and discussion of sovereign wealth funds, and who have been enthusiastic in supporting the idea of this volume. We also thank Nicole Mies for support in producing the manuscript. Fry and McKibbin acknowledge financial support for this project under Australian Research Council Grant DP0664024. O'Brien acknowledges the financial support of the Australian Research Council under LP0884046.

R. Fry and W. McKibbin, Canberra
J. O'Brien, Sydney
June 2010

List of Contributors

Christopher Balding, Peking University

Rachael Bassil, Mallesons Stephen Jaques

Adrian Blundell-Wignall, OECD

David G Fernandez, J.P. Morgan

Renée Fry, Australian National University

Greg Golding, Mallesons Stephen Jaques

Stephen Grenville, Lowy Institute for International Policy

Julie Kozack , International Monetary Fund

Doug Laxton, International Monetary Fund

Warwick McKibbin, Australian National University & Lowy Institute
for International Policy

David Murray AO, The Future Fund Board of Guardians
and the International Forum of Sovereign Wealth Funds

Justin O'Brien, University of New South Wales, Sydney

Avinash Persaud, Intelligence Capital

Krishna Srinivasan, International Monetary Fund

David Vines, University of Oxford

Gert Wehinger, OECD

Introduction

Sovereign Wealth Funds in an Evolving Global Financial System

Renée Fry, Warwick McKibbin and Justin O'Brien

The global financial crisis has required unprecedented government intervention to stabilize credit markets. The Obama administration in the United States has engaged in substantial efforts to stave off the forced nationalization of some of the most familiar names in American corporate finance. The collapse of investor confidence prompted the United Kingdom (and other countries, most notably Ireland and Iceland) to go further, accepting state ownership of strategically important banking entities. Both sets of responses are necessary prudential responses to the progressive revelation of individual, corporate and collective regulatory misjudgment. The consequences of these responses are yet to be fully understood.

While the need for liquidity during the crisis has been marked and pressing, considerable debate remains on whether the provision of capital from state-backed asset pools represents an opportunity or a threat, most notably because of the rise of China. Despite the polarizing nature of the debate, fuelled largely by hypothetical concerns rather than empirical evidence, sovereign wealth funds and other pools of state-backed capital have been stabilizing forces in global markets. Indeed, they were instrumental in ameliorating the early stages of the crisis.

In early 2008, for example, many leading financial institutions in Europe and the United States secured additional financing through rights issues largely underwritten by funds operating out of the Middle East and Southeast Asia, particularly Singapore, and China. Recipients included the Swiss giant UBS as well as Bank of America, Citigroup and Merrill Lynch. State-backed asset pools invested $24.8 billion in the first two months of 2008, just under half the total amount dispersed in 2007. Since January 2007, $60.7 billion of a total of $72.9 billion has been invested across the global financial sector (Burton 2008). Moreover, moving forward, foreign investments by the state-owned enterprise sector will play a major role in stimulating the Chinese economy, widely regarded as critical to international recovery. Both forms of state capitalism raise, however, a series of exceptionally complex geo-political as well as commercial considerations that though muted by the effects of the global financial crisis remain unresolved.

There is now widespread discussion on the need for a fundamental redesign of the domestic and international regulatory architecture (e.g. Bernanke 2008; Geithner 2008a; 2008b; Greenspan 2008; Lomax 2008; McCreevy 2008). The deliberations of the G20, through successive summits in Washington, London, Pittsburgh, and most recently, Seoul, reflects cognizance of a changed economic balance of power.

Debate initially centered on a perceived lack of transparency and accountability (see, for example, Strine 2007; Truman 2008). It was far from clear, however, whether the risks identified — the risk of the transmission of financial market shocks, the exercise of soft power, the need to protect legitimate national interests and governance deficiencies — represented pressing dangers or thinly veiled protectionism. The debate is reflected in polarization within the European Union. The European Commission itself has recognized that state-controlled capital pools form an essential transmission belt within the engine of financial globalization (Commission of the European Communities 2008). Those most in need of capital have been relatively sanguine. This is particularly evident in the United Kingdom, whose economy was expected to shrink by more than 3.7% in 2009 (IMF 2009). The UK sent its then Business Secretary, Lord Mandelson, a former EU Trade Commissioner, to the Gulf to drum up investment. Lord Mandelson made it clear that few barriers to entry would be imposed: "We welcome sovereign wealth fund investments, unlike some other countries that are hesitant, and we strongly encourage investments from the UAE and others into Britain. We need liquidity in the system, we need funds to flow, we need credit to flow" (Reuters 2009). Greece accepted substantial Chinese investment in the port city of Piraeus, a critical part of Athens' infrastructure, without domestic contestation. Other European countries, such as France and Germany, determine that national icons should remain if not in national hands then not under the control of foreign state-controlled actors. Within the European Union, particularly Germany, there is increasing concern about the intentions of Russia. The more muscular foreign policy adopted by Moscow heightens skittishness precisely because of the difficulty in differentiating business and government interests. The suspicions that Russia is prepared to deploy its energy reserves strategically in order to advance political objectives, for example, are reinforced by the revolving door between Gazprom and the Kremlin (Kramer 2008; see more generally Aslund 2008, but also Goldthau 2008).

Successive administrations in the United States have adopted an ambivalent approach, particularly with regards to foreign direct investment coming from China.

Non-controlling investments have been guardedly welcomed, particularly if not accompanied by voting rights, a compromise which gained significant traction in the academic literature (see Gilson and Milhaupt 2008). At the same time, however, unease about the implications for national security has periodically surfaced. This is most notable in cases involving investment from corporations with links to the Chinese military. Huawei, for example, voluntarily pulled out of a deal involving the acquisition of telecommunications company 3Com because of a media debate about the potential transfer of dual-use technology.

Indeed, policymakers in Washington, London, and Brussels remark candidly, if privately, that the core dilemma, particularly for the United States, is how to engage Beijing within the global trade and regulatory architecture. The chair of the influential United Kingdom Treasury Select Committee, John McFaul, for example, argued in 2008 that "there is a paranoia, particularly in Washington, about China" (Interview with Justin O'Brien, Glasgow, 7 April 2008). At the same time one of the most senior European regulators, Charlie McCreevy, the then Commissioner for Internal Market and Services, has remarked it is important "to be brutally frank. This is not about Singapore or Norway or even the Gulf sovereign wealth funds; this is about how to deal with the power of China." (Interview with Justin O'Brien, Brussels, 15 April 2008)

Given the stated need to address the transparency and accountability deficit, it is somewhat surprising that the mainstream media largely ignored the publication of an industry-designed and International Monetary Fund-brokered code of conduct, the "Generally Accepted Principles and Practices" (Santiago Principles 2008). If anything, however, the regulation of the state-owned enterprise sector of the state-backed asset pool has become even more volatile. In Australia, for example, the policy debate has focused not just on the impact of foreign ownership of natural resources on competition but also, more nebulously, the country's way of life (see Swan 2008a; 2008b). Failure to clarify these matters has put increasing strain on relations between the Australian and Chinese governments. The Rio Tinto executive was subsequently convicted, the BHP Billiton deal collapsed and, at the time of writing, Rio and Chinalco have reignited their fraught and contested courtship.

The arrest of senior Rio Tinto representatives in Shanghai in the northern summer of 2009 and subsequent leveling of commercial espionage charges underscores the sensitivity. The controversy followed from the collapse of a planned investment by a Chinese state-owned enterprise, Chinalco, in Rio Tinto, a dual-listed Anglo-Australian mining conglomerate. The Australian government maintained that it was agnostic on the investment. The decision by Rio to pursue a strategic link with BHP Billiton just weeks before the Australian government was due to provide formal adjudication on the Chinalco investment allowed the Australian government to retain its stated neutrality. It prompted exceptionally negative reaction in the

Chinese media, leading many to surmise that political considerations lay behind the Shanghai arrests.

The unresolved policy issue pivots on two interconnected considerations. For recipient countries, does the shoehorning of explicit political issues into economic policy run counter to the stated aims of financial liberalization? For donor countries, have they, or indeed should they take cognizance of these concerns and if so, how? To explore the key issues on the rise of sovereign wealth funds, a conference was organized by the Centre for Applied Macroeconomics in the College of Business and Economics at the Australian National University and the Lowy Institute for International Policy in Sydney. Most of the chapters in this volume were presented at that conference. The first section outlines the nature and historical evolution of sovereign wealth funds and their impact on the global economy. The second section identifies and evaluates the potential risks associated with the expansion of their influence and how these concerns have been dealt with in the regulatory arena, with particular reference to foreign investment review processes in the United States and Australia through two extended case studies.

1.   The Rise of Sovereign Wealth Funds

Sovereign wealth funds have been in existence for many years. As the sector has expanded so has the range of entities that fall within the ambit of state-controlled pools of capital. This is more than a question of semantics. Establishing whether to regulate a particular asset class requires, in the first instance, an agreed definition of what constitutes the sector. The first section, therefore, provides some order to the debate. It does so by putting some parameters around the different kinds of asset pools that make up the state-backed capital universe, of which the sovereign wealth fund and state-owned enterprise sectors form two distinct subsets. The heterogeneity creates, as Stephen Grenville points out in Chapter 1, an immediate policy conundrum as "amalgamating the different motivations would make it impossible to attribute any degree of behavioral homogeneity (and analytical relevance) to this disparate grouping. Policies that are appropriate for one type of institution may well be quite inappropriate for another." It is therefore essential to drill further into how different types of sovereign wealth funds operate before assessing the nature, if any, of threats posed by these various asset pools. This necessitates understanding not only the stated rationale but also factors such as source and degree of funding, size and capacity for growth, and relative transparency and accountability.

The changing dynamics of trade and capital flows provide a clear rationale for resource-rich countries to manage earnings and minimize potential disruptions caused by sudden currency or commodity price fluctuations. In Chapter 2 Kozack, Laxton, and Srinvasan trace the growth of state-backed asset pools, particularly in East Asia in response to the 1997–98 Asian financial crisis. The crisis required many countries to accept emergency aid from the International Monetary Fund (IMF). The conditionality requirements of the aid packages had profound social and political as well as economic implications. As the affected economies rebounded, policymakers across the region determined never again to submit to such invasive oversight. The building of enormous currency reserves, which were invested in part — but not exclusively in capital markets in New York and London — formed an integral part of that defensive strategy.

Unlike the traditional stabilization funds, which tend to invest in easily convertible treasury bonds, the larger sovereign wealth funds tend to adopt longer-term investment horizons. Moreover, prior to the global financial crisis there was an increasing propensity to diversify into a broad range of equities and alternative asset classes, including, for example, private equity funds and real estate. Governmental asset holdings have now eclipsed hedge funds and private equity in funds under management. The total investment pool (without leverage) is estimated at $1.75–2.5 trillion — taking into account the fall in equity prices as a consequence of the global financial crisis. The pool could reach as much as $12 trillion by 2015 (see also Fernandez, Chapter 4). The critical question is whether this will give the sector significant power to move global or regional markets. Kozack, Laxton, and Srinivasan emphasize that intra-regional transfers within and between emerging economies, particularly in East Asia, are likely to be much more prominent. The authors maintain that geographically, sovereign wealth funds located in East Asia — led by China — could potentially grow tremendously in size with limits determined primarily by political considerations, namely the share of foreign currency inflows allocated to the sovereign wealth fund.

Christopher Balding confirms the regional bias component by investigating the portfolios of major funds in Chapter 3. He finds an "unmistakable preference for domestic and regional equity investment." Balding, however, does not equate this to an attempt to exercise "soft power." The equity component is mainly blue-chip and (prior to the global financial crisis) perceived to be low-risk investment vehicles. As Balding points out, "portfolios generally seem designed to mirror broad market returns and not assume excess risk," precisely the kind of investment strategy one would expect to be followed if one was operating the fund for purely commercial considerations. At the same time, however, Balding plays down the capacity of the sector, or indeed any one component of it to exercise a material effect on global finance. On these grounds alone, he argues, there is little empirical evidence on which to justify imposing additional regulatory restraints.

David Fernandez in Chapter 4 agrees that the impact of sovereign wealth funds on the trajectory of global equity markets is likely to be minimal. Rather, the threat and opportunity relates to the interaction between the sector and financial intermediaries, particularly hedge funds and private equity providers. He estimates the current level of sovereign wealth fund exposure to alternative investments (i.e. not equities or bonds) to be 3.75% of the total. Fernandez predicts that the sector's "share in total alternatives will rise to at least 10% and possibly approaching 17% by the end of 2013. On average, sovereign wealth funds' share in alternatives is likely to triple over five years to about 13%." The interlinked governance and investment principles proposed to alleviate the risk of political imperatives trumping economic ones in both lender and recipient nations in the context of an invigorated state capitalism will be explored more fully below. First, however, it is necessary to evaluate more fully whether any of the concerns are in fact justified.

The hypothesized risks associated with sovereign wealth funds can be broken into three core areas: the risk of the transmission of financial market shocks; the exercise of soft political power; and the need to manage national security. Until the publication of the Santiago Principles (2008), it was impossible to assess the impact that particular funds were likely to have on each risk factor. The size, scale, and degree to which investment strategies were disclosed differed dramatically. Differences in transparency made it difficult to gauge whether inappropriate or misguided investment expansion could potentially generate economic or political distortions. There was no evidence, however, that this risk was or remains anything more than hypothetical. Investment bankers in London and New York speak positively of their experience with the major funds. One investment banking research director suggested that the sector has become a magnet for rising stars within the asset management industry (Interview with Justin O'Brien, London, 19 July 2008). Indeed, Fernandez shares the assessment, arguing that symbiotic linkages are likely to be strengthened as the sector deploys increasingly sophisticated asset management strategies. Moreover, he argues that this is likely to ensure stability as each has an interest in securing stability, if only to protect initial capital investments and future returns.

The larger funds have already emphasized the quality of their internal controls and external advice. A leading Singaporean fund, Temasek Holdings, for example, sent its executive director to a congressional hearing to impress upon US lawmakers how the fund is insulated from political influence. Temasek Holdings, noted Israel (2008), has an eight-member majority-independent board structure, supplemented by a high-profile international advisory panel. Similarly, the ranking civil servant responsible for the oversight of the Norwegian Government Pension Fund Global, Europe's largest sovereign wealth fund, emphasized its own well-developed controls and the need for regulatory restraint (Skancke 2008; see also Chesterman 2007). The Government Pension Fund Global, as Balding (Chapter 3) points out, invests in a wider range of asset classes, with risk tolerance levels set and monitored by the Ministry of Finance (Norwegian Ministry of Finance 2006, 38–43 & 85–88). However, notwithstanding the expertise, there is no way of knowing in advance of an escalating trade or political dispute whether the existence of sovereign wealth funds provides a moderating influence.

A second wider source of concern centers on the complex relationship between sovereign wealth funds and financial engineers. While the IMF has broadly welcomed sovereign wealth funds, it has pointed out that "as sovereign funds grow in importance, they effectively become a significant unregulated set of intermediaries that may or may not invest with hedge funds in the future." (Johnson 2007, 1) A consequence is the potential for market manipulation. Again, there is no evidence that sovereign wealth funds have either funded or directly engaged in such strategies. Indeed, as Fernandez points out, "while the tenor of the public policy debate focuses on ways that sovereign wealth funds might behave irresponsibly relative to other investors, it should be noted that none in the sector has participated in any hostile takeover."

Paradoxically, the rhetoric of recipient countries reinforces the dynamic interplay between sovereign wealth funds and private equity. Some sovereign wealth funds have sought to head-off criticism of disguised motives by developing indirect conduits, most notably through a deepening of collaborative ventures. The Chinese Investment Corporation has contributed to a major fund established by JC Flowers. The Government Investment Corporation of Singapore has emerged as a key underwriter of a similar fund established by Texas Pacific Group. It is a thought that is captivating private equity mandarins. The Abu Dhabi Investment Authority will, in time, "effectively replace Wall Street," according to Guy Hands, the head of Terra Firma, a leading private equity provider (Arnold 2008, 1). Although tinged with hyperbole, it is indicative of growing interdependence. The linkage magnifies, however, the problems of transparency associated with the acquisition and divestiture of portfolio companies.

2. The Policy Debate

Sovereign wealth funds represent a shift in market dynamics precisely because of the potential fusion of political and commercial imperatives. As noted above, for the larger established funds there is no evidence that investment strategies differ in substance from those of traditional pension funds. Indeed, it is arguable that any short-term attempt to destabilize the market would be counter-productive to long-term interests, precisely because the initial exit could be easily traced. At the same time, however, the boom in commodity prices compounds the perception that investment strategies could be used to advance the potential exercise of political "soft power" (Nye 2005). A number of plausible concerns arise in this regard.

Corporate takeovers and the acquisition of strategic stakes (particularly if accompanied by board rights) give state actors potential access to proprietary intellectual capital. Without appropriate and enforceable checks and balances, misuse of this information could be disseminated to a wider range of national champions (see Tafara 2008). A related risk is that the investment could influence strategic banking imperatives (for example, by skewing lending priorities toward projects favored by donor countries), thus undermining the efficacy of specific corporate governance controls (Allen and Caruana 2008, 14).

While there is no evidence that any sovereign wealth fund has ever been used to further political ambitions, ascertaining the motives of secretive or authoritarian governments is a notoriously imprecise exercise. Notwithstanding the advantages of increased disclosure in helping to divine intent, it is important to emphasize the point made by Stephen Grenville (Chapter 1) that sovereign wealth funds form only one component of state economic influence. The lack of transparency worsens when strategic investments derive from state-controlled corporations. It clouds over completely when the acquisition comes from business oligarchs with discernible but informal links with authoritarian regimes. The point here is that any attempt to restrict sovereign wealth fund activity could lead to the expansion of even more opaque investment mechanisms.

There is no mistaking the anger felt by many in the sovereign wealth fund sector about the debate over its regulation. The Abu Dhabi Investment Authority, for example, has cautioned that "in a world thirsty for liquidity, receiving nations should be mindful of the signals sent through protectionist rhetoric and rash regulation" (Otaiba 2008). Similar sentiment is evident in Beijing. The vice president of the China Investment Corporation, Jesse Wang, has expressed irritation at the calls for a code of conduct, saying it was "unfair" and that "the claims that sovereign wealth funds are causing threats to state security and economic security are groundless." (Ruan 2008; Wong 2008; see more generally Schwartzman 2008, 13).

In Chapter 5 Avinish Persaud stresses the essentially political nature of the debate, arguing that "the ability of countries to save or spend more than local saving or investment opportunities allow is a measure of the success of the global economy, not a failing." Moreover, he maintains that "it is also reasonable, that until domestic financial systems deepen in developing countries to such an extent that they can disintermediate and recycle long-term savings, the state should manage the national savings." This leads him to conclude that "the economic legitimacy of the state managing national savings, especially by way of index funds, in Norway, a highly developed economy, is harder to justify than the state managing national savings in China. But this is seldom questioned." The heterogeneity of the sector made the negotiating process in calibrating a generally accepted set of principles and practices exceptionally difficult to manage, a point emphasized in Chapter 7 by David Murray, the Chairman of the Australian Future Fund and head of the International Working Group. For Murray, it is exceptionally ironic that the sovereign wealth fund sector was called upon to invest in failing banks, a position that would, by its very nature, represent non-commercial investment strategies.

At the same time, the creation of substantial barriers to entry on grounds that planned investments may threaten the national interest lacks coherence or consistency, a theme explored by Adrian Blundell-Wignall and Gert Wehinger in Chapter 6. They argue that disclosure and transparency, while to be applauded, miss the essential point of contestation. As they put it, "the issue remains on the table as to what legitimate objections there might still be to the free flow of investment from these pools of capital (and/or state funding and debt). That is: even if 'the window is cleaned' and full transparency is achieved, and even if governance practices move into line with appropriate guidelines, would there still be some legitimate objections to the free flow of capital left on the window sill? The answer in practice for most OECD countries is 'yes'; and these objections most often take the form of concerns about 'national security' and essential security interests." The authors point out that there is a disconnect between stated policy and actual decision-making, noting, diplomatically, "OECD member countries have agreed that the national security clause of the OECD investment instruments should not be used as a general escape clause from their commitments to open investment policies. However, much more work needs to be done to achieve better consistency in practice."

The restrictions can be complete, partial or entail a review process, which, in turn, may or may not privilege broader security concerns. Unless the process is governed by clearly enunciated and applied guidelines, however, there is a danger that policy is susceptible to political and economic populism. The implications of that populism on the integrity of investment review processes are examined in two extended case studies in final part of the book. In Chapter 8 Justin O'Brien evaluates the changing definition of national security in the United States. He argues that the current legal framework, codified in the Foreign Investment and National Security Act (2007), has not resolved an existential conflict between the commercial and national security-related agencies that are represented in the Committee on Foreign Investment in the United States. As such, the investment process remains a politically charged arena. Moreover, the underpinning legislation specifically calls on the Committee to take into consideration "the relationship of the acquiring country with the United States, specifically on its record of cooperating in counter-terrorism efforts" (GAO 2008, 34). As O'Brien points out, this has proved exceptionally problematic for Chinese-domiciled corporations and other state-backed asset pools, even those operating outside the military environment. It is questionable, therefore, absent a fundamental overarching agreement on how to deal with expanded state reach, whether Chinese-controlled investment vehicles, in particular, can gain ongoing political support in Washington (see Associated Press 2008; Bayh 2008). Administration support now appears conditional on adherence to a further generic set of principles outside the formal legal and regulatory guidelines, which adds to uncertainty and is arguable contrary to OECD guidelines that demand equity of treatment to investors, irrespective of source.

The second case study in Chapter 9 centers on an analysis of Australian response provided by Greg Golding and Rachel Bassil, practicing lawyers in Sydney with extensive experience interacting with the Foreign Investment Review Board. Golding and Bassil argue that transparency deficit governing inward foreign direct investment from state-backed asset pools lies in the difficulty of deriving intentions behind the policy requirement that all applications involving a foreign government or agencies operating on its behalf. They note that the "policy has no legislative force, but adherence to its requirements is achieved in practice by a number of means, including by refusal to grant necessary ministerial or other approvals under other Australian legislation and by the prospect of on-going resistance from the Australian government to the relevant investor, including the likelihood that future applications under the Act might be refused." The resulting ambiguity lies at the heart of the increasingly acrimonious disputes over a potential bifurcation between stated aims and the reality governing applications emanating from China.

There are, of course, sound policy reasons for calls for greater transparency within the sovereign wealth fund sector. Greater disclosure could provide an early warning system of volatile build-ups of capital within particular sectors. Greater oversight reduces the potential of sudden capital withdrawals causing or amplifying financial crises. Thirdly, it serves broader development aims, including a hoped for increase in the transparency of overarching domestic fiscal policy in emerging markets. Sovereign wealth funds already have an obligation to follow requisite rules and regulations in the recipient jurisdiction. Greater exposure and commitment to the substance of these rules and the regulatory framework can act as a reverse transmission belt. As a result, it has the potential to improve the quality of the corporate governance regime in the donor country. This is particularly the case for countries in which the wider accountability regime is either undeveloped or untested. Fourthly, requiring sovereign wealth funds to render explicit their investment strategies reduces perception that foreign policy objectives trump commercial ones. This, however, is ultimately a subjective judgment, which, if misapplied, could intensify rather than ameliorate tension.

The regulation of sovereign wealth funds forms only one part of the problem and the solution. The IMF is exceptionally cognizant of the sensitivities involved. It has signaled that a heavy-handed one-sided approach could backfire. The IMF Deputy Managing Director, John Lipsky, has argued that "if there were a sense that somehow 'best practices' were decided by someone else and dictated [to the funds], that could be extremely counter-productive" (Davies 2008).

While there is growing recognition that some improvement in the transparency of sovereign wealth funds is required, this can only be secured by similar refinements to investment review processes in recipient countries. There is, however, an unacceptable degree of ambiguity in the proposals emanating from Brussels, Washington, and Canberra. Each maintains political discretion over ill-defined "strategic interests." The search for accountability is therefore a symbiotic process that requires careful sequencing. Sovereign wealth funds need to address deficiencies in their own governance. How the sector responds will speak volumes about commitment to the principles of free trade or narrow mercantile capitalism. If, however, proposals to regulate sovereign wealth funds are used merely as a cover for a nascent protectionism, the cause of financial liberalization will be set back. In such a scenario, both lender and recipient will bear the consequences.

References

Allen, M, & Caruana, J, 2008, *"Sovereign Wealth Funds: A Work Agenda"*, International Monetary Fund: Washington DC.

Arnold, M, 2008, "Wealth Funds Fill Bank Gap for Buy-Out Groups", *Financial Times*, 28 February.

Aslund, A, 2008, Russia Energy and the European Union: Perspective on Gazprom. Speech delivered to the European People's Party, European Parliament, Brussels, 15 May.

Associated Press, 2008, "Lawmakers Want CFIUS Rules Clarified", *Wall Street Journal*, 14 March.

Bayh, E, 2008, "Time for Sovereign Wealth Fund Rules", *Wall Street Journal*, 13 February.

Bernanke, B, 2008, Risk Management in Financial Institutions. Speech delivered at Federal Reserve Bank of Chicago, Chicago, 15 May.

Burton, J, 2008, "Wealth Funds Exploit Credit Squeeze", *Financial Times*, 24 March.

Chesterman, S, 2007, "The Turn to Ethics: Disinvestment From Multinational Corporations For Human Rights Violations: The Case of Norway's Sovereign Wealth Fund", *American University International Law Review*, vol. 23, 3, pp. 577–615.

Commission of the European Communities, 2008, *A Common European Approach to Sovereign Wealth Funds*, Commission of the European Communities, Brussels.

Davies, B, 2008, "US Pushes Sovereign Funds to Open to Outside Scrutiny", *Wall Street Journal* (New York), 26 February, A1.

GAO, 2008, Foreign Investment: Laws and Policies Regulating Foreign Investment in 10 Countries, available at http://www.gao.gov/products/GAO-08-320, accessed 29 November 2010.

Geithner, T, 2008a, Reducing Systemic Risk in a Dynamic Financial System. Speech delivered at Economic Club of New York, New York, 9 June.

Geithner, T, 2008b, The Current Financial Challenges: Policy and Regulatory Implications. Speech delivered at Council on Foreign Relations, New York, 6 March.

Gilson R & Milhaupt C, 2008, "Sovereign Wealth Funds and Corporate Governance: A Minimalist Response to the New Mercantilism", *Stanford Law Review*, vol. 60, pp. 1345–1370.

Goldthau, A, 2008, "Resurgent Russia? Rethinking Energy Inc.", *Policy Review* 147 (online edition). Full text available at http://www.ssrn.com/abstract=1137616, accessed 29 November 2010.

Greenspan, A, 2008, "We Will Never Have a Perfect Model of Risk", *Financial Times*, 17 March.

International Monetary Fund (IMF), 2009, *World Economic Outlook*, April.

International Working Group on Sovereign Wealth Funds (IWG), 2008, Sovereign Wealth Funds: Generally Accepted Principles and Practices (The Santiago Principles), available at http://www.iwg-swf.org/pubs/gapplist.htm, accessed 29 November 2010.

Israel, S, 2008, Evidence to House Committee on Financial Services, United States Congress, Washington DC, 5 March.

Johnson, S, 2007, "The Rise of Sovereign Wealth Funds", *Finance and Development*, vol. 44, no. 3, pp. 56–57.

Kramer, A, 2008, "As Gazprom's Chairman Moves Up, So Does Russia's Most Powerful Company", *International Herald Tribune*, 11 May (online edition).

Lomax, R, 2008, The State of the Economy. Speech delivered at the Institute of Economic Affairs, London, 26 February.

McCreevy, C, 2008, International Financial Crisis: Its Causes and What to Do About It. Speech delivered at Alliance of Liberals and Democrats for Europe, Brussels, 27 February.

Norwegian Ministry of Finance, 2006, *On the Management of the Government Pension Fund in 2006* (Report No. 24). Oslo: Norwegian Ministry of Finance.

Nye, J, 2005, *Soft Power: The Means to Success in World Politics*, New York: Perseus Books.

Otaiba, Y, 2008, "Our Sovereign Wealth Plans", *Wall Street Journal*, 19 March.

Reuters, 2009, "Mandelson Encourages Sovereign Wealth Fun Investment", 8 April, available at http://uk.reuters.com/article/motoringAutoNews/idUKLNE53704220090408, accessed 29 November 2010.

Ruan, V, 2008, "China's Investment Fund Pushes Back", *Wall Street Journal*, 7 March.

Schwartzman, S, 2008, "Reject Sovereign Wealth Funds at Your Peril", *Financial Times*, 20 June.

Skancke, M, 2008, Evidence to House Committee on Financial Services, United States Congress, Washington DC, 5 March.

Strine, L, 2007, "Towards Common Sense and Common Ground: Reflections on the Shared Interests of Managers and Labor in a More Rational System of Corporate Governance", *Journal of Corporation Law*, vol. 33, no. 1, pp. 1–20.

Swan, W, 2008a, Australia, China and This Asian Century. Speech delivered at Australia-China Business Council, Melbourne, 4 July.

Swan, W, 2008b, Interview with ABC Radio National, 14 May.

Truman, E, 2008, "A Blueprint for Sovereign Wealth Fund Best Practices", *Peterson Institute for International Economics Policy Brief*, 08-3.

Tafara, E, 2008, Evidence to House Committee on Financial Services, United States Congress, Washington DC, 5 March.

Wong, E, 2008, "An Emboldened China Scolds US over Economy", *International Herald Tribune*, 17 June.

Section 1: Structure and Impacts on the Global Economy

Chapter 1

What is a Sovereign Wealth Fund?

Stephen Grenville

As Humpty Dumpty said in *Alice in Wonderland*, "a word means what you chose it to mean, neither more nor less." Semantic freedom makes amusing nonsense, but poor analysis. It bedevils discussion of sovereign wealth funds, because different people have used the term with different meanings and, more importantly, with different intentions. Just look at the diversity of origin and motivation behind institutions that are commonly described as sovereign wealth funds. There is Singapore's Temasek Holdings, which embodies a conscious long-term policy strategy of sovereign foreign investment by a small country seeking diversification of its nation's assets. China's China Investment Corporation is a more or less accidental outcome of an exchange rate strategy which may or may not persist. Then there are also the non-renewable resources funds (e.g. the Abu Dhabi Investment Authority) with their resource-depletion and inter-generational issues. There are also government pension funds (c.f. Australia's Future Fund and many others), which in practice behave in the same way as private funds, seeking diversification by investing some part of their funds overseas.

If we take a wide definition of sovereign wealth funds, it would encompass the full range of these different institutions. But amalgamating the different motivations would make it impossible to attribute any degree of behavioral homogeneity (and analytical relevance) to this disparate grouping. Policies that are appropriate for one type of institution may well be quite inappropriate for another. Just as seriously, even this wide definition of sovereign wealth funds *excludes* pools of capital, which raise the same analytical and policy issues. The most notable exclusion here, if we are concerned to analyze investor behavior, is investment from foreign state-owned enterprises. At the same time, it leaves to one side the often-related issues involved with foreign official reserve holdings (which are, incidentally, larger than the sovereign wealth funds).

Having identified a group with this mish-mash of motivations, a major international effort has been mounted to find some policy issues relevant to this grouping. In the end the prescriptions are so general, so motherhood and so mundane as to be largely content-free (Truman 2007). The recommendation is for more transparency and good governance, and to beware of doing anything that would stand in the way of the free flow of international capital. Who could deny the desirability of these criteria, but why don't they also apply to other forms of foreign investment — for instance, hedge funds. Let's leave aside arguments about whether sovereign wealth funds cause greater market-disruption than hedge funds. Why not have transparency and good governance for both or, for that matter, everyone?

From an economic viewpoint, the concept of sovereign wealth funds is analytically empty and we need to break out of this dead end. A better approach is that adopted by Blundell-Wignall (Chapter 6), who takes a wider array of "government-related pools of capital," and subdivides this into behaviorally homogeneous sub-groupings. These "pools of capital" are state-owned enterprises; sovereign wealth funds; social security reserve pension funds; sovereign pension reserve funds; and official foreign exchange reserves. Different purposes require different amalgamations of these categories. For many purposes, the inter-generational resource funds should be treated as an individual grouping, with their own characteristic behavior. The now-unfashionable commodity stabilization funds are probably also a *sui generis* "stand-alone" analytical category. Blundell-Wignall's two pension fund categories might usefully be combined together. Whether a distinction should be made between the motivation of Temasek-style funds and China Investment Corporation-style funds might depend on the specific purpose of the analysis.

The interesting issues begin when these "pools of capital" are juxtaposed against a series of foreign investment issues, including national security, national interest and, most relevant for the Australian debate, the special issues raised by investment in depleting natural resources. These are complex issues (setting royalties or rates of exploitation optimally over time in response to changing circumstances; preventing tax-avoiding profit transfer; dealing with competition issues that might arise out of vertical integration): Are they harder if the owner of the resource is a sovereign government? If the answer is yes then the focus should be on sovereign foreign investors in general, not just sovereign wealth funds.

All these issues are in the realm of economics. But foreign investment is an inherently and intensely political issue, where narrow economics won't be enough. Each country will want to maximize the value of its resource endowment over time and spend the wealth in ways that will be equitable between generations. But there will also be non-economic objectives (reluctance to "sell the farm" or to become just "hewers of wood and drawers of water"), which, however irrational in narrow economic terms, should be accommodated in policy. At the same time we have to acknowledge the desire of China and others to achieve long-term security of resource supply, just as the Japanese have always put high value on security of food supply. It is in everyone's interest to ensure that resource supply remains open for *all* our international customers, not just those who own the source of supply. Reaping the full benefits of international specialization requires more than open markets and transparency: there needs to be institutional infrastructure (in the Douglass North sense of rules and accepted practices) which gives all players the firm assurance that they have security of supply and the ability to adapt to changing circumstances.

Given the inherently political nature of foreign investment, it is no coincidence that politicians are getting involved in the big natural resource deals, lobbying behind the scenes beforehand and standing in the spotlight at the deal-signings and sod-turnings. So the answer is not to attempt to purge the sovereign involvement, or to force sovereign commercial entities into a pure-market straitjacket. It is to identify where rules are needed and beneficial, and where they are not. These are political-economy issues which have to be sorted out in a variety of forums, some international, setting uniform rules for the whole world, others bilateral and on-going, where the special circumstances of the two countries will matter and may well change over time, requiring flexibility of adjustment.

This brief summary cannot explore the full complexity of this set of problems, some purely economic, some in the realm of political economy. But it can attempt to dispose of one fundamental issue. In this line-up of policy and analytical issues, none maps uniquely into the sovereign wealth fund concept. Every issue has as much applicability to investment by foreign state-owned enterprises as it does for sovereign wealth funds. At the same time, few of these vexed issues have much to do with the investment of foreign pension funds, whether owned by governments or not. So we need to abandon the current vogue for treating sovereign wealth funds as a stand-alone category for policy-making, and put the constituent "pools of funds" into a wider analysis.

Reference

Truman, E, 2007, "Sovereign Wealth Funds: The Need for Greater Transparency and Accountability", Peterson Institute for International Economics Policy Brief PB07–06, August.

Chapter 2

Sovereign Wealth Funds and Global Capital Flows: A Macroeconomic Perspective

Julie Kozack, Doug Laxton and Krishna Srinivasan[1]

2.1. Introduction

A by-product of the rapid increase in global imbalances in the run-up to the 2008 financial crisis is the growing presence of sovereign wealth funds in international capital markets. Large current account surpluses in several Asian and oil-exporting countries — reflecting the savings-investment imbalances in these countries and the sharp increase in oil prices between 2000 and mid 2008 — translated into a rapid accumulation of foreign reserves by central banks. Coinciding with this accumulation of reserves was a reduction in these countries' public debt, making them (significant) net creditors to the rest of the world. The combination of higher levels of international reserves and lower public — and often external — debt led to significant improvements in the standard reserve adequacy measures for several of these countries.

Reserve accumulation reached a point where many countries had come to believe that they had a sufficient cushion against financial or economic shocks. Although many of these countries still had enormous development needs,

[1]This paper should not be reported as representing the views of the IMF. The views expressed in this paper are those of the authors and do not necessarily represent those of the IMF or IMF policy. We are grateful to Chanpheng Dara and Susana Mursula for excellent research assistance. We are also grateful for comments and suggestions from participants at the Conference on Sovereign Wealth Funds in an Evolving Global Financial System, hosted by the Centre for Applied Macroeconomic Analysis, The Australian National University and the Lowy Institute for International Policy, Sydney, September 2008, as well as for useful discussions with Simon Johnson, Udaibir Das, Adnan Mazarai, Alison Stuart, and David Hofman.

absorptive capacity was limited. Thus, quickly spending the oil or export windfall was neither appropriate nor feasible. Moreover, there was a growing sense that turning "resources in the ground" into financial assets was an important way to transfer wealth across generations. As a result, many countries sought to enhance the return on these large pools of funds. Instead of continuing to invest conservatively through sustained reserve accumulation with resources largely held in government securities, assets were transferred to sovereign wealth funds with broader investment mandates. This is reflected in the sharp increase over the past decade in the number of such funding mechanisms.

Notwithstanding the impact of the financial crisis and associated sharp decline in equity prices, sovereign wealth fund assets are still believed to be sizeable. Assets under management of sovereign wealth funds are estimated to range from \$1.75–2.5 trillion at the end of 2008 — down from nearly \$2–3 trillion at the end of 2007.[2] Public information is not readily available on the investment strategies of many sovereign wealth funds, including the share of risky assets in their overall portfolios and the currency composition of their investments. However, most observers believe that sovereign wealth funds are conservative investors, with a long-term investment horizon. Before the crisis, given their size and projected growth, sovereign wealth funds were well placed to play a more prominent role in global finance. Since then, however, many sovereign wealth fund portfolios have suffered large losses and may turn their focus, at least temporarily, to domestic matters as the crisis increasingly affects their home economies.

From a policy perspective, the growing influence of the sector in the global financial landscape has posed concerns ranging *inter alia* from a lack of transparency concerning the size and composition of their assets, their investment behavior and possible changes that could affect global capital flows and financial stability, and other related issues concerning their governance structure and accountability. While these are valid concerns, progress has been made on several of these issues, notably in the context of the design of the *Generally Accepted Principles and Practices for Sovereign Wealth Funds*.[3]

---

[2] For the purposes of this chapter, the list of sovereign wealth funds include the 26 IMF member countries with sovereign wealth funds that comprise the International Working Group of Sovereign Wealth Funds (IWG) plus Brunei Darussalam, Kazakhstan, Malaysia, and Oman. IWG member countries are Australia, Azerbaijan, Bahrain, Botswana, Canada, Chile, China, Equatorial Guinea, Islamic Republic of Iran, Ireland, Korea, Kuwait, Libya, Mexico, New Zealand, Norway, Qatar, Russia, Singapore, Timor-Leste, Trinidad and Tobago, the United Arab Emirates, and the United States. Permanent observers of the IWG are Oman, Saudi Arabia, Vietnam, the OECD, and the World Bank.

[3] Sovereign Wealth Funds: Generally Accepted Principles and Practices, "The Santiago Principles", developed by the International Working Group of Sovereign Wealth Funds, October 2008.

This chapter discusses the recent proliferation of sovereign wealth funds and their potential effects on global financial markets. Thus far, sovereign wealth funds have not been a destabilizing force to the global financial system. To the contrary, some major funds made significant investments in global financial institutions in the early stages of the current financial crisis, although these actions were overtaken by events as the crisis intensified in late 2008. That said, even benign shifts in the risk appetite and investment behavior, including changes in the currency composition of their assets, could have an impact on global capital flows and asset prices. Given the current and potential size of sovereign wealth fund assets and their growing prominence in global financial markets, this chapter is a first attempt at analyzing the possible impact of shifts in sovereign wealth fund portfolios or strategic asset allocations on global capital flows and asset prices.

Using both illustrative scenario analysis and model-based simulations, we gauge the effect of relatively modest shifts in sovereign wealth fund behavior on capital flows, major currencies, and global interest rates, as well as on key macroeconomic variables such as consumption and investment. The chapter is organized as follows: Section 2 provides a brief overview of sovereign wealth funds and their objectives; Section 3 discusses what we know and don't know about sovereign wealth funds; Section 4 explores the implications of the growing presence of sovereign wealth funds for global capital flows and assets prices; and Section 5 concludes.

2.2. What are Sovereign Wealth Funds?

Sovereign wealth funds are not a new phenomenon. Some have been around for decades, arising out of a desire to increase the return on countries' stocks of financial assets to meet broader financial or social goals. Broadly speaking, there have been three waves of sovereign wealth fund formation. The first and second waves, spanning the periods from 1950 through the 1960s, and from 1970 through the 1980s, respectively, led to the establishment of one or two large sovereign wealth funds — such as the Kuwait Investment Authority in 1953 and the Abu Dhabi Investment Authority in 1976 — and several small ones.

The sovereign wealth funds formed over these two periods reflected little diversity, and were based largely on revenues arising from oil and commodity exports. In contrast, the third wave of sovereign wealth fund formation, spanning the period from 1990 to the present, was marked by both a significant increase in the number of sovereign wealth funds and total assets under their management, as well as an increase in their diversity. While commodity exporters formed many of the sovereign wealth funds during this stage, others — such as China's and

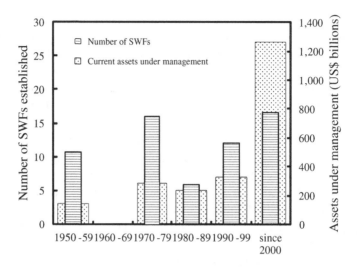

Fig. 2.1   SWF Formation.[a]

Source: Market Reports.
[a]Assets under management are the assets currenlty managed by the SWF established in each time period.

Korea's — were unrelated to commodity wealth. More generally, they reflected a significant increase in countries' holdings of foreign assets, most notably international reserves.

2.2.1. Rationale Behind Establishment

The establishment of sovereign wealth funds has hinged on a desire to increase the returns on vast foreign assets accumulated in recent years. For commodity exporters — especially oil producers — sovereign wealth funds often have a stabilization component designed to save current revenues from high commodity prices to be used later on if prices decline. This arose from a desire to avoid the boom-bust cycles of the past, and has been put into practice in many of these countries in recent months following the collapse in oil prices. At the same time, however, the very high level of foreign exchange reserves accumulated by emerging economies through mid 2008 led many of these countries to redefine their stabilization funds — which typically have narrow investment mandates targeting liquid assets — into sovereign wealth funds with broader investment goals. This appears to have occurred for two reasons. First, some component of the increase

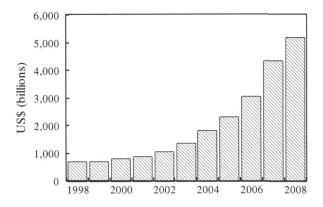

Fig. 2.2   Emerging Economy Reserves.

Source: IMF.

in commodity — and particularly oil — prices were deemed to be permanent.[4] Second, for both commodity exporters and several Asian manufacturers, there was a perception that reserves had become "excessive" — greater than what might be needed as a cushion in a financial crisis — and that higher returns should be sought. Indeed, reserves in emerging economies increased from $0.5 trillion in 1998 to around $5 trillion in 2008.

Standard measures of reserve adequacy improved significantly in recent years in emerging economies as a group. Import cover reached about ten months by the end of 2008 in non-Japan Asia, while reserves exceeded short-term external debt by a factor of ten. In oil exporting countries, the improvement was far more dramatic as surging oil prices led to massive increases in foreign assets. Import cover rose to about 12 months and reserves were more than 70 times short-term external debt. Looking across countries, the picture of reserve accumulation is more mixed. For many countries with long-established sovereign wealth funds (such as United Arab Emirates, Kuwait, and Norway), reserve adequacy measures remained broadly unchanged. For these countries, the rationale for establishing their sovereign wealth funds was not based on rapid reserve accumulation over the past decade. By contrast, reserve adequacy indicators improved tremendously in recent years in some other countries. Those with strikingly large build-ups of gross reserves include Russia and China. The current crisis is, however, calling into question standard measures of reserve adequacy. In particular, large external

---

[4] It is generally believed that commodity prices will rebound as the global economy recovers, as evident from upward sloping futures curves, particularly for oil.

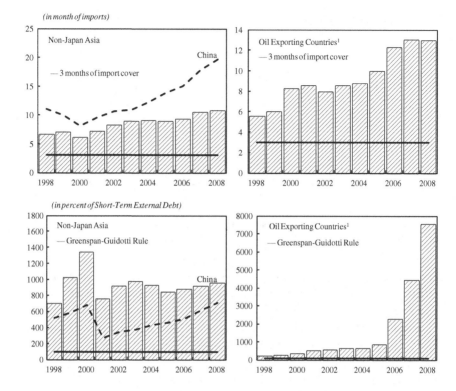

Fig. 2.3   Gross International Reserves.
Source: IMF, World Economic Outlook.
[1]Oil exporting countries are: Algeria, Angola, Azerbaijan, Bahrain, Congo, Ecuador, Equatorial Guinea, Gabon, Iran, Kuwait, Libya, Nigeria, Norway, Oman, Qatar, Russia, Saudi Arabia, Syria, Turkmeistan, United Arab Emirates, Venezula, and Yemen.

borrowing by major corporations along with reliance on external borrowing by banking systems has exposed several sovereign wealth fund countries to rollover risk at a time when they are facing slumping commodity prices and sharply lower capital inflows. Taken together, this implies that in an increasingly globalized world economy, even very large reserve cushions can be quickly eroded.

2.2.2.   *Objectives and Types*

Sovereign wealth funds typically have one of several objectives: (i) insulating the budget and economy from excess volatility in revenues; (ii) helping monetary authorities sterilize unwanted liquidity; (iii) building up savings for future generations; (iv) accumulating funds to meet future public pension obligations;

(v) increasing the return on reserves; and/or (vi) promoting economic and social development. Based on these objectives, there is a sense that sovereign wealth funds can be distinguished by four types, depending on their goals and objectives (IMF 2008).

Stabilization funds are established by commodity exporters with a view to stabilizing fiscal revenue over commodity price fluctuations. They have become increasingly attractive on account of high commodity prices and a desire to avoid the boom-bust cycles of the past. Examples include Russia's Reserve Fund and Chile's Economic and Social Stabilization Fund, and other commodity-based funds.

Reserve investment corporations — such as the one set up by Korea — aim to narrow the disparity between the return on reserves and the return on central bank liabilities, while still holding assets that can be counted as reserves.

Savings or development funds are typically long-term investment vehicles for sovereign holdings of foreign assets. They tend to arise in cases where the increase in foreign assets is deemed to be permanent, or where a large stock of assets already exists that is no longer needed for stabilization purposes. Abu Dhabi Investment Authority, Kuwait Investment Authority, Singapore's Temasek Holdings and Government of Singapore Investment Corporation, and China Investment Corporation appear to fall into this category. Norway's Government Pension Fund Global — originally instituted as a stabilization fund — was later converted into a savings fund as its resources grew larger than what was necessary for stabilization purposes.

Finally, contingent pension reserve funds provide (from sources other than individual pension contributions) for contingent unspecified pension liabilities on the government's balance sheet. These funds also tend to have a long-term investment horizon. Australia's Future Fund and New Zealand's Superannuation Fund are examples of this type of sovereign wealth fund.

2.3. What Do We Know About Sovereign Wealth Funds?

2.3.1. *Assets Under Management*

Data provided by sovereign wealth funds through regular reporting and, where such data is not available, indications by market participants allows for an approximate valuation of the total assets under management. Taken together, these various sources suggest that sovereign wealth fund assets under management total $1.75–2.5 trillion (Table 2.1). Assets under management are highly concentrated among the five largest sovereign wealth funds, which account for around 66% of estimated total assets. Looking across regions, nearly 40% of sovereign wealth funds are located in the Middle East and Africa, with another 25% in non-Japan Asia and

Table 2.1 Estimates of SWF Assets Under Management[a] End-2008 (in billions of U.S. dollars).

Name of Fund		Date Established	Assets (range)	
			Lower	Upper
Oil and Gas Exporting Countries				
UAE (Abu Dhabi)	Abu Dhabi Investment Authority	1976	250	627
Norway	Government Pension Fund-Global[b]	1990	330	330
Kuwait	Kuwait Investment Authority	1953	228	228
Russia	Reserve Fund[c]	2008	137	137
	National Wealth Fund[c]	2008	88	88
Qatar	Qatar Investment Authority	2005	60	70
Libya	Libyan Investment Authority	2006	65	65
United States	Alaska Permanent Reserve Fund	1976	30	30
Brunei Darussalam	Brunei Investment Authority	1983	30	35
Kazakhstan	National Fund	2000	27	27
Canada	Alberta Heritage Savings Trust Fund	1976	12	12
Oman	State General Reserve Fund	1980	8	8
Bahrain	Reserve Fund for Strategic Projects	2006	1	1
Mexico	Oil Income Stabilization	2000	6	6
Azerbaijan	State Oil Fund	1999	11	11
Timor-Leste	Petroleum Fund	2005	4	4
Trinidad & Tobago	Heritage and Stabilization Fund	2007	3	3
Other Commodity Exporters				
Chile	Economic and Social Stabilization Fund	2006	20	20
Chile	Pension Reserve Fund	2006	3	3
Botswana	Pula Fund	1993	7	7
Asian Manufacturing Exporters				
Singapore	Government Investment Corp.	1981	70	300
	Temasek	1974	84	84
China	China Investment Corporation	2007	190	190
Korea	Korea Investment Corp.	2005	25	25
Malaysia	Khazanah Nasional BHD	1993	16	16
Pension Reserve Funds				
Australia	Future Fund	2006	42	42
Ireland	National Pensions Reserve Fund	2001	23	23
New Zealand	Superannuation Fund	2001	7	7
Total			**1,800**	**2,400**

Sources: Annual or quarterly reports of SWFs, SWF websites, analyst reports, media reports.
[a]Does not include reserve assets. Does not include estimates for the Islamic Republic of Iran or Equitorial Guinea.
[b]Formerly known as the Petroleum Fund.
[c]The Reserve Fund and National Wealth Fund were funded initially with transfers from the Stabilization Fund of Russian Federation, after which it ceased to exist.

(percent share)

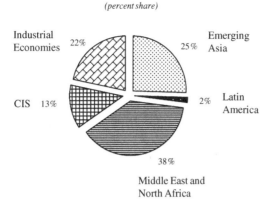

Fig. 2.4   SWFs by Region.

Source: Author's calculations.

(percent share of assets under management)

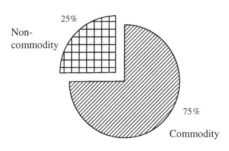

Fig. 2.5   SWFs by Type.

Source: Author's calculations.

about 20% in advanced economies. The remaining 15% are concentrated in the Commonwealth of Independent States, with a small share in Latin America. Commodity exporters account for roughly 75% of estimated assets under management.

There is no doubt that sovereign wealth funds are large — even when compared to the size of other investment vehicles (such as hedge funds and private equity) and various capital markets. In particular, sovereign wealth fund assets under management likely exceed those of hedge fund and private equity assets combined, especially given the very sharp contraction in hedge fund assets over the past year. Assets under management are also large when compared to the size of some capital markets. Sovereign wealth fund assets under management represented about two times the gross capital flows to emerging economies in 2008. This suggests that significant growth in sovereign wealth fund assets — if channeled in substantial part to emerging economies — could eventually represent a large share of new flows to these countries. When compared to the size of emerging economy capital markets, sovereign wealth funds are about 10% the size of stock market capitalization and 20–30% the size of debt markets in these countries. To be sure, markets, particularly stock markets, in these countries had been growing rapidly — stock market capitalization more than doubled between 2006 and 2007. Part of this large increase in market capitalization was likely due to increased investment by sovereign wealth funds and other investment vehicles associated with rapidly rising commodity wealth (Wiegand 2008). At the same time, stock market capitalization in these countries declined in 2008 and into 2009 as equity markets sold off sharply as the financial crisis intensified.

For advanced economy markets, which are much larger, sovereign wealth fund assets represent a smaller, but still substantial share of market size. They range from 4–6% of advanced economy stock market capitalization, 3–4% of advanced economy debt markets, and 1.5–2% of total advanced economy capital market size. When compared to the United States — which has the deepest and most liquid financial markets — estimated sovereign wealth fund assets are 25–35% of the US public debt market and 8–10% of the US corporate debt market.

Sovereign wealth funds have the potential to grow rapidly over the next decade, although the crisis is clearly affecting key revenue sources through reduced capital inflows and lower commodity prices. Based on projections regarding the size of external surpluses in sovereign wealth fund countries — along with assumptions about annual returns and the share of the external surplus that is allocated to the sovereign wealth fund (rather than continued reserve accumulation) — a range of estimates for the future size of sovereign wealth funds is calculated.[5]

---

[5]The range is based on projections of foreign currency inflows over 2009–2014, calculated as the sum of each country's current account balance and net private capital flows less reserve accumulation, drawn from the IMF's *World Economic Outlook* (April 2009). It is assumed that all new flows into sovereign wealth funds are invested abroad, earning the LIBOR rate of interest (lower bound of range) or LIBOR +200 bps (upper bound of range). For countries with relatively new sovereign wealth funds (i.e. those established after 2003), new flows are calculated as the sum of the current account balance and net private capital flows. From our sample, these countries include Bahrain, Chile, China, Korea, Libya, Qatar, Russia, Timor-Leste, and Trinidad and Tobago. For these cases, it is assumed that 50–100% of new resources flow to their sovereign wealth funds, with the 50% assumption forming the lower bound of the range of estimates and the 100% assumption forming the upper bound. For China, prospective foreign exchange inflows are assumed to be equal to the sum of the current account balance and net private capital flows less half of the current projected reserve accumulation.

Based on these calculations, sovereign wealth funds could grow to $4–6 trillion by 2014. This is around 33% lower than previous estimates, given revised projections regarding the size of external surpluses in these countries (see IMF 2008). Funds of commodity exporters could grow by 75%, to reach $2.25–3 trillion, while other funds could increase by between four and five times to $1.5–3 trillion, led by China and Singapore.

Geographically, sovereign wealth funds located in East Asia — led by China — could potentially grow tremendously in size, although the ultimate outcome depends on the share of foreign currency inflows allocated to sovereign wealth fund reserves. In the Middle East and advanced economies, sovereign wealth funds are projected to grow to nearly twice their current size, while those in the Commonwealth of Independent States and Latin America would remain roughly flat over time, as the sharp deterioration in current account balances would reduce amounts available to sovereign wealth funds.

2.3.2. *Transparency and Investment Strategy*

Sovereign wealth funds provide a range of information regarding their structure, governance, accountability framework, and investment behavior — with some disseminating significant information across all of these areas and others providing little or no information (see Truman 2007). With limited disclosure by some of these funds, it may become increasingly difficult to track the build-up of global financial vulnerabilities. It is generally believed that sovereign wealth funds follow a conservative investment strategy, and that they are "buy and hold" investors. But, in the run-up to the crisis, press reports and market commentary suggested that some had become more aggressive in their investment plans, with greater focus on maximizing returns. For example, Qatar Investment Authority sought to use leverage to finance a large buyout deal, while Norway shifted into a higher share of equity holdings and increased its exposure to emerging economies (see *Financial Times* 2007). Moreover, several sovereign wealth funds reportedly invested in private equity and hedge funds, indirectly financing highly leveraged strategies. In addition, the recent proliferation of sovereign wealth funds — and the need to quickly prove that these new funds can indeed outperform the return on reserves — seemed to suggest that the newer funds were likely to follow a more aggressive investment strategy than the more established funds.

There is significant differentiation among sovereign wealth funds regarding the information available on their strategic asset allocations. Some sovereign wealth funds provide significant detailed information on investment benchmarks and changes in strategy. Other sovereign wealth funds simply indicate that they will cover a broad swath of riskier assets, including equities, derivatives, and investments with hedge funds and private equity funds. Market participants note that sovereign wealth funds and oil exporters are increasingly investing directly into capital markets, rather than through banks. They also suggest that, in some cases, many of the investments are domestic rather than foreign, involving the purchase of real estate.

In terms of currency composition, available information again varies widely. Norway publishes its currency composition on its website, but some other sovereign wealth funds provide limited or no information. It is generally believed that a gradual shift from reserve holding to sovereign wealth fund holdings by sovereigns would lead to a reduction in their overall share of US dollar assets. This is because it is believed that sovereign wealth funds have a lower share of US dollar assets than official reserves (Setser and Ziemba 2007).

The ongoing financial crisis has had a dampening impact on sovereign wealth fund activity, with several large funds reporting large negative returns and a change in investment strategy. Market reports suggest that many of those that produce regular financial statements witnessed negative returns varying from 7 to 20% in 2008, with weak investment performance being particularly acute for those that have a high concentration of equities in their portfolio and with large exposures to "alternative investments." As a result, some sovereign wealth funds may be changing their investment behavior, with a shift away from investments in advanced economies, including notably from financial services, accompanied by a greater inclination to invest in domestic markets and emerging economies (Monitor Group 2008). Moreover, sovereign wealth funds in countries that have been hit hard by the financial crisis — such as Kazakhstan and Russia — are facing significant drawdowns as their "rainy day" resources are being used to finance fiscal expansion. Although the source of financing is less clear in many Middle Eastern economies, it is possible — if not likely — that some sovereign wealth fund resources may also be used to support the domestic economy.

2.4. Implications for Global Capital Flows and Asset Prices

Against this background, a key issue concerns the impact of the growing presence of sovereign wealth funds on the pattern of global capital flows, asset prices, and financial stability more generally. As noted above, sovereign wealth funds typically have medium- to long-term investment horizons, suggesting that they are less likely to make abrupt portfolio shifts, which could affect market stability. Indeed, sovereign wealth funds were a source of initial capital injections into systemically important financial institutions, suggesting that they can and indeed did play a stabilizing role in global financial markets. That said, even a gradual shift toward greater portfolio diversification of reserve assets by sovereigns, including through sovereign wealth funds, could have implications for the flow of funds between countries and the absolute and relative price of assets.

From a global macroeconomic perspective, three factors point to the possibility of a more subdued outlook for US capital inflows in the coming years as investors seek to diversify their portfolios. First, the financial crisis has been associated with a "safe haven" dynamic, which has dramatically increased demand for US dollar assets, particularly government securities. As this dynamic fades, investors may view US assets as riskier — particularly given the sharp losses on credit and equity instruments since the crisis erupted. Investors may also come to view government debt as increasingly risky, given the very large issuance already in the pipeline to finance the fiscal expansion and the longer-term fiscal pressures associated with entitlements. Both of these factors could lead to an increase in the country risk premium on US assets. Second, independent of risk-return considerations for global portfolios, global demand for US assets could contract sharply if national saving in US creditor countries, such as China and Japan, falls following their large fiscal stimulus packages. This could reduce capital inflows into the United States. Third, global demand for dollars relative to other currencies (particularly euros), which had already begun to ease in recent years, may decline further over the long term, as investors seek to diversify the currency exposure of their portfolios. This could put downward pressure on the dollar. Taken together, these shifts in investor sentiment and behavior could have an impact on the US dollar and US interest rates, as well as on capital inflows to other countries, particularly emerging economies.

Prior to the crisis, many commentators believed that a shift into riskier assets would lead to less demand for dollar assets, although most were of the view that this shift would be gradual and would not lead to a disorderly depreciation of the dollar. Others argued that the growing role of sovereign wealth funds would not affect the dollar very much, given that the depth and breadth of US financial markets were unparalleled. More specifically, observers subscribing to this view suggested that a greater appetite for riskier assets would simply lead to a shift in the composition of dollar assets — away from US government securities and into equities or alternatives. Before the crisis, some market participants believed that — like the US dollar — the impact on US Treasuries would be gradual and would not generate a disorderly outcome. Others were more skeptical and took the view that the shift from a conservative line of investing to one of greater risk taking would necessarily bode poorly for US Treasuries. Even without a large currency shift in reserve holdings, if new flows were geared away from Treasuries, interest rates in the United States would rise. In the event, the financial crisis led to a massive reduction in risk appetite and increased demand for US assets — particularly Treasury securities.

Before the collapse of Lehman Brothers in September 2008, nearly all commentators believed that the rising presence of sovereign wealth funds in global capital markets would be favorable to emerging economy and high-yield corporate assets. As sovereign wealth funds looked to diversify their holdings and sought higher returns, capital would flow into riskier asset classes, including those of emerging economies. As a result of the crisis, however, capital flows to emerging economies contracted sharply, particularly in the fourth quarter of 2008, and it remains to be seen whether capital flows will ever recover to their pre-crisis levels.

2.4.1. *Stylized Portfolio Analysis*

Despite the recent impact of the crisis on capital flows and risk appetite, it is still worthwhile to better understand the potential impact that portfolio shifts by sovereign wealth funds could have on global capital flows — even if the effects are viewed as improbable in the short term. Thus, we seek to estimate the potential impact of a diversification of sovereign reserves through sovereign wealth funds. In the scenario, sovereign wealth funds diversify their assets across two spectra: asset class and geography. First, sovereign wealth funds could diversify away from low-risk, low-return assets, such as government securities, into equities and other high(er)-risk instruments, such as private equity and real estate. Second, sovereign wealth funds could also focus more on emerging economies, with attendant implications for capital flows to advanced economies, particularly the United States. This may be increasingly likely if the significant deterioration in the fiscal positions of many advanced economies gives rise to longer-term sustainability concerns, thereby shifting perceptions of risk-return tradeoffs. Such an exercise is, however, challenging because of the lack of reliable information for several large sovereign wealth funds, notably concerning their asset allocations. To examine the possible implications of the growing presence of sovereign wealth funds, illustrative scenarios of asset allocation were constructed for countries that are in the process of shifting away from holding reserves to more diversified assets through sovereign wealth funds.

Two stylized, diversified portfolios — replicating Norway's Government Pension Fund (GPF-Global) and that of a more diversified sovereign wealth fund — were calibrated and compared with a stylized portfolio of foreign exchange reserve assets, with a view to assessing likely changes in the pattern of global capital flows and the impact on asset prices.[6] To complement this scenario analysis, the exercise

---

[6]The stylized portfolio of a diversified sovereign wealth fund is based on market reports concerning asset allocation and currency composition. The Norway-like portfolio is based on publicly available data

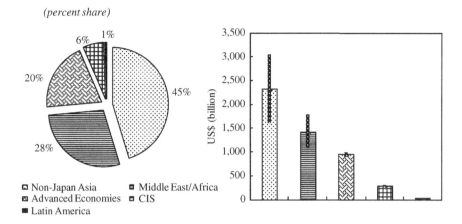

(percent share)

□ Non-Japan Asia   ▣ Middle East/Africa
▣ Advanced Economies ▫ CIS
■ Latin America

Fig. 2.6   SWF Projections by Region.
Source: IMF staff estimates.

also estimates the impact of a modest shift away from dollar assets in the current stock of reserves for the ten largest emerging economy reserve holders. Such a shift is within the realm of possibility, especially given recent statements by officials from some emerging economies raising concerns about the dollar's future as a reserve currency (see *Financial Times* 2009).

The analysis assumes that countries that have either recently established sovereign wealth funds or announced their intention to establish one will channel a portion of their prospective foreign exchange inflows to their respective sovereign wealth funds. The prospective foreign exchange flows are calculated as the sum of each country's current account balance and net private capital flows, based on *World Economic Outlook* (IMF 2009) projections for 2009–2014.[7] The analysis provides for a lower bound — which assumes that countries that have recently established sovereign wealth funds will transfer 50% of newly available foreign currency inflows to their investment vehicle — and an upper bound — which assumes that, in addition, countries that are contemplating setting up sovereign wealth funds transfer 100% of newly available foreign currency inflows. The upper bound also assumes that 15% of the stock of existing reserves of the top 10 emerging market

from Norges Bank, as of the end of December 2008. The reserves portfolio is based on the IMF's COFER database, which records end-of-period quarterly data on the currency composition of official foreign exchange reserves. Aggregate COFER data is used to derive a stylized reserves portfolio, assuming that assets are allocated exclusively to government bonds according to the COFER currency composition.
[7]For China, prospective foreign exchange inflows are assumed to be equal to the sum of the current account balance and net private capital flows less than half of the current projected reserve accumulation.

(a) Foreign exchange reserve assets

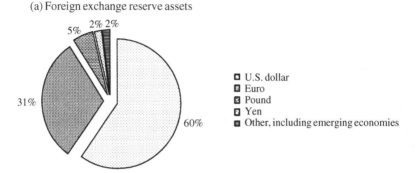

- ☐ U.S. dollar
- ☒ Euro
- ☒ Pound
- ☐ Yen
- ☒ Other, including emerging economies

Source: Author's calculations, based on COFER data.

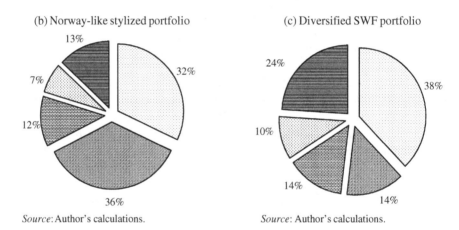

(b) Norway-like stylized portfolio

(c) Diversified SWF portfolio

Source: Author's calculations.   *Source*: Author's calculations.

Fig. 2.7   Currency Composition of Stylized Portfolios.

reserves holders is shifted from reserves to sovereign wealth fund holdings over the period 2009–2014. It is assumed that all new flows into sovereign wealth funds are invested abroad.

A note of caution is, however, warranted. As in many illustrative exercises, the results are highly sensitive to the underlying assumptions. For instance, by focusing largely on new sovereign investments, the exercise provides only a partial picture of the possible magnitude of the impact on capital flows and asset prices arising from the diversification strategy. Moreover, other sovereigns (and not just the top ten emerging market reserves holders as assumed in the exercise) may choose to diversify their existing stock of their reserve assets. That said, this limited exercise provides a sense of the direction and magnitude of the possible impact on markets.

The analysis suggests that the pattern of global capital flows could change significantly, with the United States facing lower capital inflows and emerging economies attracting substantially larger inflows. Relative to reserve assets, which are predominantly dollar-denominated and generally held in the form of US Treasury or agency securities, the stylized sovereign wealth fund portfolios are more diversified across both asset classes and currency exposures. This suggests lower inflows into government bond markets, with attendant implications for interest rates. The shift away from reserve assets could have the most significant effect on markets in the United States, if countries diversify away from dollar holdings.

Estimates show that inflows into the United States could decline by 0.5–0.75% of US GDP per year on average, depending on the number of countries in the sample and the assumption made regarding the currency composition of reserves for the ten largest emerging economy reserve holders. The results also hinge on the asset allocation strategy that is used to model investments by the prospective sovereign wealth funds. Portfolios that are more weighted to emerging economies — such as the stylized diversified portfolio — would result in lower flows into both dollar and euro assets, while flows to emerging economies would tend to increase substantially. However, the adverse effect on demand for euro assets fades as large emerging economy reserve holders shift out of US dollar assets and into euros and other currencies. By contrast, a portfolio similar to Norway's — which is heavily weighted to investments in Europe — would suggest somewhat lower investment in dollar assets even before the reserve shift is taken into account and a less sizeable, but still positive, inflow to emerging markets.

2.4.2. *Model Simulations*

To quantify the implications of potential changes in the pattern of capital flows on interest rates and exchange rates, simulations were undertaken using an annual version of the Global Integrated Monetary Fiscal Model (GIMF).[8] The change in the pattern of capital flows is modeled as a shock to portfolio preferences, as investors shift out of US assets in favor of more diversified portfolios. More specifically, the shock is modeled as an increase in the country risk premium on US

---

[8]GIMF is a multi-country dynamic stochastic general equilibrium model that has been designed for studying macroeconomic policy issues that emphasize stock-flow consistency. The model is based on an overlapping generations setup, which produces a well-defined steady state where countries can be either net creditors or debtors, depending on their savings behavior (see Kumhof and Laxton 2007). The simulations are based on extended version of the model includes separate models for the United States, the euro area, Japan, emerging Asia, and "remaining countries" (for the code used to produce these simulations, see www.douglaslaxton.org).

(a) Norway-like portfolio   (b) Diversified SWF portfolio

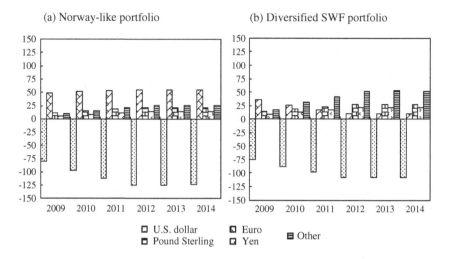

□ U.S. dollar   ◙ Euro
□ Pound Sterling   □ Yen   ▤ Other

Fig. 2.8   Change in the Pattern of Capital Flows, by Currency.
Source: IMF staff estimates.

assets. Three variants based on different magnitudes of the shock are presented in
Figures 2.9 and 2.10 — labeled as low, moderate and high. The low case assumes a
50 basis point permanent increase in the US country risk premium and is associated
with the lower bound of the change in the pattern of capital flows. The high case
assumes a shock that is 150 basis points and would represent a more extreme shift in
portfolio preferences than those presented in the previous section. The text below
focuses on the moderate variant, which assumes a 100 basis point shock and is
associated with the upper bound of the change in pattern of capital flows computed
in the previous section.

The model results point to significant, but manageable, effects on exchange
rates, current account balances, and trade balances in three economic regions —
the United States, the euro area, and emerging Asia.[9] All results are shown as
deviations from a baseline.

The increase in the US country risk premium would induce a temporary depreciation of the US dollar in real effective terms and an improvement in the current
account balance. The US dollar would immediately depreciate by about 7% in real
effective terms. This would induce an improvement in the current account balance
by about 0.5% of GDP in the first year. Intuitively, in the short run, the real exchange

---

[9]The results focus on emerging Asia rather than emerging economies as a group because of the model's
structure, which does not (at this time) contain a separate block for emerging economies as a group or
by regions outside of Asia.

(a) Current account balance

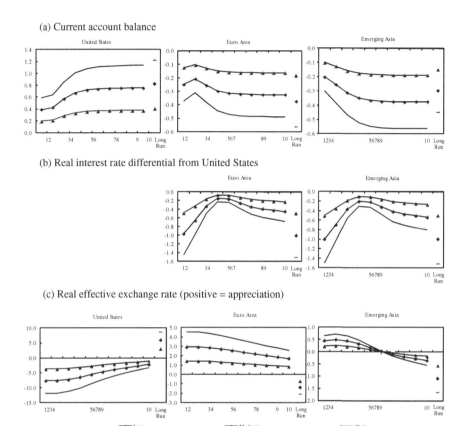

(b) Real interest rate differential from United States

(c) Real effective exchange rate (positive = appreciation)

Fig. 2.9   Model Simulations.

Source: IMF staff estimates.

Note: Deviations from baseline; x-axis in years.

rate must depreciate in the United States to generate an improvement in the trade balance that is consistent with savings behavior and capital flows. Over time, the depreciation in the real exchange rate would result in a further improvement in the current account balance, which would eventually stabilize at a value that is 0.75% higher than in the baseline. However, this longer-term improvement in the current account would result in a significant improvement in the net foreign asset position, reducing US interest obligations to the rest of the world. To equilibrate this process, the real exchange rate must therefore appreciate in the long run (relative to baseline) to generate a decline in the trade balance. Essentially, the composition of the current account changes over time — the initial improvement would arise

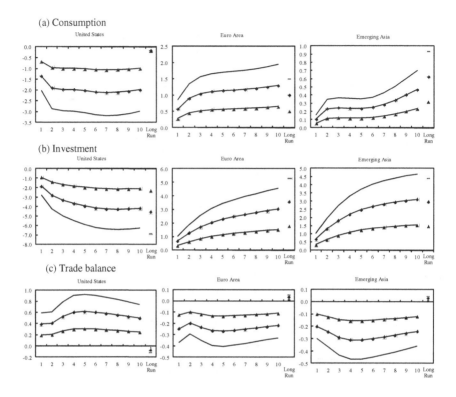

Fig. 2.10   Model Simulations.

Source: IMF staff estimates.
Note: Deviations from baseline; x-axis in years.

from an improvement in the trade balance, while the long-run improvement would arise from lower interest payments as the stock of net foreign assets improves.

In the euro area and emerging Asia, the shock to the US country risk premium would induce a temporary real effective appreciation of the euro and emerging Asian currencies. The euro would appreciate in real effective terms, initially by about 3% and by smaller amounts over time. In emerging Asia, the dynamics are more rapid, given the region's openness to trade. Currencies initially appreciate by 0.5% in real effective terms, but relatively quickly begin to depreciate. In the long run, current account balances deteriorate by less in the euro area and emerging Asia — by around 0.5% and 0.25%, respectively. As in the United States, the composition of the current account balance would change over time, reflecting the impact of the real exchange rate path on the trade balance and the associated change in the net foreign asset position. Thus, over time, the exchange rate must depreciate in real effective terms to induce an improvement in the trade balance to offset the decline in interest earnings on net foreign assets. In these simulations, the real exchange rate has to adjust by more in the euro area than in emerging Asia because the latter (as a region) is more open.

According to the model results, real interest rate differentials between the euro area and emerging Asia vs the United States would fall. When real exchange rates stabilize at their long-run values, a permanent increase in the country risk premium of 100 basis points will also be reflected in a 100 basis point decline in real interest rate differentials between the rest of the world (in this case, the euro area and emerging Asia) and the United States. However, over the transition path, where the real exchange rate is still adjusting to generate a path for the trade balance that is consistent with portfolio preferences, real interest rate differentials in the rest of the world (relative to the United States) would decline by less than 100 basis points.[10] Higher interest rates in the United States and lower interest rates in the rest of the world would shift production to the rest of the world. As a result, investment would decline in the United States and rise in the euro area and emerging Asia. This would lead to lower levels of permanent income and consumption in the United States, and higher levels elsewhere.

While these simulations provide important analytical support to the qualitative assessment made earlier in the chapter, it is important to note that they deliberately abstract from a number of real-world issues. First, they assume that nominal exchange rates are flexible and adjust instantaneously to be consistent with risk-adjusted asset returns and fundamentals. Second, the model assumes that there is only one type of bond traded internationally and that it is denominated in US dollars. Third, valuation effects that would be associated with a sudden decline in the value of the US dollar are not taken into account. Including valuation effects in the analysis would require extending the model to include different types of asset classes. For example, modeling emerging Asia as a net-creditor country would tend to weaken its consumption responses, as a depreciation in the US dollar would result in a negative valuation effect on their stock of financial assets that are denominated in US dollars.

2.5. Conclusion

Although the financial crisis has generally taken sovereign wealth funds out of the media headlines they are still key players in global finance. Given their size and

---

[10]The model has an overlapping generations structure, which allows it to have a well-defined steady state where countries or economic regions can be either net creditors or debtors. This feature is critical because it is possible to consider permanent shocks to study the transition from one steady state to another.

scope, it is plausible that their actions would have implications for global capital flows and asset prices. In particular, even a gradual shift toward greater portfolio diversification of foreign assets by sovereigns, including through sovereign wealth funds, could have implications for the flow of funds between countries and the absolute and relative prices of assets. Using illustrative scenario analysis combined with model-based simulations, this chapter is a first attempt at better understanding the implications of portfolio allocation decisions of sovereign wealth funds on global capital flows and asset prices. While it may seem implausible in the near term, the analysis suggests that the pattern of global capital flows could change significantly if countries shift away from US dollar assets, including through more diversified sovereign wealth fund portfolios. In the scenario analysis, advanced economies would face lower capital inflows and emerging economies would attract substantially larger inflows. The results of the model-based simulations show that such a change in the pattern of global capital flows would lead to higher US interest rates (lower interest rates elsewhere) and a depreciation of the US dollar (an appreciation of other currencies). These findings are consistent with the economic intuition prevailing before the crisis and may yet come to pass as the global economy gradually recovers and risk appetite returns.

References

Anderlini, J, 2009, "China Urges Switch from Dollar as Reserve Currency", *Financial Times*, March 24.

International Monetary Fund (IMF), 2008, *Sovereign Wealth Funds — A Work Agenda*, March.

International Monetary Fund (IMF), 2009, *World Economic Outlook*, April.

Kerr, S, 2007, "Qatar Optimistic on Sovereign Wealth Fund Access to Credit", *Financial Times*, September 20.

Kumhof, M, & Laxton, D, 2007, "A Party Without a Hangover? On the Effects of U.S. Fiscal Deficits", International Monetary Fund Working Paper 07/202.

Monitor Group, 2008, "Sovereign Wealth Fund Investment Behaviour", December 2008.

Setser, B, & Ziemba, R, 2007, "What Do We Know About the Size and Composition of Oil Investment Funds?" RGE Monitor, April.

Truman, E, 2007, A Scoreboard for Sovereign Wealth Funds. Paper presented at the conference on China's Exchange Rate Policy at Peterson Institute for International Economics, Washington DC, October 19.

Wiegand, J, 2008, "Bank Recycling of Petro Dollars to Emerging Market Economies During the Current Oil Price Boom", International Monetary Fund Working Paper 08/180.

Chapter 3

A Portfolio Analysis of Sovereign Wealth Funds

Christopher Balding

3.1. Introduction

Due to sustained global growth and sound macroeconomic fundamentals, commodity-based economies accumulated significant excess foreign exchange earnings and reserves. In an effort to avoid boom and bust cycles, sterilize foreign currency inflows, smooth long-term consumption and investment, and improve reserve returns, countries created sovereign wealth funds to manage their holdings. Due primarily to high commodity prices, sovereign wealth funds are estimated to control assets in excess of $3 trillion and could see their holdings rise to $12–15 trillion by 2015 (Morgan Stanley 2007). To place these numbers in context, the market capitalization of all publicly listed national investment brokerages and money center banks in the United States is $1.4 trillion while annual revenues top $500 billion.[1] In other words, sovereign wealth funds could currently purchase all national investment brokerages and money center banks listed on US exchanges and still have more than $1.6 trillion left to spend.

The speed and size with which these funds grew caught policy-makers off guard and caused many to question the economic logic of state-owned investment firms. Former US Treasury Secretary Larry Summers (2007) summarized the position of many when he argued that the

> logic of the capitalist system depends on shareholders causing companies to act so as to maximize the value of their shares. It is far from obvious that this will over time be the only motivation

---

[1] Calculated using Bloomberg data accessed 18 March 2008.

43

of governments as shareholders. They may want to see their national companies compete effectively, or to extract technology or to achieve influence.

Critics have argued that without proper global regulation of sovereign wealth funds, they may gain access to national security secrets, influence politics, create chaos in foreign economies, or destabilize international financial markets (see Summers 2007; Truman 2007; Luft 2008). Governments struggle to deal with sovereign wealth funds for two reasons. First, sovereign wealth funds are government-linked entities raising the fear of politically motivated large-scale investments designed to pursue policy objectives of the state rather than economically driven decisions (see Yeung 2000; Feng *et al.* 2004; Ramirez and Tan 2004; Yeung 2004; Sam 2007). Second, many sovereign wealth funds disclose little information about their activities. For both economic and political reasons, many sovereign wealth funds, similar to investment banks and hedge funds, resist releasing information about their investment decisions, portfolio, or performance. Consequently, critics and friends alike wonder about their purpose and activities. Critics go so far as to charge sovereign wealth funds with threatening the stability of the international financial system by accident or design, for example through unsupervised derivatives trading strategies or willful destruction of companies for political purposes. The concerns surrounding sovereign wealth funds arise from worries surrounding the political management of large funds and their impact on cross-border investment.

This chapter focuses on the portfolio construction of sovereign wealth funds. Using specific holdings data where available and broader financial data, this paper analyzes the specific portfolios of Singapore and Norway and studies other sovereign wealth funds with more general data. The aim is to determine if they act as economically driven investors and how they allocate capital between asset classes and geographic regions. I find that they appear to act as investors and the common estimates fail to accurately control for certain financial assets and therefore skew their estimates of sovereign wealth funds. The chapter is divided into three sections. First, the problem of a lack of definition clarity is addressed. Second, utilizing data and estimates of the portfolio holdings of major sovereign wealth funds, I analyze their portfolios to deduce whether they act as economic driven investors. Third, I analyze the implications for the findings based upon the behavior of sovereign wealth funds.

3.2. The Problem of Definition

While some sovereign wealth funds own significant amounts of publicly listed equity and control state owned enterprises, this returns to a simple question: What

Table 3.1   Comparison of Entities with Alternative Sovereign Wealth Fund Definitions.

| | Definitions | | | | | | | |
| | International Monetary Fund | | | | | Truman | | Balding |
Fund Name	SWF	Stable	Savings	Reserve	Devel.	Pension	SWF	SWF
calPERS	X					X	X	X
United States Social Security Trust						X	X	
Saudi Arabian Monetary Agency							X	
Russian Stabilization Fund	X	X					X	X
Virginia Revenue Stabilization Fund							X	
Gazprom							X	
Singapore Airlines	X		X		X		X	X
United States Public Utilities					X		X	

is a sovereign wealth fund? Table 3.1 presents a brief sampling of whether some publicly controlled assets qualify as sovereign wealth funds.

It is important to emphasize a few points. First, the definition of a sovereign wealth fund is important. Different definitions can include or exclude similar assets resulting in divergent estimates. Second, similar assets should be treated similarly throughout estimates. State-owned enterprises, foreign exchange reserves, stabilization, and pension funds should be counted consistently. Third, many countries have similar entities or assets even if they are included in sovereign wealth funds estimates. Whether stabilization funds, state-owned enterprises, or pension holdings, most states have these entities. Fourth, ownership structure should not define a sovereign wealth fund holding. For instance, a state-owned enterprise under the umbrella of a sovereign wealth fund owned by the state should only count if a state-owned enterprise not under the umbrella of a sovereign wealth fund also counts. Fifth, researchers, governments, and policymakers must resist the temptation to create the largest number possible. As Truman (2007) notes, "the broadest definition of a sovereign wealth fund is a collection of government-owned or government-controlled assets." Sixth, as a question of economic accounting, it seems dubious to include public pensions in sovereign wealth fund holdings. The offsetting pension liability creates at best only a minor net economic benefit and in most cases no net wealth gain or a financial deficit. While debt used for leverage or other investment purposes remains sole and separate, these funds are completely offset by accompanying liabilities of mandated spending. Otherwise the only thing being counted are all government assets rather than sovereign wealth funds. Research should resist simply listing and counting all government assets, or if it does, at least count consistently. In the future, calculations should either include state-owned assets and foreign exchange reserves from all countries, or exclude these assets from countries with sovereign wealth funds. At the very least, estimates of sovereign wealth funds should clearly note what the calculation does or does not include. Primarily, it is important to make fair comparisons about assets and investments.

To better understand how a sovereign wealth fund may impact foreign economic policy it helps to understand what it is. Numerous definitions have been proposed for what constitutes a sovereign wealth fund, as can be seen in Table 3.2. Sovereign wealth fund estimates may include foreign exchange reserves, stabilization funds, development funds, and state-owned enterprises. Sovereign wealth funds are a heterogeneous group and may serve various purposes. A sovereign wealth fund is a pool of capital controlled by a government or government-related entity that invests in assets seeking returns above the risk-free rate of return. Contained within that definition, three distinct aspects create the definition of a sovereign wealth fund (see Table 3.2).

First, a sovereign wealth fund is a pool of capital. It normally derives its capital base from natural resource earnings, but Singapore and China built theirs from continued fiscal surpluses and foreign reserves accumulation. Kuwait, Abu Dhabi, Norway, Saudi Arabia, Russia, Chile, and Oman are among the nations that channel funds from commodity royalties into a sovereign wealth fund. Originally created as stabilization funds to reduce the boom and bust tendency of commodity dependent economies, states created clear rules of fund savings, investment strategies, and scenarios under which the government could access fund capital to smooth out economic downturns. The legislation required strict price mechanisms and government revenue caps to place commodity revenue into the stabilization fund. With price mechanisms based on low commodity prices from the late 1990s through 2002, the high oil and metals prices of recent history proved a boom for the sector and have rapidly expanded its capital base.

Second, a government or government-linked entity similar in stature to an independent central bank exercises control over the sovereign wealth fund, although the exact relationship varies from country to country (see Habibi 1998; Petersen and Budina 2003; Amuzegar 2005; Kalyuzhnova and Kaser 2006; Mehrara and Oskoui 2007). Countries generally place the fund far enough from the potential meddling of political pressures but not so far as to relinquish control over such a potentially powerful body. No major country completely incorporates its sovereign wealth fund activities into governmental bodies such as the finance ministries; neither do they remove the government from at least an oversight role.

Table 3.2   What is a Sovereign Wealth Fund?

Author/Institution	Definition of sovereign wealth fund and other government investment entities
Balding (Chapter 3)	**Sovereign wealth fund** a pool of capital controlled by a government or government-related entity that invests in assets, seeking returns above the risk-free rate of return
Fotak and Megginson (2008)	**Sovereign wealth fund** a pool of domestic and international assets owned and managed by government to achieve a variety of economic and financial objectives, including the accumulation and management of reserve assets, the stabilization of macroeconomic effects and the transfer of wealth across generations **Commodity stabilization fund** national investment funds whose main purpose is to offset revenue declines due to falling commodity prices or production levels **State budget stabilization fund** a fund imposing restrictions on deposits and withdrawals of funds usually to avoid political interference
International Monetary Fund (2008)	**Sovereign wealth fund** special investment fund created or owned by government to hold foreign assets for long-term purposes **(Commodity) stabilization fund** set up by countries rich in natural resources to insulate the budget and economy from volatile commodity prices (usually oil). The funds build up assets during the years of ample fiscal revenues to prepare for leaner years **Savings fund** intended to share wealth across generations. For countries rich in natural resources, savings funds transfer non-renewable assets into a diversified portfolio of international financial assets to provide for future generations or other long-term objectives **Reserve investment corporation** established as a separate entity either to reduce the negative cost-of-carry of holding reserves or to pursue investment policies with higher returns **Development fund** allocate resources for funding priority socioeconomic projects, such as infrastructure **Pension reserve fund** have identified pension and/or contingent-type liabilities on the government's balance sheet
Blundell-Wignall, Hu, and Yermo (2008)	**Sovereign wealth fund** an asset pool owned and managed directly or indirectly by a government, to achieve national objectives
McKinsey Global Institute (2007)	**Sovereign wealth fund** has a diversified portfolio that ranges across equity, fixed income, real estate, bank deposits, and alternative investments, such as hedge funds and private equity **Central bank** an entity whose primary investment objective is stability, not the maximization of returns. They hold foreign reserves mainly in the forms of cash and long-term debt, currently largely US Treasury bills **Government investment corporation** invests directly into domestic and foreign corporate assets, shunning the portfolio investment approach of sovereign wealth funds. They operate like private equity funds that actively buy and manage companies, either alone or with a consortia of other investors

(Continued)

Table 3.2   (*Continued*)

Author/Institution	Definition of sovereign wealth fund and other government investment entities
Truman (2007)	**Sovereign wealth fund** a descriptive term for a separate pool of government-owned or government-controlled assets that includes some international assets. Truman includes all government pension, as well as non-pension, funds to the extent that they manage marketable assets
Organization for Economic Cooperation and Development (2008)	**Sovereign wealth fund** an asset pool owned and managed directly or indirectly by a government to achieve national objectives. They may be funded by: (i) foreign exchange reserves; (ii) the sale of scarce resources such as oil; or (iii) from general tax and other revenue. Their objectives, which are not always easy to attribute to a particular fund (and some may have more than one) may include: (i) to diversify assets; (ii) to get a better return on reserves; (iii) to provide for pensions in the future; (iv) to provide for future generations when natural resources run out; (v) price stabilization schemes; (vi) to promote industrialization; and (vii) to promote strategic and political objectives **Social security reserve fund** set up as part of the overall social security system, where the inflows are mainly surpluses of employee and/or employer contributions over current payouts, as well as, in some cases, top-up contributions from the government via fiscal transfers and other sources **Sovereign pension reserve fund** established directly by the government (completely separated from the social security system) to meet future deficits of the social security system. Its financial inflows are mainly from direct fiscal transfers from the government
Martin Weiss (2008)	**Sovereign wealth fund** owned and managed by national governments

Governments typically control appointment to key positions such as managing directors, senior executives, board members, or auditing functions. Recruitment is not limited to the bureaucracy. Candidates can come from the private sector and in some instances foreigners are recruited to provide management or corporate expertise. For instance, some countries use respected international auditors, outside fund managers, imported foreign talent, and board members to demonstrate their professionalism and independence. Countries also resist yielding control of such large firms. To date no country has privatized its sovereign wealth fund, though many such as Temasek Holdings of Singapore and the Abu Dhabi Investment Authority, have publicly listed subsidiaries. States generally institute well-defined rules for withdrawals and set standard investment objectives. As sovereign wealth funds outgrew stabilization imperatives, for example, rules were promulgated whereby funds accumulated cash when commodity price level remained above a pre-defined price such as a long-term average, and governments could withdraw a defined amount of fund capital when prices dropped. In short, governments can't bring themselves to relinquish control of such large pools of capital, but they also see the need to remove it from political manipulation.

A sovereign wealth fund seeks returns above the risk-free rate of return rather than purchasing a basket of currencies or risk-free assets such as government securities. This stems from divergent factors. First, governments and sovereign wealth funds pay an implicit cost of capital. Consequently, holding foreign exchange reserves of a declining currency or low yielding government securities, which fail to cover the implicit cost of capital, creates an economic loss on reserves. For instance, between currency and inflation costs, the Chinese government entity State Administration of Foreign Exchange and the newly created Chinese Investment Corporation face a high cost of capital. Whereas governments previously deposited money in global banks and low-risk fixed income securities, the decision to pursue higher returns stems at least in part from a desire to cover the cost of capital for countries with large foreign currency holdings.

Second, countries increasingly treat their accumulated financial capital or foreign exchange reserves less as low risk capital or currency reserves to cover international trade requirements and more as capital that needs to earn higher rates of return than cash and government securities. Funds work with investment banks, hedge funds, private equity firms, and internal staff to seek out higher yielding investment opportunities. Countries with high levels of foreign reserves are no longer content to accept money market returns offered from large international banks. The Singaporean funds for example declare their desire to "achieve good long-term returns" on "Singapore's foreign reserves" (Government Investment Corporation of Singapore 2010); China diverted foreign currency reserves from the Central Bank to provide the China Investment Corporation with $200 billion to start their fund recognizing the potential for higher returns and their high cost of capital; Kuwait succinctly declares its purpose is to "achieve a rate of return on the investment that, on a three-year rolling average, exceeds composite benchmark(s)" (Kuwait Investment Authority 2010). This not only represents a significant shift in the investment strategy of central banks and stabilization funds; it may also mean that the distinction between central bank and sovereign wealth fund may be blurring. The importance of the move to higher risk, higher return assets by sovereign wealth funds cannot be underestimated.

Third, states use their sovereign wealth fund to diversify their economies and improve their human capital. Some sovereign wealth funds, explicitly or implicitly, state investment in the domestic or regional economy as an objective. Analysis of holdings confirms the validity of this objective. States may use their sovereign wealth fund to make much needed infrastructure investments, for example, while others use the fund to remake their economies specializing, for instance, in financial services rather than outsourcing this lucrative and specialized work. Smaller city-states such as Abu Dhabi and Qatar, with large per capita sovereign wealth numbers, remade their cities into large financial service centers importing specialized financial talent from around the world. Others focus more on the diversification of their economy away from a commodity-dependent economy. In almost all cases, sovereign wealth funds have also been increasingly professionalized, importing world-class talent to improve the quality of financial management and domestic human capital. There are numerous reasons for doing so, but a common feature is that countries are no longer content to park financial capital in assets that earn a negative real return in foreign markets.

3.3. Sovereign Wealth Fund Portfolio: Behind the Curtain

To analyze sovereign wealth funds and their potential impact, it is important to formulate a hypothesis concerning geographic preferences and asset class investments. First, if financial empirics hold, we would expect sovereign wealth funds to invest heavily in domestic and regional markets demonstrating home bias. Research indicates investors retain a significant home and regional bias when making investment decisions. For instance, we would expect Singaporeans to invest primarily in Singapore and regional Asian markets, using Europe and the United States primarily as diversification outlets. Second, sovereign wealth funds should diversify their holdings between a risk-adjusted portfolio comprised of stocks, bonds, and alternative investments. Due to their nature as guardians of national wealth, we would also expect sovereign wealth funds to target safe liquid assets such as blue-chip stocks, highly rated corporate debt, and sovereign securities while allocating a small portion of the portfolio to more risky investments such as growth stocks, private equity, and hedge fund activities. In short, we would expect them to invest more in low-risk liquid assets and less in higher-risk and lower-liquidity securities like private equity.

To compile an investment profile of sovereign wealth funds I use both direct and indirect data. First, using direct holdings data from the Thomson One Banker and Bloomberg, which provide ownership information on publicly listed equity securities and private equity transactions from exchanges and deal information

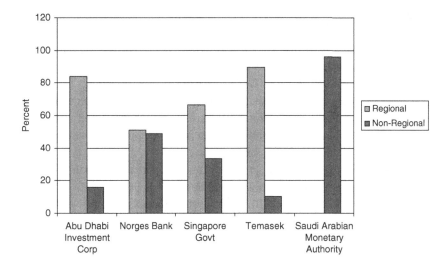

Fig. 3.1   Sovereign Wealth Fund Public Equity Geographic Profile.

Source: Thomson One Banker.

around the world, this chapter analyses investment holdings of sovereign wealth funds, focusing on the largest funds.[2] Second, using financial flow data from central banks, international organizations, national treasuries, and other financial data, I compiled indirect data on where funds flowed from and where they flowed to. Based upon the aggregated data from Bloomberg and Thomson One Banker, sovereign wealth funds clearly act with regards to their equity holdings as financial theory would predict. Figure 3.1 presents the geographic allocation of equity investments held by major sovereign wealth funds.

The major funds demonstrate an unmistakable preference for domestic and regional equity investment.[3] Only in the case of Norway and Saudi Arabia are domestic and regional equities not dominant and each require further explanation. As of April 2008, more than 80% of equities held by the Norwegian fund are in Europe and North America. Furthermore, it has voiced a clear preference for liquid

---

[2]According to a variety of sources the largest sovereign wealth funds by country come from Abu Dhabi, Singapore, Norway, Saudi Arabia, Kuwait, China, and Russia. (The Chinese Investment Corporation and Russian Stabilization Fund are not included in Figures 3.1 & 3.2 because the Russian Stabilization Fund does not invest in equity securities and the Chinese Investment Company has not built a portfolio or track record.) Collectively these funds control approximately 91% of all sovereign wealth fund capital and are also the best placed to increase capital in the future.

[3]For Norway I considered all European holdings as regional. Singapore holdings were classified as regional for Australia and Asia excluding the Middle East. Gulf sovereign wealth fund holdings were classified as regional for the Middle East and North Africa.

well-developed markets with a high level of corporate governance and therefore may be reluctant to make large investments in less developed markets. The Saudi Arabian example, although included as part of the larger group, does not represent larger investment patterns as it only covers roughly a quarter of 1% of estimated Saudi state-controlled assets or $700 million. Whereas the other funds listed have made large investments in the global equity markets, I find no evidence that the Saudi Arabian fund has made similar investment in equities. Based upon their investment in global equities, sovereign wealth funds do appear to act as expected in their geographical allocation of assets.

Critics also allege that sovereign wealth funds may also assume unnecessary risk and concentrate their portfolios in equities with high growth prospects as well as excessive downside risk. To mitigate this, financial theory implies that sovereign wealth funds should make conservative, low risk, and liquid investments. In equities, these stocks are referred to as large cap or blue chip stocks. The equity allocation of major sovereign wealth funds is presented in Figure 3.2.

It is inferred from their preference for large capitalized stocks that sovereign wealth funds tend to concentrate on lower risk investments.[4] In only two instances

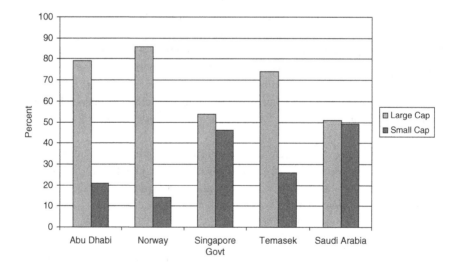

Fig. 3.2   Sovereign Wealth Fund Equity Allocation.

Source: Thomson One Banker, April 2008.

---

[4]The information from Thomson One Bank divided stocks into five categories: mega, large, mid, small, and micro. For purposes of this study, I divided the stocks into mega and large cap stocks and then combining mid, small and micro cap stocks into the small cap stock category.

are the ratios between large and small cap stock close, one being the Saudi Arabian Monetary Agency (which as noted previously consists of only $700 million in equities) and the other being the Government of Singapore Investment Corporation (where a 10% differential exists).[5] While experts may argue over the perceived risk of specific equities held in any given portfolio, it is unmistakable that sovereign wealth funds design their portfolios to assume low levels of risk. An examination of the public equity holdings of two Singaporean funds for which good records exist — Temasek Holdings and Government Investment Corporation — indicates a conservative portfolio of global equities. The top 25 companies by market cap out of the approximately 200 equity securities in the Singaporean holdings comprise approximately 84.56% of their portfolio.[6] Internationally, Government Investment Corporation and Temasek Holdings hold major positions in British Petroleum, Merrill Lynch, Vodafone, Barclays, Standard and Chartered, China Construction Bank, Anglo-American, Rio Tinto, Barclays Bank, and Taiwan Semiconductor. Singaporean sovereign wealth fund holdings, therefore, display a clear preference for large cap companies and a low risk portfolio.[7]

Norges Bank, the Norwegian Central Bank and manager of the Government Pension Fund, the sovereign wealth fund that holds the largest number of equity securities and also the most geographically dispersed, exhibits a similar tendency. As of April 2008, the top 1200 stocks by market capitalization in their portfolio of 4800 equities comprise 91.43% of the Government Pension Fund portfolio. Norges Bank holds significant positions in ExxonMobil, General Electric, and Microsoft in the United States; British Petroleum, HSBC Holdings, and Vodafone in the United Kingdom; Total, Nestle, and Nokia in Europe; and China Mobile, Toyota Motor, and Mitsubishi Financial in Asia. These 1200 companies have an average market capitalization of $30 billion. Other sovereign wealth funds that hold equity portfolios, such as Abu Dhabi and Kuwait, demonstrate similar risk appetites frequently holding the same companies.

Portfolios generally seem designed to mirror broad market returns and not assume excess risk. Based upon an analysis of the equity holdings of the largest sovereign wealth funds, they do not appear to hold anything more than average market risk applicable to every equity market participant. Two other points pertain to the Norwegian sovereign wealth fund. First, the Norwegian sovereign wealth fund

---

[5]The small difference between large and small cap stock also stems from the Singaporean focus on regional stocks as there is not simply the number of large cap stocks available.

[6]Due to omissions in the Thomson One Bank data covering Singaporean holdings, the numbers are probably higher than indicated.

[7]Data compiled for Singaporean sovereign wealth fund in April 2008.

is the only country that publicly invites tenders for equity and fixed-income managers. It currently employs, among others, Legg Mason, T Rowe Price, Barclays, and Lehman Brothers to manage their equity and fixed-income investment by geographic and sector profile. Second, the Norwegian sovereign wealth fund specifically states that it does not invest in private, unlisted equity, hedge fund, or options. Though some portfolio managers might disagree and allocate some capital of the overall portfolio to these activities, Norwegian managers cannot be faulted for prudent financial management.

Singaporean sovereign wealth fund managers Temasek Holdings and Government Investment Corporation, along with related subsidiaries, invest in private equity and venture capital investments as part of their overall portfolio. A few notable points about their non-traditional investments need highlighting. First, Temasek Holdings and Government Investment Corporation partner with well-known investors. JP Morgan, Deutsche Bank, Northwest Mutual Life, and Sequoia Capital are only a partial listing of co-investors in private equity and venture capital investments with Singaporean sovereign wealth funds. In other words, Singaporean sovereign wealth funds do not appear to assume risks other sophisticated investors do not also assume. Second, Singaporean sovereign wealth funds allocate private equity capital as a portion of the overall portfolio targeting high risk and return investments, totaling less than approximately $2 billion in invested capital in a total portfolio of more than $300 billion. Spread throughout Asia, North America, and Europe, Singaporean sovereign wealth fund private equity investments use relatively small amounts of capital in early-stage investments throughout a variety of industries, though more concentrated in technology and financials. When considered as a part of the total portfolio, the portfolio allocation to venture capital and private equity investment does not appear to be an excessive assumption of risk. Third, Singaporean private equity investments have enjoyed a reasonable number of failures and notable successes, as would be expected in higher-risk investments, such as one subsidiary's early investment in PayPal. Venture capital and private equity investment carry a higher-risk profile and the bankruptcies associated with Singaporean sovereign wealth fund private equity investments should be considered as part of the entire portfolio, both within private equity and the range of investments, rather than individually. In short, when considered as part of the whole, though total return statistics are currently unobtainable, the Singaporean sovereign wealth fund private equity investment record seems both rational and respectable.

Equity holdings, however, do not comprise a portfolio. As previously noted, based upon their most widely stated purpose as sovereign wealth funds, one would reasonably and theoretically expect to find low-risk investments with a regional focus. Using data compiled from the US Treasury, the IMF Coordinated Portfolio Investment Survey (CPIS), International Financial Statistics (IFS), and Bloomberg, this paper estimates sovereign wealth fund debt security holdings for Singapore and Norway. For purposes of estimation, I assume that the geographic and risk profile of debt holdings mirror the overall country and equity holdings.[8] Sovereign wealth funds demonstrate a distinct preference for low-risk debt securities as a major portion of their portfolio. For instance, Norway the country for whom the best sovereign wealth fund specific data exists, allocates a near constant 55% of its portfolio to debt securities. According to CPIS in 2001, the Norwegian sovereign wealth fund allocated 59% of its assets into debt securities, while in 2005 this number dropped slightly to 54%. Additionally, industrial country debt comprised 98.85% of their debt portfolio in 2001, dropping to 96.86% of debt securities in 2005, while regional debt securities in the Norwegian portfolio grew from 57.88% of the portfolio to 66.1%.[9] Finally, Norwegian sovereign wealth fund assets grow in near perfect unison with overall foreign portfolio investment (Norges Bank 2008). In 2001, Norwegian sovereign wealth fund assets comprised 65.85% of all Norwegian foreign debt securities. In 2005, that number dropped to 65.84%, a change of 0.01%.

No other sovereign wealth fund makes public its amount or allocation of debt holdings, however, extrapolating from the IMF and US Treasury, it is possible to reasonably estimate debt holdings. For instance, though Singapore does not break out the holdings of its two sovereign wealth funds, it is possible to estimate their debt holdings using their known equity holdings and subsequently extrapolating. Based upon the known value of Singaporean sovereign wealth fund equities and the extrapolated estimate of debt securities in portfolio, this paper estimates that the Singaporean sovereign wealth funds hold debt securities totaling nearly $180 billion, though this number under plausible assumptions could be $80 billion higher.

Furthermore, neither Singapore nor Norway appears to have invested their debt portfolio in risky issues. Though debt holders are not specifically listed as

---

[8]This estimation assumption rests on two ideas. First, the geographic portfolio composition of sovereign wealth fund holdings will resemble the country's holdings. Second, the sovereign wealth fund investment philosophy will remain relatively constant for risk allocation between debt and equity securities. In short, if sovereign wealth fund holdings comprise a significant percentage of total foreign holdings, then they must resemble to some degree the overall asset allocation of the country as it would be statistically difficult for the overall holdings of a country to differ significantly from its sovereign wealth fund.

[9]As a point of comparison, the IMF statistics used here were compared against US Treasury statistics. Due primarily to time frame issues, the comparison is not exact, but the numbers do come rather close. For instance, the IMF reports $12 and $40 billion in equity investments in the United States for 2001 and 2005, respectively. The US Treasury, with a six-month lag, reports $12 and $43 billion, respectively.

Table 3.3   Norwegian and Singaporean Sovereign Wealth Fund Estimates.

| | Norway Singapore SWF Comparison | | | |
	Norway Total	Norway Percentage	Singapore Total*	Singapore Percentage*
Debt	$203,735	57.76	$186,383	60.00
Equity	$148,972	42.24	$124,255	40.00
Portfolio	$352,707	100.00	$310,638	100.00

Source: Thomson One Banker and Norges Bank.
*Estimated from known equity holdings and estimated asset allocation.

equity holders, it is not an unreasonable assumption that sovereign wealth fund holdings mirror the broader country and narrower equity holdings. Though it is an inexact measurement, due to the sheer size of sovereign wealth fund as a percentage of the countries assets, it is unlikely that country holdings would fundamentally differ from the sovereign wealth fund or from the geographic allocation of equity investment.

For instance, according to the IMF CPIS data, Germany, the United States, Japan, Italy, and France comprise the top five holdings of debt securities held by Norway; the United Kingdom, United States, Australia, Malaysia, and Germany comprise the top five holdings of debt securities held by Singapore. Though no known public record detailing Norwegian and Singaporean sovereign wealth fund debt holdings exists, it does not seem unreasonable to assume, based upon country-wide statistics and equity investments, that their primary holdings are in investment grade corporate and government securities with a small portion allocated to high yield, emerging market, and distressed debt.

Russia has taken a similar low-risk approach to sovereign wealth fund portfolio management. Though the Russian stabilization fund as of April 2008 exceeds $150 billion, it holds by law only fixed-income securities of AAA credit quality issuers from low risk countries denominated in dollars, euros, and sterling (Ministry of Finance 2008). Pressure may exist to diversify the Russian fund into both domestic and international equities, but currently the Russian Stabilization Fund holds a clear low-risk mandate with respect to its investment policy. In fact, estimates of Russian sovereign wealth fund holdings include only the debt holdings, excluding the state holdings of Gazprom and Rosneft, which would add more than $200 billion to the total holdings. The Russian sovereign wealth fund has adopted a low-risk approach with clearly defined rules to investment management. Though possible to criticize the underlying securities or debate investment policy, Russia appears to have allocated their debt portfolio towards low-risk offerings.

Finally, I turn to countries with the least amount of public data about their sovereign wealth funds: Abu Dhabi, Saudi Arabia, and Kuwait.[10] Before turning to their known holdings, it is important to consider the estimated size of their holdings. The United Arab Emirates, Saudi Arabia, and Kuwait comprise three of the top five estimated sovereign wealth funds by assets under management with estimates ranging as high as $1.9 trillion in capital.[11] Together, these three funds comprise 63% of the major funds and 52% of all sovereign wealth funds. To put their estimated assets in perspective, $1.9 trillion is approximately 45% of the value of the entire Dow Jones Industrial Average; Abu Dhabi, Saudi Arabia, and Kuwait sovereign wealth funds may hold assets nearly 50% greater than all of the foreign reserves in China for a population 2.5% as large.[12] Based upon a careful review of the data there is little reason to believe the outsized claims of the capital base or their current impact on the international financial system.

Focusing on the estimates of the size of the sovereign wealth funds of Abu Dhabi, Saudi Arabia, and Kuwait, there is little reason to believe that these funds hold liquid capital approaching the amount estimated. According to the US Treasury, oil-exporting countries, not broken out by country, only held $308 billion of debt and equity securities in the United States.[13]

The nine countries included under the "Middle East Oil Exporting" title ranked behind Belgium, the Netherlands, and Canada. Ireland passed Middle East Oil Exporting countries in terms of investment in the United States between 2006 and 2007. While their $308 billion in US investment holdings may seem significant in absolute terms, when placed in context the number seems small. For instance, assuming for a moment the entire amount labeled "Middle East Oil Exporter" came from a sovereign wealth fund, the $308 billion comprises 16% of estimated Gulf sovereign wealth fund assets and 3.2% of foreign investment in the United States. Furthermore, neither the European Central Bank or the Japanese Ministry of Finance consider the financial holdings of oil exporters significant enough to list separately and even if they comprised the entire investor pools classified as "Other" in Japanese and European financial data, these holdings could not begin to reconcile the common estimate of $1.9 trillion in assets. UK statistics tell a similar story to that of the United States (as illustrated in Table 3.5).

---

[10]It should be emphasized that less data about direct holdings of equities exists for Abu Dhabi, Saudi Arabia, and Kuwait. To better understand their impact and size, I will utilize other financial data.

[11]Author's calculation from common estimates of sovereign wealth fund holdings.

[12]Calculated using Bloomberg and IMF International Financial Statistics data on 1 May 2008.

[13]It is worth noting and emphasizing that the United States and some international organizations either do not report on individual oil exporting states or group them together under the heading "oil exporters."

Table 3.4   U.S. Treasury and IMF Listing of Foreign Investment in the United States.

Country	Treasury Department Total Investment 2007 Preliminary			IMF Portfolio Investment 2006 Preliminary		
	Total	Equity	Debt	Total	Equity	Debt
JAPAN	$1,196,536	$220,199	$976,337	$797,608.04	$224,135.99	$573,472.05
UNITED KINGDOM	$980,630	$421,019	$559,611	$816,890.67	$340,776.80	$476,113.87
CHINA	$922,046	$28,519	$893,527	N/A	N/A	N/A
CAYMAN ISLANDS	$740,197	$279,474	$460,723	$59,094.00	$1,538.00	$57,556.00
LUXEMBOURG	$703,442	$234,553	$468,889	$417,048.11	$213,233.08	$203,815.02
CANADA	$475,196	$347,208	$127,988	$313,947.48	$236,901.23	$77,046.25
BELGIUM	$396,431	$24,592	$371,839	$54,877.99	$21,708.05	$33,169.94
IRELAND	$342,028	$81,120	$260,908	$397,387.63	$139,471.62	$257,916.01
SWITZERLAND	$328,982	$174,288	$154,694	$118,890.44	$63,354.09	$55,536.34
NETHERLANDS	$321,378	$184,919	$136,459	$305,526.46	$209,697.59	$95,828.87
MIDDLE EAST OIL-EXPORTERS*	$308,394	$139,393	$169,001	N/A	N/A	N/A
GERMANY	$265,770	$99,579	$166,191	$179,094.88	$71,173.31	$107,921.57
BERMUDA	$238,482	$90,384	$148,098	$282,093.76	$39,747.40	$242,346.36
FRANCE	$221,164	$131,529	$89,635	$253,640.29	$92,161.99	$161,478.30
SINGAPORE	$175,358	$107,946	$67,412	$37,087.85	$15,800.87	$21,286.98
AUSTRALIA	$165,387	$96,594	$68,793	$117,250.88	$81,143.86	$36,107.02
RUSSIA	$147,699	$203	$147,496	$4,684.00	$75.00	$4,609.00
KOREA, SOUTH	$137,870	$5,355	$132,515	$30,409.39	$5,180.23	$25,229.16
HONG KONG	$137,816	$30,549	$107,267	$64,867.31	$15,536.66	$49,330.65
TAIWAN	$121,003	$10,888	$110,115			

(Continued)

Table 3.4 (Continued)

Country	Treasury Department Total Investment 2007 Preliminary			IMF Portfolio Investment 2006 Preliminary		
	Total	Equity	Debt	Total	Equity	Debt
NORWAY	$109,371	$56,459	$52,912	$96,242.49	$46,458.95	$49,783.55
BRITISH VIRGIN ISLANDS	$107,802	$66,527	$41,275	N/A	N/A	N/A
MEXICO	$107,432	$18,778	$88,654	$9,621.66	$3,785.03	$5,836.63
BRAZIL	$106,384	$1,481	$104,903	$1,284.28	$713.38	$570.90
SWEDEN	$99,005	$59,623	$39,382	$93,465.05	$65,053.82	$28,411.22
JERSEY	$67,397	$13,321	$54,076	$132,545.69	$11,037.95	$121,507.74
ITALY	$50,189	$25,720	$24,469	$103,635.74	$31,808.93	$71,826.81
DENMARK	$49,803	$31,295	$18,508	$48,560.96	$31,555.45	$17,005.51
Major Investors	$9,023,192	$2,981,515	$6,041,677	$4,735,755.03	$1,962,049.27	$2,773,705.77
U.S. TOTAL	$9,771,725	$3,129,523	$6,642,202	$6,254,227.00	$2,096,152.00	$4,157,452.00

Source: United States Treasury and the International Monetary Fund.
*Bahrain, Iran, Iraq, Kuwait, Oman, Qatar, Saudi Arabia, United Arab Emirates.

Table 3.5   UK Pink Book Financial Statistics and IMF Investment in the United Kingdom.

	Pink Book 2004				IMF 2006		
Country	Liabilities	Net Investment	Liabilities Dollars	Net Investment Dollars	Portfolio	Equity	Debt
America	£924,974	−£55,874	$1,720,452	$(103,926)	$1,075,579	$673,978	$401,601
Germany	£446,986	−£107,937	$831,394	$(200,763)	$147,775	$37,945	$109,830
Netherlands	£250,055	£63,652	$465,102	$118,393	$110,459	$67,263	$43,196
Switzerland	£249,670	−£110,567	$464,386	$(205,655)	$51,432	$25,994	$25,439
France	£237,478	£37,359	$441,709	$69,488	$246,678	$83,639	$163,039
Japan	£213,462	£48,577	$397,039	$90,353	$145,272	$52,107	$93,165
Ireland	£207,110	−£62,958	$385,225	$(117,102)	$308,485	$104,214	$204,271
Luxembourg	£124,994	£34,488	$232,489	$64,148	$195,898	$107,557	$88,341
Belgium	£95,198	£2,978	$177,068	$5,539	$31,010	$11,303	$19,707
Hong Kong	£83,821	−£28,002	$155,907	$(52,084)	$71,970	$48,147	$23,824
Singapore	£77,468	−£34,740	$144,090	$(64,616)	$40,674	$3,851	$36,823
Gulf Countries	£33,358	−£7,464	$62,046	$(13,883)	$–	$–	$–
Norway	£27,325	£916	$50,825	$1,704	$42,880	$25,166	$17,714
Russia	£23,146	−£6,779	$43,052	$(12,609)	$1,047	$191	$856
China	£10,050	−£1,065	$18,693	$(1,981)	$–	$–	$–
Saudi Arabia	£16,226	−£11,085	$30,180	$(20,618)	$–	$–	$–
SEFER + SSIO (**)	N/A	N/A	N/A	N/A	$108,071	$4,837	$103,234
SWF Country Total	£187,573	−£60,217	$348,886	$(112,004)	$156,571	$77,355	$79,217
Major Investor Total	£3,010,236	−£238,501	$5,619,657	$(443,612)	$2,577,231	$1,246,192	$1,331,039
UK Total	£4,071,589	−£110,868	$7,573,156	$(206,214)	$3,177,767	$1,516,407	$1,658,418

Source: UK Pink Book Statistics and the International Monetary Fund.

Gulf country holdings, excluding consideration of ownership, comprise less than 1% of investment in the UK in 2004 (the last available year of statistics). Finally, research provides in great detail the equity holdings of sovereign wealth funds such as Norway and Singapore, but Saudi Arabia, Kuwait, and Abu Dhabi collectively hold $38 billion or 2% of estimated assets in listed equities. Though these sovereign wealth funds invest in hedge funds, private equity funds, or privately managed funds operated by partners, which might not require foreign registration of securities, it is doubtful that this would account for the difference between current estimates and verified holdings. Using the most liberal allowances for total sovereign wealth fund holdings, it is difficult in accepted international financial statistics to account for widely cited estimates of assets under management for Abu Dhabi, Saudi Arabia, and Kuwait. Even allowing for significant measurement errors and flawed ownership data, it is difficult to reconcile differences of such enormity.

If foreign asset ownership data does not justify the widely cited numbers of assets under management by Abu Dhabi, Saudi Arabia, and Kuwait, then it is important to ask: Are there additional numbers that might justify the differences? Two possibilities exist to reconcile the differences between the common estimates and verified financial statistics. First, if one includes foreign exchange reserves, it becomes plausible to estimate that the sovereign wealth funds of Abu Dhabi, Saudi Arabia, and Kuwait hold assets under management totaling $1.9 trillion. Using IMF data from the IFS, it becomes possible to slightly narrow the differences in estimates. According to the IFS, Industrial Countries hold $1.44 trillion in foreign exchange holdings with more than $1 trillion of that held in US dollars. Developing countries hold $4.27 trillion, nearly three times the reserves held by industrial countries. However, according to the IMF (as presented in Table 3.6), the United Arab Emirates, Saudi Arabia, and Kuwait have foreign reserves excluding gold totaling only $87 billion as of June 2007.

In terms of total foreign reserves excluding gold, the Gulf sovereign wealth fund countries rank behind countries like Malaysia, Algeria, Mexico, Thailand, and Libya. Conversely, China, Russia, and Singapore collectively hold $1.9 trillion. It seems incongruous with estimates of assets that the United Arab Emirates, Saudi Arabia, and Kuwait — all of which comprise three of the top five sovereign wealth funds — should hold such a relatively small amount of international debt, equity, and reserves. Second, Gulf estimates include a significant amount of domestic state-owned companies. Despite their estimated size, Gulf sovereign wealth funds and their home country financial data, show little evidence of having accumulated financial positions to justify their estimated size in standard international financial instruments such as foreign exchange, debt, and equity holdings. Moreover, there

Table 3.6   Total Foreign Reserves Global Ranking.

Total Reserves July 2007 (Millions of U.S. Dollars)

Global Rank	Country	2007Q2
1	China	$1,334,590
2	Japan	$897,568
3	Russia	$397,398
4	Korea	$250,628
5	India	$206,579
6	Euro Area	$205,930
7	Brazil	$146,815
8	Singapore	$144,056
9	Hong Kong	$136,267
10	Malaysia	$98,071
11	Algeria	$91,091
12	Mexico	$77,864
13	Thailand	$71,268
14	Libya	$69,153
15	Turkey	$68,375
16	Australia	$65,434
17	Norway	$56,658
18	United States	$55,086
19	Poland	$52,286
20	Indonesia	$49,406
21	Germany	$43,265
22	France	$43,082
23	United Arab Emirates	$42,999
24	Nigeria	$42,627
25	United Kingdom	$42,356
26	Argentina	$41,977
27	Canada	$39,341
28	Switzerland	$38,130
29	Denmark	$31,183
30	Czech Republic	$31,014
31	Romania	$29,663
32	Italy	$29,511
33	Israel	$29,070
34	Egypt	$26,982
35	Sweden	$26,103
36	South Africa	$25,495
37	Ukraine	$25,383
38	Saudi Arabia	$23,908
39	Philippines	$23,455
40	Hungary	$22,774

Source: International Monetary Fund.

Table 3.7   United Arab Emirates and Kuwaiti Financial Data.

Central Bank of the United Arab Emirates (Millions of Dollars)

Monetary Survey

	2000	2007	% Change
Net Domestic Assets	$7,215	$110,384	1430.01%
Foreign Assets	$38,726	$131,472	239.50%
Foreign Liabilities	$7,399	$87,815	1086.87%
Net Foreign Assets	$31,327	$43,657	39.36%
Net Foreign Assets to Net Domestic Assets	434.21%	39.55%	

Bank Assets

	2000	2007	% Change
Total Assets	$81,086	$333,043	310.73%
Total Domestic Assets	$56,182	$279,428	397.36%
Foreign Assets	$24,904	$53,615	115.29%
Foreign Assets to Total Assets	30.71%	16.10%	
Foreign Assets to Total Domestic Assets	44.33%	19.19%	

Central Bank of Kuwait Financial Asset Data (Millions of Dollars)

Domestic Banks

	April 2003	April 2008	% Change
Local Bank Assets	$59,253	$134,101	126.32%
Foreign Banking Assets	$7,831	$27,623	252.74%
Foreign Banking Liabilities	$6,288	$24,081	282.98%
Net Foreign Banking Assets	$1,543	$3,542	129.51%
Net Foreign Assets to Total Bank Assets	2.60%	2.64%	

Sharia Compliant Investment Holdings

	April 2003	April 2008	% Change
Local Assets	$2,917	$25,515	774.62%
Foreign Assets	$644	$5,300	723.25%
Foreign Liabilities	$91	$2,491	2650.47%
Net Foreign Assets	$553	$2,810	407.82%
Net Foreign Assets to Total Bank Assets	18.97%	11.01%	

(*Continued*)

is significant reason to believe that Gulf sovereign wealth funds are investing more in the home economies than internationally (see Table 3.7).

For instance, between April 2003 and April 2008, Kuwaiti asset holdings demonstrated no shift toward foreign assets. Kuwaiti domestic banks and investment foreign asset holdings, while increasing rapidly, did not significantly alter the foreign domestic asset profile. The percentage of total foreign assets to

Table 3.7   (*Continued*)

Conventional Investment Holdings			
Local Assets	$12,522	$35,963	187.20%
Foreign Assets	$7,503	$15,361	104.73%
Foreign Liabilities	$5,279	$8,134	54.09%
Net Foreign Assets	$2,224	$7,227	224.95%
Net Foreign Assets to Total Bank Assets	17.76%	20.10%	
Total			
Total Local Assets	$74,692	$195,579	162%
Total Foreign Assets	$15,978	$48,285	202%
Total Foreign Liabilities	$11,658	$34,706	198%
Total Net Foreign Assets	$4,320	$11,026	155%
Total Foreign Assets to Total Local Assets	21.39%	24.69%	
Net Foreign Assets to Total Local Assets	5.78%	5.64%	

Source: Kuwait Central Bank and Central Bank of the United Arab Emirates.

total local assets increased from 21.4 to 24.7% and net foreign assets to total local assets dropped slightly from 5.8 to 5.6%. The United Arab Emirates exhibit a similar trend. According to the United Arab Emirates Central Bank Monetary Survey, between 2000 and 2007, total foreign assets increased 240% but net domestic assets increased 1430%. Net foreign assets from 2000 to 2007 increased less than 40% for an annual growth rate of less than 4%. The Monetary Survey and Bank Asset data indicate that total and net foreign asset holdings by the United Arab Emirates have risen significantly slower than similar domestic measures and have fallen significantly as a portion of the portfolio of assets held by the United Arab Emirates. The data presented here implies two key points. First, as we would expect given investor home bias, Kuwait and the United Arab Emirates appear to be investing significantly more at home than abroad. Second, estimates of sovereign wealth funds include large amounts of state-owned enterprises to justify their valuations.

Subsidiaries of Middle Eastern sovereign wealth funds are private companies frequently with cross-ownership of other companies owned directly or indirectly by the state, inflating asset estimates. Middle Eastern sovereign wealth fund subsidiaries frequently have cross-shareholdings or joint venture with other state-owned enterprises. For instance, the Abu Dhabi Investment Authority (ADIA) partnered with the state owned Abu Dhabi National Oil Company (ADNOC) to create the International Petroleum Investment Company (IPIC). Estimates of the ADIA include its ownership stake of the IPIC in their asset valuation. However, if the IPIC was a wholly owned subsidiary of the ADNOC rather than a joint venture with ADIA, it would not count as a sovereign wealth fund holding even though Abu Dhabi owns both ADIA and ADNOC. Due to state-centered economies and overlapping shareholdings, the government of a Middle Eastern sovereign wealth fund country will frequently own different sides of a transaction or in some way be involved in most major transactions. The companies owned by sovereign wealth funds tend to focus on investing in the domestic economy and partner with other large government-managed firms in the region. While Middle Eastern sovereign wealth funds make headline-grabbing foreign investments in financial services and tourism, the bulk of their managed investments appear to stay in the natural resources, energy, and gas and oil sector, industries they know well. ADIA subsidiaries have invested heavily in oil, gas, energy, and generation through a large number of subsidiaries spread throughout the world, though the most significant investment focuses on Canadian oil. ADIA has used a lengthy list of subsidiaries so that most news articles demonstrate no indication that the ultimate parent company is a Middle Eastern sovereign wealth fund. Finally, Gulf sovereign wealth funds purchase private securities and use outside managers or funds to placate political sensitivities and avoid accompanying publicity. While rumors run rampant about outside managers and private securities used by Gulf sovereign wealth funds, no reliable information exists to support these claims. However, by working backwards from accepted international financial statistics, no reason exists to believe that Gulf sovereign wealth funds are flooding foreign markets.

3.4. Implications of the Findings

The data presented implies that the facts of how and where countries invest seem boring compared to the hype. Direct and indirect data imply that countries use their sovereign wealth funds primarily to invest in their domestic economies, not make foreign investments. While Norway holds only 2.43% of listed equities in Scandinavian markets, most others invest the majority of their assets in domestic and regional assets. Foreign equities held by the Kuwait Investment Office of London totals only $21.5 billion.[14] Considering the Kuwaiti Investment Authority controls an estimated $250–300 billion, their holdings of foreign equities appears restrained.[15] Singapore follows a similar pattern (see Table 3.8).

Of the listed equities held by Singaporean sovereign wealth funds, 65% are Singaporean companies. Temasek and Government Investment Corporation combined

---

[14]The best available data from Thomson One Banker did not include a known $6 billion investment in Citigroup.
[15]Estimate of Kuwaiti sovereign wealth fund size comes from the IMF and other sources.

Table 3.8   Singaporean Sovereign Wealth Fund Geographic Public Equity Holdings.

	Total	Singapore	Regional	Non-Regional
GIC Total	$12,602	$–	5,989	$6,613
GIC %	100.00%	0.00%	47.52%	52.48%
Temasek Total	$111,622	$80,350	$16,596	$14,676
Temasek %	100.00%	71.98%	14.87%	13.15%
Singapore Total	$124,225	$80,350	22,585	$21,289
Singapore %	100.00%	64.68%	18.18%	17.14%

Source: Thomson One Banker.

hold roughly equal amounts of regional equities and non-regional equities.[16] Singaporean sovereign wealth fund non-regional equity investments total $22 billion. Singaporean and Kuwaiti sovereign wealth funds are estimated to manage sized investment pools. They also seem inclined to invest internationally at similar levels. Furthermore, they appear to be acting as rational investors assuming general market risk that all market participants accept. While investment managers may argue over the specific basket of equities and asset allocation between stocks and bonds, sovereign wealth funds hold broadly diversified baskets of equities balanced with debt securities and some alternative investments. Sovereign wealth fund portfolios appear to act as economically driven investors.

   These findings imply that estimate inconsistency may be a problem when calculating the size of a sovereign wealth fund. What assets are included under the umbrella of sovereign wealth fund holdings is vitally important for both a fair estimation of their size and understanding of their potential impact. Two specific types of estimation mistake occur. First, many estimates fail to properly count state-owned industries. While few would argue that France via EDF and Gaz de France owns a sovereign wealth fund with nearly $300 billion in assets, most seem willing to make that argument when counting the oil, gas, electrical, and airline assets of Middle Eastern and Asian sovereign wealth funds. In fact, most state-owned companies from Europe, Russia, and Japan are in the same industries as the major industrial holdings of Middle Eastern and Asian sovereign wealth fund, yet are not credited as such. Estimates correctly list the Russian sovereign wealth fund as controlling approximately $150 billion in assets, while they omit the more than $200 billion in listed equity the government of Russia owns via its holdings in Gazprom and Rosneft.

---

[16]For our purposes, regional equity for Singapore is defined as Australasia and non-regional equity is everything else.

The different estimation methods are magnified in largely state-owned economies. For instance, due to the number of state-owned companies frequently included in the calculation of Abu Dhabi's sovereign wealth fund, these estimates may better represent some fractional value of national assets. Estimates of the Chinese sovereign wealth fund exclude the value of the many state-owned enterprises even for listed equities. Before estimating the value of sovereign wealth fund, it would help to utilize similar methods across countries and decide on an accounting treatment of state-owned enterprises on sovereign wealth fund valuations.

Second, estimations of the size of sovereign wealth funds use inconsistent methods of accounting for foreign reserves. For instance, while sovereign wealth fund estimates include the more than $200 billion in unlabeled foreign securities held by the Saudi Arabian Monetary Agency, they exclude these funds when calculating the holdings of other central banks not counted as operating a sovereign wealth fund. For instance, China, Japan, and South Korean government-linked entities all hold large amounts of long-term US government and agency debt not counted as sovereign wealth fund holdings. The Saudi Arabian Monetary Agency may be allocating $200 billion to low-risk foreign government and multilateral debt or to high-risk international equities. However, its mere existence should not qualify it for inclusion into a sovereign wealth fund as it probably includes significant amounts of commonly accepted central bank assets or collateral such as government or highly rated debt. The inclusion of any foreign exchange reserves or foreign securities held by central banks into sovereign wealth fund estimates should be treated carefully and as uniformly as possible to provide for fair treatment and comparison across countries. Unless risk-based capital regulations extend to central bank assets, it would seem preferable without good reason to exclude their assets from sovereign wealth fund estimates.

Finally, what defines and qualifies as a sovereign wealth fund? As most countries with sovereign wealth funds appear to be using natural resource earnings to diversify and invest in their domestic economy, should that count as a sovereign wealth fund? Many countries throughout the world hold listed equities of domestic companies (see Table 3.9).

If we count all state-owned listed equities, the total comes in at $1.2 trillion. For instance, France holds listed equities valued at $281 billion primarily in Electricite de France, Gaz de France, France Telecom, Renault, Thales, and Air France among others. Russia is second with $246 billion, with oil and gas giants Gazprom and Roseneft comprising the two largest assets. Italy holds $67 billion worth of listed equities with the two largest holdings, ENI and Enel. However, when excluding domestic companies owned by governments, the listed foreign equity owned by

Table 3.9   State-Owned Listed Equities Worldwide.

Counting Assets of All State Owned Listed EquitiesÉ		Counting Assets of All State Owned FOREIGN Listed EquitiesÉ	
Country	Dollars	Country	Dollars
France	281,301	France	$–
Russia*	246,337	Russia	$–
China**	142,712	China	$7,500
Singapore	123,168	Singapore	$40,957
Norway	122,296	Norway	$119,324
Italy	66,524	Italy	$–
Germany	61,083	Germany	$–
Japan	54,997	Japan	$–
Abu Dhabi	37,117	Abu Dhabi	$5,570
Sweden	21,969	Sweden	$–
Kuwait	18,834	Kuwait	$15,425
Belgium	10,456	Belgium	$–
UK	2,535	UK	$–
Saudi Arabia	709	Saudi Arabia	$709
Total	$1,190,038	Total	$189,486
Non-SWF Country State Owned Listed Equities	$745,202	Non-SWF Country State Owned Listed Equities	$–
Total SWF Listed Equity Assets	$322,540	Total SWF Listed Equity Assets	$189,486
		Does not include investments made by government linked companies	

Source: Thomson One Banker.
*Russia in this table is not counted as a SWF country because the listed equities are not held by the SWF.
**This number represents only listed equities held directly by the Chinese Ministry of Finance and the SWF.

governments drops substantially to under $200 billion with 84.6% of that owned by Norway and Singapore.

3.5.   Conclusion

Sovereign wealth funds have been subject to much hype and little factual analysis. This study has attempted to address the lack of factual analysis by combining both direct and indirect statistics to secure a more reliable understanding of how sovereign wealth funds invest and their impact on international finance and investment. The study comes to three basic conclusions. First, based upon the facts and analysis presented here, there is little reason to believe that they are large relative to international investors or have a large impact on international financial markets. Second, sovereign wealth funds have to date acted as rational economically driven investors diversifying their portfolio by asset class and geographic region. Third, estimates of sovereign wealth fund size are inaccurately calculated by counting assets they exclude from other countries resulting in a misleading understanding of their size. Consequently, it would seem unreasonable to place regulatory or legal burdens on sovereign wealth funds not applied to similar domestic firms. Though countries would be wise to follow the development of sovereign wealth funds, the data does not currently support measures to restrict cross-border investment.

References

Amuzegar, J, 2005, "Iran's Oil Stablization Fund: A Misnomer", *Middle East Economic Survey*, vol. 48, no. 47.

Blundell-Wignall, A, Hu, Y, & Yermo, J, 2008, "Sovereign Wealth Fund and Pension Issues", OECD Working Papers on Insurance and Private Pensions, No. 14, OECD Publishing.

Feng, F, Qian, S, & Tong, W, 2004, "Do Government-Linked Companies Underperform?", *Journal of Banking and Finance*, vol. 28, pp. 2461–2492.

Fotak, V & Megginson, W, 2008, "The Financial Impact of Sovereign Wealth Fund Investments in Listed Companies", unpublished manuscript.

Government Investment Corporation of Singapore, 2010, "About Us Overview", available at http://www.gic.com.sg/about/overview, accessed on 12 November 2010.

Habibi, N, 1998, "Fiscal Response to Fluctuating Oil Revenues in Oil-Exporting Countries of the Middle East", *Economic Research Forum Working Paper*.

International Monetary Fund, 2008, "Sovereign Wealth Funds — A Work Agenda", Monetary and Capital Markets & Policy Development and Review Departments, 29 February.

Kalyuzhnova, Y, & Kaser, M, 2006, "Prudential Management of Hydrocarbon Revenues in Resource Rich Transition Economies", *Post Communist Economies*, vol. 18, pp. 167–187.

Kuwait Investment Authority, 2010, "Objective and Strategy", available at http://www.kia.gov.kw/En/About_KIA/Objective_Strategy/Pages/default.aspx, accessed on 12 November 2010.

Luft, G, 2008, Sovereign Wealth Funds, Oil, and the New World Economic Order. Speech delivered before the House Committee on Foreign Affairs, May 21.

McKinsey Global Institute, 2007, "The New Power Brokers: How Oil, Asia, Hedge Funds, and Private Equity Are Shaping Global Capital Markets", October 2007.

Mehrara, M, & Oskoui, KN, 2007, "The Sources of Macroeconomic Fluctuations in Oil Exporting Countries: a Comparative Study", *Economic Modelling*, vol. 24, pp. 365–379.

Ministry of Finance, 2010, "Investment Management", available at http://www1.minfin.ru/en/nationalwealthfund/management/, accessed on 12 November, 2010.

Morgan Stanley Research Global, 2007, *How Big Could Sovereign Wealth Funds Be by 2015?* 3 May.

Norges Bank, 2008, *Government Pension Fund Global Annual Report 2008*.

OECD, 2008, "Sovereign Wealth Funds and Recipient Country Policies", *OECD Investment Committee Report*, 20 April.

Petersen, C, & Budina, N, 2003, "Governance Framework of Oil Funds: The Case of Azerbaijan and Kazakhstan", prepared for the *Workshop on Petroleum Revenue Management*.

Ramirez, C, & Tan, LH, 2004, "Singapore Inc. Versus the Private Sector: Are Government-Linked Companies Different?", *IMF Staff Papers*, vol. 51, pp. 510–528.

Sam, CY, 2007, "Corporate Governance Reforms in the Post-1997 Asian Crisis: Is There Really a Convergence to the Anglo-American Model?", *Global Economic Review*, vol. 36, pp. 267–285.

Summers, L, 2007, "Sovereign Funds Shake the Logic of Capitalism", *Financial Times* 30 July.

Truman, E, 2007, "Sovereign Wealth Funds: The Need for Greater Transparency and Accountability", Peterson Institute for International Economics Policy Brief PB07–06, August.

Weiss, M, 2008, "Sovereign Wealth Funds: Background and Policy Issues for Congress", *Congressional Research Service Report*, 3 September.

Yeung, HW, 2000, "Local Politics and Foreign Ventures in China's Transition Economy: The Political Economy of Singaporean Investments in China", *Political Geography*, vol. 19, pp. 809–840.

Yeung, HW, 2004, "Strategic Governance and Economic Diplomacy in China: The Political Economy of Government-Linked Companies from Singapore", *East Asia*, Spring 2004, vol. 21, pp. 39–63.

Chapter 4

The Implications of Sovereign Wealth Fund Investment on Capital Markets: A Bottom-Up View

David G. Fernandez

4.1. Introduction

The buzz around sovereign wealth funds has been turned down a notch, but they remain a hot topic. The accusations of sovereign wealth funds having hidden agendas remain, but with the very public losses suffered by some during the recent financial turmoil, such talk has even less credibility. And given that most of those losses were from investments in US, UK, and European financial institutions, hope that sovereign wealth funds would be the saviors of Wall Street has also faded. At its base, four trends continue to keep sovereign wealth funds in focus. First, there is the phenomenal rise of foreign reserves, chiefly among oil-exporting countries as well as some of the current account surplus countries in Asia. Second, there is the relatively recent establishment of large sovereign wealth funds in geopolitically important countries like China and Russia. Third, there are some high-profile investments by foreign government entities in companies in the United States and Europe that are viewed to be of strategic or even national security importance. Lastly, there are the multi-billion dollar investments in some of the world's leading financial institutions followed by subsequent losses and partial divestment.

It is important to remember that sovereign wealth funds are nothing new. Indeed, many of the established funds have been around for several decades. It is the sheer size and growth of these funds, and the unease about their ultimate intentions, that have raised a number of issues about their potential impact on financial markets, competitiveness, corporate governance, and even national security. This chapter provides some background to sovereign wealth funds. It analyzes their potential market impact and the related political debate. Although the label "sovereign wealth fund" is used as though they are a homogeneous group, there are huge differences between the more than 50 funds in terms of purpose, size, funding source, structure, degree of transparency, and asset allocation.

Sovereign wealth fund assets are highly concentrated, with the top ten funds accounting for 80% of total assets. About two-thirds of sovereign wealth funds are commodity based. With around $3 trillion in total assets, sovereign wealth funds have become an important investor group, bigger than hedge funds and private equity combined. Despite recent losses, sovereign wealth funds will grow further. However, the past year has shown that growth projections can easily be overstated. Sovereign wealth fund growth is largely the result of oil price movements and Asian surplus savings. How these forces play out going forward needs to be analyzed on a country-by-country basis, just like the return that each sovereign wealth fund is likely to generate in the future. The bottom-up analysis used here shows that sovereign wealth fund assets are likely to continue to grow, but are unlikely to surge into double-digit trillion dollar figures over the next five years.

It is believed that, despite the market downturn, sovereign wealth funds are likely to increase in size by 50–130% in the next five years, raising questions about their potential impact on the relative pricing between bonds and equities. But sovereign wealth funds' share in either market is too small and unlikely to change significantly. Moreover, their investments are well diversified. This stands in contrast to the investment strategies developed by central banks, which are highly concentrated around the much smaller government bond market.

Sovereign wealth funds have become more active in primary and merger and acquisition transactions and this trend is likely to continue despite recent losses in these sectors. Political issues aside, this is not bad news since sovereign wealth funds are likely to be stable providers of long-term funding. The largest growth and asset allocation impact will probably be in alternative investments. Some sovereign wealth funds have large exposures to alternatives, especially private equity, and more will join, which is likely to make alternatives the biggest growth area for sovereign wealth funds. Given their absolute size and relatively limited resources, efficiency is a legitimate concern. Not surprisingly, the majority of sovereign wealth funds use external managers to fill the skill gap and diversify investment risks. Financial market support from sovereign wealth fund growth, however, seems unlikely to ease political concerns. Progress on "best practices" for sovereign wealth funds and for recipient countries is encouraging. Even though some key countries may resist the IMF-led effort on best practices for sovereign wealth funds, their actual actions in terms of disclosure practices, investment approach, and market behavior, are more in line with best practices than the rhetoric suggests.

4.2. Sources and Purpose

Sovereign wealth funds are broadly defined as special government asset management vehicles that invest public funds in a wide range of financial instruments. Unlike central banks, which focus more on liquidity and safe-keeping of foreign reserves, most sovereign wealth funds have the mandate to enhance returns. They are allowed to invest in riskier asset classes, including equity and alternative assets, such as private equity, property, hedge funds, and commodities. It is not always easy to differentiate between "pure" sovereign wealth funds and other forms of public funds, such as conventional public-sector pension funds or state-owned enterprises. For example, it is not entirely clear why Norway's Government Pension Fund and Australia's Future Fund are usually classified as sovereign wealth funds, while the Stichting Pension Fund (ABP) in the Netherlands and the California Public Employees' Retirement System (CalPERS) are viewed as conventional pension funds.

Sovereign wealth funds are, however, usually distinguished by their funding sources and purpose. In terms of funding, three sources stand out. Commodity sources are largely oil and gas related, although some funds are also based on revenues from metals and minerals (e.g. Chile). Most commodity revenues are generated either directly through state-owned companies or commodity taxes. Commodity revenues are viewed as "real wealth" as they typically have no corresponding liability on the government's balance sheet. Fiscal sources can come from fiscal surpluses, proceeds from property sales and privatizations or transfers from the government's main budget to a special purpose vehicle. Most fiscal sources are "real wealth," although some have liabilities. China, for example, is funding the transfer of foreign reserves from the central bank to the China Investment Corporation by issuing government bonds. Lastly, foreign reserves represent often "borrowed wealth" as the reserve build-up in many countries stems from sterilized foreign exchange interventions, in which case the central bank issues interest bearing liquidity notes to fund the interventions and mop up the excess liquidity. However, part of the foreign reserves may also represent "real wealth," thanks to asset appreciation and the accumulation of interest income. The share of foreign reserves managed by sovereign wealth funds is typically viewed as excess reserves, as it exceeds the portion of foreign reserves deemed necessary for the conduct of foreign exchange policy and precautionary reasons.

The classification based on purpose usually can be broken down into four types of funds. First are the revenue stabilization funds, designed to cushion the impact of volatile commodity revenues on the government's fiscal balance and the overall economy. Second are the future generation (savings) funds, which are meant to invest revenues or wealth over longer periods of time. In some cases, these funds are earmarked for particular purposes, such as covering future public pension liabilities. Next are holding funds which manage their governments' direct investments in companies. These may be domestic state-owned enterprises and private companies as well as private companies abroad. Holding funds typically support the government's overall development strategy. Lastly, generic sovereign wealth funds often cover one or several of the previous three purposes, but their size tends to be so large that the main objective becomes optimizing the overall risk-return profile of the existing wealth. These funds often manage part of the "excess" foreign reserves. Table 4.1 provides some typical examples of the four main fund purposes and their funding sources.

In reality, however, the current universe of sovereign wealth funds cannot be neatly summarized as suggested in the above matrix. Besides the above-mentioned four main purposes, some sovereign wealth funds serve a number of other motives. For commodity-based economies, sovereign wealth funds help diversify the revenue base and shield the domestic non-commodity sector from the risk of sharp currency revaluations, so-called "Dutch disease." Sovereign wealth funds also help enforce fiscal discipline and transparency, especially where funding and spending is governed by specific rules. This role is particularly important for newly emerging commodity economies that historically lacked fiscal discipline and transparency. A few countries use their sovereign wealth funds as catalysts to promote the development of the domestic financial sector. Finally, some countries use their investment pools to pursue strategic interests by investing in specific sectors that are viewed as important for the overall economic development of the country (e.g. skills transfer).

Sovereign wealth funds differ in many other aspects besides objectives and funding sources. With regard to ownership and governance, all sovereign wealth funds belong to the public sector, but some are directly owned, while others are statutory entities. All sovereign wealth funds have a board, but some are entirely government controlled, while others have mixed representations from the government and private experts and a few are even independent from the government yet answerable to the legislature (e.g. Australia's Future Fund).

When it comes to disclosure, standards vary between full transparency (e.g. Norway) and absolute secrecy. However, disclosure is becoming more accepted as best practice and some notoriously secretive funds have started to reveal information about their fund size, performance, and basic asset allocation. The more

Table 4.1   Examples of Sovereign Wealth Fund Sources and Purposes.

Purposes/sources	Commodity Revenues	Fiscal Sources	Foreign Reserves
Revenue stabilization	Russia: Reserve Fund Kuwait: Reserve Fund Mexico: Oil Stabilization Fund		
Future generations/public pensions	Russia: National Welfare Fund Kuwait: Future Generation Fund Norway: Government Pension Fund	Australia: Future Fund New Zealand: Super Fund	
Management of government holdings	Abu Dhabi: Mubadala Saudi Arabia: Public Investment Fund	Singapore: Temasek Malaysia: Khazanah Vietnam: State Capital Investment Corporation	China: Bank holdings managed by China Investment Corporation
Wealth or risk/return optimization	Abu Dhabi Investment Authority Brunei Investment Authority Qatar Investment Authority	Singapore: Government Investment Corporation	Singapore: Foreign reserves managed by Government Investment Corporation Korea: Foreign reserves managed by Korea Investment Corporation China: Foreign reserves managed by China Investment Corporation

Source: JP Morgan.

recently launched funds also show a higher degree of transparency than some of the long-established funds.

Regarding the institutional structure of sovereign wealth funds, the main difference is between sovereign wealth funds that act as separate entities with their own balance sheet (e.g. Abu Dhabi Investment Authority; Temasek) and those that act as agent for one or several public-sector entities (e.g. Government Investment Corporation; Korea Investment Corporation). In some cases, the central bank acts as the agent that manages the assets of the sovereign wealth fund (e.g. Norway; Saudi Arabia Monetary Authority).

The asset allocation itself depends partly on the purpose, that is, stabilization funds tend to invest in liquid and less risky instruments, while future generation funds tend to invest in higher-yielding asset classes. In total, the largest share of sovereign wealth fund assets is invested in public securities (bonds and stocks), but the share of alternatives (private equity, property, hedge funds, and commodities) is rising. The majority of sovereign wealth fund assets are invested in foreign markets, but there are notable exceptions of funds that invest partially or largely in the domestic market (e.g. Temasek; Khazanah). More recently, since the onset of the global financial and economic turmoil, some sovereign wealth funds (e.g. Abu Dhabi Investment Authority; Qatar Investment Authority; Kuwait Investment Authority) focus more on stabilizing their domestic economies, including buying shares of local banks and/or making deposits in local banks to boost liquidity.

In theory, sovereign wealth funds can choose their own currency allocation. In practice, many sovereign wealth funds are constrained by their country's foreign exchange policy regime. While many countries target the dollar in some shape or form, their sovereign wealth fund's ability to diversify into other currencies is limited. Most sovereign wealth funds have performance benchmarks, which are used in different ways. Some have overall portfolio benchmarks (index or total return), while others use separate benchmarks for each asset class. The majority of benchmark indices are based on market indices, but many are customized. In the past, most sovereign wealth funds tried to outperform their benchmark indices, but a number of funds are moving to passive benchmark tracking, especially in equity. A few funds are also using portable alpha strategies.

Depending on their size and resources, some funds perform many activities internally and outsource only some operations (e.g. Government Investment Corporation). Others outsource essentially all front and back office operations and focus entirely on the strategic asset allocation, manager selection, and basic control functions (e.g. Australian Future Fund; New Zealand Superannuation Fund).

4.3. Current Size and Future Growth: A Bottom-Up Approach

Part of the reason for the intense interest in sovereign wealth funds relates to their size. Estimating the aggregated size of all sovereign wealth funds is not without difficulty. While some sovereign wealth funds provide timely updates of their total assets under management, others, including some of the largest funds, provide little if any information.

Using a broad definition of sovereign wealth funds, but excluding conventional public pension funds which are already paying benefits (such as ABP and CalPERS), there are currently more than 50 funds in operation with total assets under management estimated to be between $2.9–3.5 trillion (see Table 4.2). Of the total size, nearly 20% of the funds are also included in official foreign reserves and should not be double-counted when calculating the combined size of official reserves and sovereign wealth fund assets. Furthermore, roughly 10% of sovereign wealth fund assets are held in local domestic assets (often state enterprises) and should not be viewed as international financial assets.

Sovereign wealth fund assets are highly concentrated. The top ten funds account for about 80% of all sovereign wealth fund assets while roughly two-thirds of all sovereign wealth fund assets are held by commodity exporting countries. East Asia and the Middle East, for example, account for around three-quarters of all sovereign

Table 4.2   Sovereign Wealth Fund Assets.*

	USD Billion	% of Total SWF Assets
Total SWF assets	3,370–3,900	100
Of which:		
Top ten SWFs	2,622–3,097	78–79
Commodity funds	2,084–2,547	62–65
East Asia	1,188–1,251	32–35
Middle East	1,184–1,644	35–42
Europe & Central Asia	~ 754	19–22
Africa	136–142	~ 4
Americas	104	~ 3
Memo items		
*Official reserves***	*8,592*	
Hedge funds and private equity	*4,200*	
Private pension, insurance and mutual funds	*72,500*	
Global financial assets	*178,000*	

Source: JP Morgan.
*Estimates are mostly based on 2009 year-end figures, but also include some mid-2010 and early 2009 figures.

wealth fund assets. Without doubt, sovereign wealth funds are large players among the new financial power brokers. Total sovereign wealth fund assets are larger than hedge fund and private equity assets combined and account for about half the size of all official foreign reserves. Yet, they are still relatively small compared to the overall investor and market universe. Sovereign wealth fund assets account for less than 3% of global financial assets and less than 6% of the assets of all private pension, insurance and mutual funds.

While coming from a relatively small base in aggregate, sovereign wealth funds will undoubtedly grow and gain more significance. Just a year ago, consensus forecasts put the annual growth rate of total sovereign wealth fund assets at about 20% for the next five to ten years. Strikingly, this rate was about the same as that of official reserves over the last five years. The peril of using past reserve growth as a guide to sovereign wealth fund growth has been made clear with the recent global financial and economic turmoil. The rise in sovereign wealth funds has much to do with the macro drivers behind the rise in foreign reserves, in particular the large current account imbalances between the United States and the surplus economies in Asia and the oil exporting countries (see Figure 4.1). However, the rebalancing of global current accounts makes it clear that analysts, who were forecasting 20% annual growth on a multi-year horizon, were making, explicitly or implicitly, an incorrect assumption that global current account imbalances would consistently grow further.

A comprehensive, bottom-up, forward projection of sovereign wealth fund assets should be built on scenarios around the following factors: (a) the oil price;

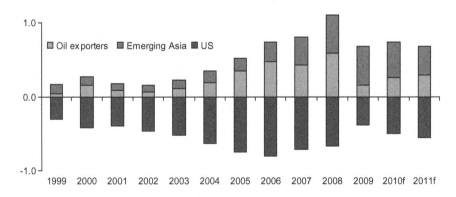

Fig. 4.1   Current Account Balances (USD billion).

Source: JP Morgan and IMF.

(b) the foreign exchange policy of surplus countries; (c) current account dynamics in the United States and its main trade partners in Asia; (d) the allocation of new reserves or other surpluses to individual sovereign wealth funds; (e) the establishment of new sovereign wealth funds; and (f) the rate of return.

Recent research undertaken by JP Morgan (JP Morgan 2008), explored the implications of two basic scenarios: one where oil prices range between $100 and $125 per barrel over the next five years, causing current account surpluses in oil exporting countries to rise as much as 50%; and a second where a US recession causes oil prices to fall to a range of $50 to $70 per barrel, where for many countries there would be few excess savings to be channeled into sovereign wealth funds.

For the surplus economies in Asia, key factors are the current account dynamic in the United States and their own current exchange policy. Given this, JP Morgan (2008) then considered two additional scenarios: one where a relatively quick recovery leaves the US current account deficit relatively unchanged at the 2007 level of around 5% of GDP (a projection consistent with the higher oil price scenario) and where the Asian surplus countries do not let their currencies appreciate faster; second, recession and a drop in oil prices squeeze the US current account deficit to about 2% of GDP, while Asian countries allow their currencies to appreciate faster. In the first scenario, Asian current account surpluses remain broadly unchanged. In the second scenario, Asian current account surpluses drop by roughly 50%.

With foreign reserve holdings exceeding reserve adequacy requirements in most countries that have sovereign wealth funds, it is reasonable to assume that a larger share of any incremental balance of payments surplus will be allocated to sovereign wealth funds. However, it would be misleading to apply a general formula or assume that central banks will reduce reserves and shift those funds to sovereign wealth funds. In the Middle East, for example, most sovereign wealth funds already get all surpluses, with official reserves staying at minimum adequacy levels. In Russia, growth of the Stabilization Fund is directly linked to the tax revenues from oil exports. In China, the decision to move reserves from the central bank to the China Investment Corporation is completely discretionary, and how soon and how much will be transferred next is likely to depend greatly on how well the China Investment Corporation performs.

Lastly, in terms of forecasting rates of return, using historic returns of leading sovereign wealth funds (such as Singapore's Government Investment Corporation and Temasek, and Norway) as benchmarks for all funds is not representative. While total sovereign wealth fund assets are relatively balanced between fixed income and equity and some residual exposure to alternatives, there are vast differences on a fund-by-fund basis, which get compounded by the size differences. In a bullish scenario, those funds with a high allocation to equity and alternatives are likely to push average returns close to double digits. But the opposite is likely as well, especially in the near term, which could result in lower, single-digit returns.

Summarizing the impact of these different factors on total sovereign wealth fund assets produces two main scenarios: (a) low inflows and returns; and (b) high inflows and returns. Given the differences in size, funding and asset allocation, these scenarios should be applied to each individual sovereign wealth fund and not the total of all sovereign wealth fund assets. In this analysis, inflow and return scenarios are projected for each fund, based on its specific circumstances and initial size estimates.

Recapping JP Morgan (2008) where the individual sovereign wealth fund projections were aggregated, two basic outcomes emerged. First, in the low inflow/return scenario, new inflows over the next five years total $0.7 trillion (which would be less than half the inflows over the last five years) and the average return is around 4%. Based on this and starting from the low end of the initial size estimates, total sovereign wealth fund assets rise on average close to 9% per year to reach $4.4 trillion in 2013. Secondly, in the high inflow/return scenario, new inflows are over three times larger than in the low inflow/return scenario (or only slightly larger than over the last five years) and average returns are close to 8%. Coming off a higher initial assets-under-management estimate, total sovereign wealth fund assets will rise by about 18% per year to come slightly above $8 trillion by 2013.

Based on our calculations, the conclusion of JP Morgan (2008) was that the consensus growth forecast for sovereign wealth fund assets of 20% per year was optimistic. Clearly that view has been vindicated. However, in hindsight, even though our growth estimates were more conservative than the consensus, we can now see that our low-case scenario was not low enough. In particular, our forecast for assets under management in 2012 in a low inflow/low return scenario is now down to $4 trillion compared to the $5 trillion forecast made in JP Morgan (2008).

Not only has the global economic and financial turmoil of the past year led to declines in assets under management, but it seems reasonable to assume that looking ahead, there are likely to be lower returns for sovereign wealth funds over the next several years across asset classes due to the likelihood of a broadly less benign investment environment (See Table 4.3 and Figure 4.2).

Table 4.3   Sovereign Wealth Fund Growth Scenarios.

	Assets Under Management 2009 (USD tn)	Inflows 2010–2014 (USD tn)	Average Return (%) 2010–2014	Assets Under Management 2014 (USD tn)	Compound Annual Growth Rate (%) 2009–2014
Low inflow/ return scenario	3.3	0.6	5.4	4.9	7.9
High inflow/ return scenario	3.9	2.6	6.4	8.9	18.0

Source: JP Morgan.

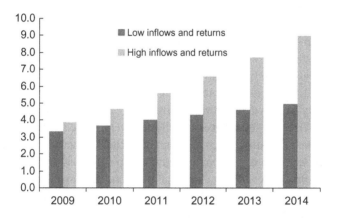

Fig. 4.2   Sovereign Wealth Fund Asset Projections (USD trillion).

Source: JP Morgan.

4.4.   Asset Allocation and Market Impact

While our forecasts of sovereign wealth fund assets in the mid-to-high single-digit trillion dollar figure may be modest compared to some other projections, it is still large in absolute terms and raises questions about sovereign wealth funds potential market impact. The popular view is that the rise of sovereign wealth funds will have distorting market implications. First, sovereign wealth funds are believed to increase the overall demand for risky assets and with that drive down their risk premia. Second, part of the growth in sovereign wealth funds is seen to come from a reduction in central bank reserves. This expected substitution effect is believed to reduce the demand for government bonds and drive up bond yields. Furthermore, there is the concern that sovereign wealth funds may abandon their traditional passive approach and become more active as both traders and shareholders.

The following analysis addresses some of these concerns by taking a closer look at current and likely future asset allocation of sovereign wealth funds. In summary, the analysis suggests that sovereign wealth funds are unlikely to have a significant distorting impact on financial markets. First, even if sovereign wealth fund assets triple over the next five to ten years, they will remain relatively small compared to the financial universe, accounting for no more than 3–4% of global financial assets. Second, while sovereign wealth funds have the mandate to take more risk and target higher returns than central banks, they remain public-sector institutions and are unlikely to turn into hedge funds and private-equity firms that engage in speculative trading and use extensive leverage. Indeed, most sovereign wealth funds will probably behave more like large institutional asset managers that have long-term horizons and broadly diversified investment portfolios.

Analyzing the investment approach of sovereign wealth funds is not without difficulty as only roughly half of all sovereign wealth funds disclose their asset allocation. Still, some basic estimates of the overall asset allocation between fixed income (mostly bonds but also some cash), public equity, and alternatives are feasible (Table 4.4). These show that essentially all sovereign wealth funds are in fixed income, of which the bulk is in government bonds and agencies. Some funds also hold credit products, ranging from high-grade corporates, asset-backed securities and mortgage-backed securities to high-yield and emerging market debt (both hard currency and local currency markets). Nearly three-quarters of all sovereign wealth funds are in public equity, which consist of mostly OECD equity markets and some emerging markets. In some cases, there are large individual stock holdings. Nearly half of all sovereign wealth funds are in alternatives, with the bulk in private equity,

Table 4.4   Sovereign Wealth Fund Current and Future Asset Allocation.

	Fixed Income	Public Equity	Alternatives
Current			
% of all SWFs	100	76	49
% of all SWF assets	45–50	40–45	9–11
Future			
% of all SWFs	100	80–100	60–80
% of all SWF assets	20–30	55–60	15–20
US endowment funds (% of assets equally weighted)	25	58	17

Source: JP Morgan.

followed by property and hedge funds, but limited exposure to commodities. In terms of total sovereign wealth fund assets, 35–40% are in fixed income, 50–55% are in public equity, and 8–10% are in alternatives. These figures are biased towards the bigger sovereign wealth funds, which have larger holdings of public equity. The average sovereign wealth fund has a higher fixed income allocation (more than 50%) and a lower public equity allocation (about 40%).

The stated intentions of most sovereign wealth funds suggest that this broad asset allocation is likely to change over the next five to ten years, with more funds moving into public equity and, especially, alternatives. Role models are sovereign wealth funds like Singapore's Government Investment Corporation, which is believed to have a portfolio consisting of 30% in fixed income, 50% in public equity, and 20% in alternatives; and Norway's Government Pension Fund, which last year increased its equity allocation from 40% to 60% and announced that it will soon start investing in some alternatives. But there are also role models outside the sovereign wealth fund spectrum, like the US endowment funds, which over the last ten years successfully increased their allocations to alternatives.

So, what impact will this have on each asset class? Intuitively, one would think that this will be negative for bonds, positive for public equity, and very positive for alternatives. A closer look, however, suggests that such allocation shift may only have meaningful implications for alternatives and little impact on the broader bond and equity markets.

4.4.1. *Fixed Income*

Sovereign wealth funds currently hold $1.3–1.6 trillion in fixed-income assets (a small fraction of that is in cash). This is about 1.6–1.9% of the global debt market (Table 4.5). Depending on the degree to which sovereign wealth funds reduce their fixed income allocations, as well as the growth in underlying sovereign wealth

Table 4.5   Share of Sovereign Wealth Fund Fixed-Income Assets in Global Debt Market.

	2009	2014		
	45–50% Fixed-Income Allocation	20% Fixed-Income Allocation	30% Fixed-Income Allocation	Average
Low assets under management scenario	1.8%	0.8%	1.3%	1.1%
High assets under management scenario	2.0%	1.3%	2.0%	1.7%
Average	1.9%	1.1%	1.6%	1.4%

Source: JP Morgan.

fund assets and debt markets, sovereign wealth funds share in global fixed income markets will vary between 0.8–2.0% by the year 2013. On average, however, the share will decline slightly over the next five years to around 1.4%.

While sovereign wealth funds are expected to reduce their overall fixed-income market share, the decline should not be expected to be large. Furthermore, a negative substitution effect is also unlikely as the majority of central banks will probably not reduce their reserves and, thus, bond holdings. In the Middle East, official reserves are already small as all surplus funds go into sovereign wealth funds. For the large reserve holders in Asia, which are also the largest holders of government bonds, it seems more likely that additional reserves will be channeled into sovereign wealth funds, but that existing reserves stay in place. Indeed, an overall reduction in official reserves seems only likely if balance-of-payment dynamics reverse and net inflows become net outflows. But sovereign wealth fund assets are unlikely to grow in such a scenario.

In contrast to central banks, which focus their investments on the much smaller market of liquid government bonds, sovereign wealth funds are likely to diversify their fixed-income portfolios. Corporate bonds, emerging market debt, and mortgage-related securities will probably form a growing part of many sovereign wealth funds' fixed-income portfolios over time. Thus, sovereign wealth funds may not add much to the demand pressure on government bonds from central banks, which would be a welcome relief.

4.4.2. Public Equity

Sovereign wealth funds currently hold $1.4–1.8 trillion in public equity. This is about 4.4–5.4% of the global equity market. Depending on the degree to which sovereign wealth funds change their equity allocations, as well as the growth in underlying sovereign wealth fund assets and stock markets, sovereign wealth funds share in global equity markets will vary between 5.4–8.5% by the year 2013 (Table 4.6). On average, the share of sovereign wealth funds in global equity markets will probably be close to two percentage points higher in five years than it is now, which seems too small an increase to have any significant impact on pricing. In essence, the total exposure of sovereign wealth funds to public equity is already very large. Especially, most of the large funds have very sizable equity portfolios and are unlikely to increase their share further. Thus, smaller funds moving into stocks or increasing their equity portfolios will not make a huge difference.

Having said that, individual funds will probably have more impact on single transactions and stocks. This is despite instances of second-guessing of equity investments (e.g. those of the last few years in US and European financial

Table 4.6   Share of Sovereign Wealth Fund Public Equity Assets in Global Stock Markets.

	2009	2014		
	40–45% Public Equity Allocation	55% Public Equity Allocation	60% Public Equity Allocation	Average
Low assets under management scenario	3.0%	4.2%	4.5%	4.4%
High assets under management scenario	3.5%	6.0%	6.5%	6.3%
Average	3.3%	5.1%	5.5%	5.3%

Source: JP Morgan.

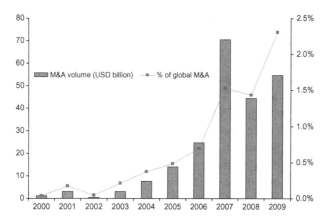

Fig. 4.3   Sovereign Wealth Fund Merger and Acquisition Volumes.
Source: Dealogic and JP Morgan.

institutions by both the public and government officials in countries such as China and Singapore). This will be particularly visible in primary and merger and acquisition transactions where sovereign wealth funds will increasingly function as the lead or anchor investor. A few years ago, sovereign wealth funds did essentially not participate in primary and merger and acquisition deals, but activity picked up in 2006–2007 and reached new heights in late 2007 and early 2008. Such activity has dropped sharply in the past year, together with the global decline in mergers and acquisitions (Figure 4.3).

4.4.3.   *Alternatives*

Given sovereign wealth funds growing risk appetite and higher return targets, alternatives are likely to experience the largest allocation increase. Sovereign wealth

Table 4.7   Share of Sovereign Wealth Fund Alternative Assets in Total Alternative Sector.

	2009	2014		
	9–11% Alternative Allocation	15% Alternative Allocation	20% Alternative Allocation	Average
Low assets under management scenario	7.5%	10.2%	13.6%	11.9%
High assets under management scenario	8.7%	16.0%	16.0%	16.0%
Average	8.1%	13.1%	14.8%	14.0%

Source: JP Morgan.

funds currently hold roughly $150–180 billion in alternatives (Table 4.7). This is about 3.7–4.5% of total alternatives. Of that, at least half is private equity. Especially some of the Gulf funds have sizable private equity portfolios. Hedge fund exposure has been smaller, but is on the rise. Sovereign wealth funds have little commodities exposure, but several have significant property holdings, often consisting of large direct investments. Depending on the degree to which sovereign wealth funds increase their allocation to alternatives as well as the growth in underlying sovereign wealth fund assets and the alternative sector, sovereign wealth funds share in total alternatives will rise to at least 10%, possibly approaching 17% by the end of 2013. On average, the sovereign wealth fund share in alternatives is likely to triple over five years to about 13%.

The main beneficiaries of the increased allocation by sovereign wealth funds to alternatives are set to be private equity firms and hedge funds. These managers offer skills, resources, and expertise that would be difficult for most sovereign wealth funds to develop on their own. Already, several major sovereign wealth funds have forged strategic relationships with some of the leading hedge funds and private equity firms. These include investments by sovereign wealth funds in the general partnership of private equity firms and hedge funds, which give them better performance participation.

The increased investments by sovereign wealth funds will be welcome news for private equity and hedge fund managers, as it will boost fees, but it is not clear whether this will have a lasting impact on the direction of the underlying markets in which these funds operate. True, more funding from sovereign wealth funds will allow private equity firms and hedge funds to operate on a somewhat larger scale, but their impact is more likely to be felt in terms of individual transactions and trading activity rather than the overall market direction. There is also talk that sovereign wealth funds may provide private equity firms with debt funding for leveraged buyout deals, replacing some of the bank financing. However, this would require the very type of credit skills and expertise that sovereign wealth funds are lacking.

It is similarly unlikely that sovereign wealth funds will have a large aggregated effect on the property market, but they may drive up prices of particular developments. Least clear is what impact sovereign wealth funds will have on commodities. The oil producers have little reason to invest in energy commodities (although a few Gulf funds are investing in exploration and refining projects in other parts of the world), but may be interested in metals, especially precious, and soft commodities. For the large funds in Asia, energy commodities may be most interesting. Despite much speculation, however, very little has happened so far, which may suggest that many sovereign wealth funds view commodities as too speculative and current prices as too high. So, the overall impact on commodity markets may be negligible, but that would not rule out some Gulf funds going on long agriculture indices and some Asian funds overweighting energy indices.

More broadly, a big beneficiary of the sovereign wealth fund growth will be the asset management industry (both traditional portfolio manager as well as alternative managers). Already, roughly 60% of sovereign wealth funds use external managers, with about half of all sovereign wealth fund assets managed externally. Most of the external mandates are equity and alternatives. Going forward, the share of externally managed sovereign wealth fund assets is set to rise as more funds move into equity and alternatives. But the biggest boost will come from the underlying asset growth. The high degree of outsourcing is not only good news for the asset management industry, but probably has also a stabilizing market impact. Sovereign wealth funds are not immune to making mistakes, but they diversify these risks by outsourcing large pools of their assets to many professional managers.

Summarizing, it seems reasonable to conclude that the rise of sovereign wealth funds, although significant, is unlikely to have material distorting effects on overall markets. This is because sovereign wealth funds will remain small relative to the market universe in which they operate. Second, they will diversify their investments across a wider range of assets and managers. This stands in contrast to central banks which focus mostly on the liquid and low-risk markets. Conversely, one could argue that sovereign wealth funds may have a stabilizing effect on markets. They are long-term investors with stable funding sources that are unlikely to be withdrawn quickly (low redemption risk). Second, as public-sector entities, sovereign wealth funds are unlikely to engage in speculative activities and use much, if any, leverage. Instead, risk management will be high on their agenda and be reflected in diversified portfolios. Combined with their higher return targets, this means that sovereign wealth funds are likely to be stable providers of long-term risk capital. Indeed, sovereign wealth funds have not been following the mainstream and compounding volatility in the current market crisis.

4.5. Friend or Enemy?

Even though it appears that sovereign wealth funds are positive and stabilizing for markets thus far, their public policy discussion is still dominated by concerns that their activities need to be restricted or more closely regulated. These concerns focus on the motives and operating style of sovereign wealth funds. From recipient countries, three main issues have emerged behind this unease.

First, the acquisition of private companies by foreign government entities raises questions about the impact of those investments on the recipient country's competitiveness and efficiency. Indeed, some industrialized countries question why they should privatize state-owned enterprises only to see them snapped up by foreign government entities. Second, since sovereign wealth funds are generally not subject to the disclosure standards that apply to regulated investors, the concern is that this lack of transparency leaves little insight of their motives and portfolios. Third, sovereign wealth funds may not make investments with the commercial intention of maximizing returns, but rather pursue the political or foreign policy interests of their countries. This then raises national security issues such as giving foreign government control or access to defense-related technologies. For their part, sovereign wealth funds have said they voluntarily restricted their investment choices to avoid criticism, while others have forthrightly complained about being singled out unfairly. One prominent sovereign wealth fund manager, for example, is quoted as saying "the consequences of imposing regulations on sovereign wealth funds will result in an adverse impact on global capital flows. [...] These regulations will not solve or prevent any future financial crisis" (Gillespie 2008). Another high-profile sovereign wealth fund official said a code of conduct for sovereign wealth funds would only "hurt feelings" (CBS 2008).

Despite such misgivings, sovereign wealth funds have generally supported the IMF-led initiative to establish a set of generally accepted principles and practices (GAPP) for sovereign wealth funds. After meetings in Norway, Singapore, and Chile, 26 countries with sovereign wealth funds in October 2008 adopted the so-called "Santiago Principles." They are intended to demonstrate that sovereign wealth funds are properly set up and that investment decisions are made based on an economic and financial basis. Among the 24 principles included in the GAPP is the provision of evidence that investment decisions are aimed at maximizing risk-adjusted financial returns, and to publicly disclose any investment decisions otherwise made. Sovereign wealth funds are also to publicly disclose their policy purpose, their source of funding, their financial information (to demonstrate economic and financial orientation), and their general approach to risk management. Highlighting the difficulty analysts still have in gathering information on sovereign wealth funds, the GAPP says that assets and investment performance of sovereign wealth funds would be reported, but only to the owner, and not necessarily to the public. However, sovereign wealth funds are also to publish an annual report and an audited financial statement.

As for recipient country guidelines, in April, the OECD published its report on recipient guidelines. The OECD's approach calls on recipient countries to apply the same principles to investments from sovereign wealth funds as they do to any investments from foreign entities. In particular, the OECD emphasizes the key principles of non-discrimination (i.e. treat foreign investors not less favorably than domestic investors) and transparency (i.e. make restrictions on foreign investment clear and accessible). The OECD investment instruments also call for progressive, unilateral liberalization, which means that members commit to the gradual elimination of restrictions on capital movements, without condition of reciprocity, and to not introducing new restrictions (known as "standstill").

However, the key issue when it comes to recipient guidelines is how to deal with national security concerns. On this score, the OECD adopts a very broad set of principles that boil down to each country determining when an investment by a foreign entity should be deemed a national security concern and how that investment should be dealt with. Specifically, each country has a right to determine what is necessary to protect its national security (self-judging). As to the application of the core OECD investment instrument of non-discrimination, if a country feels application of this principle does not adequately safeguard its national security, then any specific measures should be based on the specific circumstances of the individual investment.

As these efforts at the macro level, led by the IMF for the sovereign wealth funds and the OECD for recipients, proceed, it is useful to keep in mind the individual stories of the motivations and investment practices. First, it should be recognized that the existence of sovereign wealth funds and their purpose are well justified. Development experts widely agree that emerging economies with large commodity sectors are best off if they stabilize volatile commodity revenues and spread the commodity wealth over several generations, rather than fueling a domestic investment and consumption bubble. Concerning the surplus economies in Asia, especially China, the principle issue is not sovereign wealth funds, but the industrial, trade, and currency policies that generate the surpluses. These economies need to reform their domestic goods and financial markets and liberalize their currencies.

However, most experts agree that this should happen gradually. Sovereign wealth funds remain an efficient way to manage the excess savings in the meantime for future generations and liabilities.

Second, although not all funds comply with the same standards, well ahead of the publication of the Santiago Principles, some basic best practices concerning governance, transparency, and accountability have emerged organically. And increasingly, other sovereign wealth funds are starting to adopt them. For example, most newly launched entities are based on legislation that defines the basic mandate of the fund, have a board of government representatives and independent experts that decides on the basic investment policy and is answerable to the legislature, and publish audited financials. Examples of recently launched sovereign wealth funds that comply with those standards include the Australian Future Fund, Korea's Investment Corporation, Russia's Stabilization Fund, and the Chilean Pension Reserve Fund.

China has yet to disclose what standards it will adopt, but the openness in which it conducted its recent high-profile investments and the way it tenders its mandates for external managers suggest that transparency and accountability are high on the agenda. Some of the recent changes among the long-established funds are also encouraging. In Singapore, Temasek is morphing into a public corporation with audited financials and the Government's Investment Corporation reported at its 25th anniversary for the first time on its long-term performance and basic asset allocation. In the Middle East, the Kuwait Investment Authority reported last year for the first time on its asset size and performance, and the Qatar Investment Authority revealed its currency allocation.

Lastly, while the tenor of the public policy debate focuses on ways that sovereign wealth funds might behave irresponsibly relative to other investors, it should be noted that none in the sector has participated in any hostile takeover. Moreover, the recent large-scale investments in financial institutions have been done with a high degree of transparency. If at all, it is not sovereign wealth funds but large state-owned enterprises and their foreign investment ambitions that should be the focus of scrutiny. Sovereign wealth funds are not set up to (and have little interest in) actively manage the operations of portfolio companies. State-owned enterprises on the other hand, have a high interest to get involved in the operations of the companies they buy to integrate them in their own operations and make them part of their overall business and development strategy.

To encourage more progress in these directions, industrialized countries are best advised to engage sovereign wealth funds, and their governments not to demonize them. Trying to address these concerns through capital flow restrictions is likely to fuel protectionist forces and may even undermine current trade negotiations.

Capital flow restrictions could also lead to distortions as they deprive companies in the industrialized countries of long-term risk capital and undermine the development efforts in emerging economies. Safeguarding national security with respect to investments from sovereign wealth funds must be done in a way that preserves open markets. Sovereign wealth funds, for their part, should recognize that heightened scrutiny of their activities is inevitable and that a transparent operating framework addresses most of the concerns currently being raised.

References

CBS News, 2008, "60 Minutes: Sovereign Wealth Fund's President Promises Transparency", 6 April, available at http://www.cbsnews.com/stories/2008/04/04/60minutes/main3993933_page4.shtml, accessed on 25 January 2011.

Gillespie, E, 2008, "No State Secret", Emerging Markets News, 6 April, available at http://www10.emergingmarkets.org/article.asp?PositionID=&ArticleID=1940913, accessed on 25 January 2011.

Morgan, JP, 2008, *Sovereign Wealth Funds: A Bottom-Up Primer*, JP Morgan Research.

Section 2: Regulation and Public Policy Issues

Chapter 5

The Political Economy of Sovereign
Wealth Funds

Avinish Persaud

5.1. Introduction: From Heroes to Villains and Then What?

The uproar over sovereign wealth funds[1] that broke out before the 2007–2009 global financial crisis was a measure of the newfound economic insecurity of Western industrialized economies. In particular, it reflected anxiety over the seeming eastward shift in economic power. When the US, French or other Western politicians worry about sovereign wealth funds, they do not have in mind the Norwegian Oil Reserve Fund, or even the investment authorities of Abu Dhabi, Kuwait, and Saudi Arabia — key Western allies. Yet these funds are the genre. They are the largest and oldest of the funds, accounting for approximately $1.5 trillion out of the approximately $3 trillion of assets held by sovereign wealth funds at the end of 2008.[2] When Western politicians worry about sovereign wealth funds, they have in mind a newly minted fund from China, Kazakhstan, or less agreeable quarters of the Middle East.

Just one year into the credit crunch, sovereign wealth funds went from villains to heroes and the earlier uproar dissipated. On 26 November 2007, Citigroup announced (with a ring of nostalgia for those old enough to remember the Latin America debt crisis) that it would sell $7.5 billion of mandatory convertible equity units with an 11% coupon to the largest sovereign wealth fund, the Abu Dhabi

---

[1]I believe the term "sovereign wealth fund" was first coined by Andrew Rozanov, an early authority on the species.
[2]My own estimates from IMF and national central bank sources.

Investment Authority. Between then and the collapse of Bear Sterns in March 2008 when the crisis appeared to take a turn for the worse, a further $40 billion of equity instruments were sold by ailing banks to sovereign wealth funds. UBS, Morgan Stanley, Merrill Lynch, and others sold stakes close to 10% to the Government of Singapore Investment Corporation, the China Investment Corporation, Temasek Holdings (another government investment corporation based in Singapore), or others.[3] Sovereign wealth funds were welcomed with open arms. All was forgiven. Never backward in spotting an opportunity, the City of London unveiled plans to bring the management of their assets to London. The new attitude to sovereign wealth funds reflects the desperation of our times. But how will sovereign wealth funds be considered when the current panic gives way to calmer times?

5.2. The Size and Management of National Savings

A number of economists used to argue that the build-up of surpluses in emerging market countries was the result of illegitimate beggar-thy-neighbor exchange rate policies.[4] Others add that these surpluses are managed by largely undemocratic governments in pursuit of mercantilist and political advantage. It was in this context, commentators argued, that opposition to sovereign wealth funds from countries "hosting" their investment targets should be viewed, and not as some unprovoked, illiberal act of financial protectionism.[5] This opposition led the IMF to pull together an International Working Group (IWG) of Sovereign Wealth Funds, which later devised the voluntary "Santiago Principles" on how sovereign wealth funds should be run (IWG 2008). The purpose of the Santiago Principles was not

---

[3]This development was awash with delightful irony. In the boom years, bankers justified their compensation packages on the basis that this was the natural order of the hard and ruthless marketplace they inhabited. In unguarded moments they might say that sovereign wealth funds from the East were trying to supplant this natural order of things with investment by dictat from foreign governments with dubious credentials. When things went wrong, bankers were bailed out by easy money from local central banks, regulatory forbearance and fresh capital from, amongst others, funds run by Chinese Communist Party apparatchiks.

[4]The savings glut idea has been ascribed to Ben Bernanke and the exchange rate manipulation idea to Fred Bergsten. By and large these related ideas are held by US-based economists, which is unsurprising as the United States has become a large deficit country, and being a large country with modest trade exposure is unfamiliar with and suspicious of fixed exchange rates. Respectable British economists held similar views about surplus countries in the 1940s when Britain moved from being a surplus to a deficit country.

[5]Western governments are vulnerable to the charge of hypocrisy given that they spent much of the 1990s arguing that emerging economies should liberalize their capital accounts and be less bothered about who is investing in their country.

to stop sovereign wealth funds investing in host countries. By 2008, when the IWG was meeting in earnest, host countries were desperate to attract any kind of financing they could. The purpose of the principles was, in the minds of the host countries, to legitimize this flow of savings. The "home" countries were by and large content to agree to non-binding principles — perhaps too keen as we shall discuss later — because they were loath to narrow the size of their investment universe at a time when good investments were hard to find.

The arguments against sovereign wealth funds and developing Asia's reserve build-up are tangled up together and rooted in politics rather than economics. Although exchange rate manipulation is often cited to give credence to opposition to Asian surpluses, exchange rates play a passive role in explaining the pattern of global imbalances. Global imbalances arose as a result of savings and investment imbalances that had less to do with exchange rates and more to do with the commodity cycle, past investment booms and crashes, and the monetary and fiscal policies of the country that issues the world's reserve currency: the United States. Indeed, countries with the largest surpluses in dollar terms had very different exchange rate regimes; from the relatively floating rates of Japan,[6] Brazil, Korea, and Chile, to the managed but flexible exchange rates of India, Russia, and Singapore, to the relatively fixed rates of China, Germany within the euro area, and the Gulf states. In 2005, when pressure against Asian reserves and sovereign wealth funds was at a peak (perhaps best illustrated by the proposed Schumer–Graham Bill in the US Senate to unilaterally impose 27.5% tariffs on Chinese imports) the counterpoint to the US current account deficit was surpluses in oil exporters, Japan and Germany — not China.[7] No commensurate tariff was proposed for Japanese or German exports to the United States.

The ability of countries to save or spend more than local saving or investment opportunities allow is a measure of the success of the global economy, not a failing. Capital autarky would represent a failure of the international financial system. It is entirely appropriate that after the over-investment boom that crashed traumatically in Asia in 1997–1998 — or the sudden rise in the prices of oil and gas from 2003–2008 — that some Asian and oil-exporting countries would choose to save more than they could invest at home. In my experience the key defining aspect of an emerging economy is one where there is limited capacity to absorb new

---

[6]Since 1998, the Ministry of Finance in Japan has intervened in the foreign exchange markets as infrequently as the US Treasury.

[7]The rise in the Chinese current account balance between 1997 and 2004, the year before the Schumer–Graham Bill, represented 6.7% of the rise of the US current account deficit over the same period. The rise in the Russian surplus represented 10.7% of the rise in the US deficit, the rise of the Japan surplus, 14.2%, and the rise of the Middle-East surpluses, 19.4% (see Genberg *et al.* 2006, 19).

investment. This is particularly the case in the Middle East where, outside of oil and gas, economic activity is shallow. Misguided attempts to use surpluses to boost domestic investment and consumption led to boom and bust.[8] But more importantly, irrespective of the level of exchange rates or what is appropriate at home or not, if the world's financial hegemon leader is over-consuming, it will draw savings from the rest of the world. The US is the one place where — as a result of being the issuer of the world's reserve currency — demand for foreign savings creates its own supply.[9]

It is also reasonable that until domestic financial systems deepen in developing countries to such an extent that they can disintermediate and recycle long-term savings, the state should manage the national savings. The rise in oil prices from 2003–2008 added over $1 trillion of savings to the Middle East, but the Middle Eastern financial markets, or those in China and to a lesser extent those in Russia and Singapore, did not have the capacity to absorb and manage this wall of liquidity in such a short time.[10] The economic legitimacy of the state managing national savings, especially by way of index funds, in highly developed economies such as Australia, France, Norway, the United States, and others,[11] is harder to justify than the state managing national savings in Abu Dhabi, Saudi Arabia, Kuwait, Libya, and Qatar.

5.3. Future Generations and the Asset Allocation Problem

Traditionally, developing country governments entrusted their central banks to manage these national savings and central bankers — picked in the first place for their risk aversion — put the savings into the least risky assets: short-dated, US government, or agency bonds or bills. While national savings were modest it was reasonable for the central bank to manage them as an expanding pool of liquidity. Many developing countries had witnessed events in the past, whether it was during the Asian financial crisis that began in July 1997 and eventually spilled over into

---

[8]The first salvo in the global financial crisis was probably the collapse in Saudi Arabian equity markets in 2006 and the resulting banking trouble, over a year before the autumn 2007 collapse of Northern Rock and IKB.

[9]This is of course the Keynesian inversion of Say's Law.

[10]The Asian financial crisis was partly caused by an excessive inflow of capital that could not be absorbed into the economy in a sustainable way and found its way into banks and real estate markets pushing down rates of return until the crash brought markets back to more sustainable levels.

[11]See, Alabama Trust Fund, Alaska Permanent Fund, Alberta's Heritage Fund, Australia Future Fund, France's Strategic Investment Fund, New Mexico State Investment Office Trust, New Zealand Permanent Superannuation Fund, Norwegian Government Pension Fund, and the Wyoming Mineral Trust.

Russia and Brazil by 1999, or the Latin American debt crisis in the middle of the 1980s, when the international markets were suddenly closed to them. Given that almost 70% of international trade and financial flows take place in US dollars, if international liquidity dried up and a country needed to pay for essential imports or meet debt repayments, the best insurance asset to have at the central bank is short-dated, high credit quality, US dollar denominated bonds. A typical asset could be a US dollar denominated bill issued by the US government with a maturity of six months. In this way the US government benefited significantly from the dollar being held as a reserve asset, allowing it to finance its deficits more cheaply and for longer than would otherwise be the case.

But once savings went beyond what was necessary for short-term liquidity insurance, this asset allocation was no longer appropriate. The obvious point is that national savings in, effectively, one asset, represents a financially dangerous concentration of risk. The dollar is the most liquid currency, but it is also exhibits substantial gyrations in value.[12] This concentration of exposure in one small part of the US government bond market is also bad for the United States. Concentrated purchases of short-dated US government paper held down the yields on the risk-free asset. This encouraged investors to buy riskier assets to obtain the yields they required to meet their pension, life insurance, or other commitments. It may not always seem so, but diversification is good for everyone — but not just any kind of diversification.

When savings are held in case of a liquidity crisis, savers have to invest in assets that offer liquidity and as a result they "pay" the liquidity premium in terms of a lower return on assets than might be obtained if immediate liquidity was not the purpose of the savings. High liquidity assets include foreign cash or short-dated government bonds in internationally acceptable currencies. When savings are being held for future generations and therefore the primary investment focus is long-term returns, holders should "earn" the liquidity premium by investing in assets that offer a higher rate of return to offset the characteristic that they cannot be sold for immediate liquidity.[13] Low liquidity assets need not offer low credit quality as well, and could be a portfolio of blue-chip equities in emerging markets or a portfolio of private equity investments in government-backed infrastructure projects. These are very different assets from the normal prevue of central bankers. It requires very different asset and risk management skills and approaches. It is why governments

---

[12] In the most recent cycle, the value of one US dollar has gone from being worth 1.17 euros in 2002 to being worth less than 0.70 euros in 2009, an almost halving of its international value.
[13] For further discussion of the difference between paying and earning the liquidity risk premia, see Persaud (2009a; 2009b).

started siphoning off part of their savings into sovereign wealth funds to be invested for the long term. The different investment objectives, instruments, and approaches had already been established by the older commodity-based funds,[14] which were from the very beginning set up not to help with short-term liquidity problems, but to provide an alternative source of income in the future when the commodity runs out.

5.4. Domestic Development Versus Liquidity

The decision to manage part of a developing country's foreign exchange reserves for future generations creates enormous pressure to spend the money at home. This pressure exists even when poverty is not prevalent, as in Norway and Australia. The arguments are both reasonable and emotive. How can a country "take" from those who are poor today in order to "give" to future generations who are likely to be wealthier? Savings invested abroad in developed country assets will yield less than investing in assets at home would, where scarce capital means the economic and social returns from investments are large. It is not surprising, therefore, that sovereign wealth funds are rare or small in democratic countries and are more prevalent in countries where there is a more autocratic form of government, less constrained in pushing through an intergenerational transfer from current to future citizens.

The reality for funds born out of large foreign exchange reserves is that these assets are tied to a foreign exchange liability. In a sense they are a loan rather than equity. The investor who has given US dollars to the central bank in order to receive the equivalent in local currency to make a local investment, has only done so on condition that if and when he or she wishes to exit the investment, they can receive dollars for their original investment and its accrued returns. Consequently, these dollar reserves could be considered to be held for safe keeping and while a proportion may be invested in assets that are not immediately liquid on the assumption that not everyone will want foreign exchange at the same time, this is not a distant probability, and they will need to be invested in assets that could be used as collateral for immediate foreign exchange liquidity. There is, therefore, very little scope for them to be used for socially useful, illiquid, local projects. But not all is lost for those looking for a developmental impact from the rise of national savings.

---

[14]For example, the Kuwait Invest Authority established in 1953, the Abu Dhabi Investment Authority established in 1976, and the Alaska Permanent Fund established in 1976.

The presence of large reserves and national savings in emerging markets appears to have produced three powerful, separate, but related development dividends. First, it is now possible to see that while emerging economies were initially coupled to the turn-down in developed countries in 2008, and while world trade and cross-border flows have collapsed,[15] economic weakness in emerging economies was far more limited than would have been expected given the experience of other crises. The counterfactual is always hard to prove but it is noteworthy that India and China are likely to post a strong 2009. Brazil and Russia — two of the most heavily affected emerging economies — are already showing signs of recovery, their path first worsened and then bettered by the fall and subsequent rebound of commodity prices.

During the boom years, the presence of large surpluses appears to have lowered the risk premia of investing in emerging economies. This is one explanation for why this period of large surpluses, often seen as a sign of repressed consumption, has coincided with big foreign direct investments, hurtling economic activity[16] and signs of overheating.[17] This dichotomy — rising savings and rapid growth — does not sit well with the idea that the solution to the US deficit is that surplus countries should grow even faster.

The third development dividend from the rise in national savings is that where assets are held for future generations and the focus is long-term returns with good credit quality, a suitable investment is private or public equity portfolios in emerging economies. While sovereign wealth funds should not invest at home, they should — from a financial perspective — invest in their developing country neighbors. If 33% of the assets of the world's sovereign wealth funds were put into emerging market equities, it would represent an appropriate, long-term, diversified investment, as well as an unprecedented $1 trillion shot in the arm for global development.[18]

5.5. Governance, Security and Management

To return to the issue that troubles many, should we not be worried over the influence on corporate decisions of foreign governments who own sovereign wealth funds?

---

[15] In 2008, world trade fell by over 15%, the largest fall since the 1930s (OECD, 2009).

[16] The five years to 2007 were the first five years on record in which the world economy has grown by over 5% per annum (IMF 2008).

[17] In 2006, Chinese and Indian policymakers were worried about inflation, not unemployment, which is one of the reasons that both countries allowed some exchange rate appreciation.

[18] Investment would flow most easily to those middle income countries with developed capital markets and not the poorest, though these countries may also benefit from private equity flows, as is already the case in commodity-rich parts of Africa.

It is interesting that the same people who ask this question often see nothing wrong with the investment activism of CalPERS and ABP Investments — the two largest public employee pension funds. Is CalPERS not a Californian sovereign wealth fund? And what about private equity firms? Why would we say no to a sovereign wealth fund investor and yes to a private equity group like Carlyle with former prime ministers and presidents on its board? Bank regulators are often national champions of their banking system and promote their banks abroad — should these highly regulated institutions be seen as purveyors of national policy? At home, we often consider the local public sector pension fund as the "good" long-term investor concerned about extra financial issues — the point here being that it is not as easy as it looks to differentiate between the kind of investors we like, the appropriate role of the state, and those investors we do not like. Non-discrimination is a good principle in trade liberalization and is also a good starting place in capital liberalization.

What makes it possible to defend this apparently laissez-faire position is that governments have more than enough instruments to protect national security if they feel it is under threat and these instruments are often used liberally. Remember Dubai Ports?[19] And going down the route of investment, protectionism is not free.[20] Being choosy about which capital you want, reduces competition and raises its cost. Limiting who can buy local assets will lower their value and, as with all protectionism, protecting local firms from foreign takeover also reduces the discipline on management.

I hesitate to offer an economic solution to what is in essence a political problem, but in those sectors where they may be legitimate concerns, one half-agreeable solution is to ask sovereign wealth funds to pass on their voting proxies either to other shareholders or to shareholder activist groups. This would deflect concerns that sovereign wealth funds are investing to use their influence for non-commercial purposes.

Deflecting concerns is also the line of the Santiago Principles, which aims to make sovereign wealth funds look like any other asset management firm. The disarming of sovereign wealth funds from their political background helps sovereign wealth funds to invest more freely and helps host countries welcome these investors.

---

[19] In case you do not, in 2006, Dubai Ports World agreed to purchase a set of US ports but US politicians kicked up a storm, arguing that it would undermine security at US ports, and the deal was dropped.

[20] While it is hard to differentiate the effects of financial protectionism on stock ratings, the story of Danone, the French dairy food manufacturer, is illustrative. In 2003 and 2005 repeated rumors of Pepsico taking over Danone in France, led the Danone share price to outperform other stocks by approximately 10% before French government officials and others would intervene to make it clear than any takeover would face tough legal, union, and other resistance.

Everyone appears to be a winner. But maybe not... The crisis of 2007–2008, and the ability of sovereign wealth funds to take stakes in beleaguered banks, showed the benefit to the financial system of a diverse set of players. Forcing sovereign wealth funds to look, feel, and behave like any other asset managers will mean they would not behave differently than other asset managers. The logical extension of some of the calls on sovereign wealth funds to look like other asset managers is that they will find it easier to simply outsource the management of their assets to other, largely developed country-based asset managers. But if sovereign wealth funds behave like all other asset managers they would not have come to the rescue of the banks. This reduction in diversity will remove a source of systemic stability. Voting proxies would preserve the diversity of the financial system while also deflecting political concerns.

We should be careful of the seemingly innocuous calls for sovereign wealth funds to look like other asset management companies and show a greater formalization of their value accounting, risk management strategies, and prudential controls. This will serve to shed sovereign wealth funds of their favorable systemic characteristics. Sovereign wealth funds can buy when everyone else is selling because they do not follow market-to-market accounting systems, market price-based risk systems, and do not need to disclose short-term performance and holding figures which could breed short-term pressures. Nor are these control mechanisms appropriate to very long-term and very large investors.

5.6. Conclusion

Diversity is good for market functioning. Remembering that governments have instruments at their disposal to deal with security concerns, recipient countries and companies should ask of sovereign wealth funds what we would be happy to ask of any investor, including individual investors, once they take a strategically sized investment in a company. What shareholders and citizens ask of the sovereign wealth funds is a different matter and while transparency is generally good, forcing sovereign wealth funds to behave like any other asset manager defeats the purpose of the exercise.

References

Genberg H, McCauley R, Park YC, & Persaud A, 2006, *Official Reserves and Currency Management in Asia*, Geneva: International Center for Monetary and Banking Studies, and London: Centre for Economic Policy Research.

A. Persaud

International Monetary Fund (IMF), 2008, *World Economic Outlook*, April.

International Working Group on Sovereign Wealth Funds (IWG), 2008, Sovereign Wealth
    Funds: Generally Accepted Principles and Practices (The Santiago Principles), October.
    Available at http://www.iwg-swf.org/pubs/gapplist.htm, accessed on 25 January 2011.

OECD, 2009, *Economic Outlook*, April.

Persaud, A, 2009a, "Devastating liquidity effects of financial regulation and market
    microstructure", in Mayes, D, Pringle, R, & Taylor, M (eds.) *Towards a New Framework
    for Financial Stability*, London: Central Banking Publications.

Persaud, A, 2009b, "Regulation, Valuation and Systemic Liquidity", *Financial Stability
    Review, Banque de France*, October.

Chapter 6

Open Capital Markets and Sovereign Wealth Funds, Pension Funds, and State-Owned Enterprises

Adrian Blundell-Wignall and Gert Wehinger

6.1. Introduction

Sovereign wealth funds have been around for a long time, but have grown quickly in recent years due to high oil prices boosting oil-producer revenues, and in response to foreign exchange market intervention in the face of large capital inflows into emerging markets. They have now become too large to ignore. It is important to be clear at the outset that possible concerns about sovereign wealth funds cannot plausibly be related to their causing financial market instability. On the contrary, sovereign wealth fund direct speculative risk-taking in the recent financial crisis has been a stabilizing influence, allowing weak banks to raise some of the capital required to avoid bankruptcy. Furthermore, compared to central banks investing all of their foreign exchange reserves in US Treasuries — arguably a contributory factor to the too-low cost of capital that caused the sub-prime crisis — sovereign wealth funds provide a ready mechanism for governments with large foreign exchange reserves to diversify their portfolios. Extremely large concentrations of high saving-country investments in Treasuries have long been a concern in respect to asset price (including exchange rate) stability.

The concern voiced most often is that governments with sovereign wealth funds may use their financial power to build strategic advantages that are against the national interest of host countries (recipients of foreign investment), typically in the areas of energy, telecommunications, high technology, and materials, where national security issues are said sometimes to arise. But when one looks for examples of sovereign wealth fund investments in the past that have demonstrably compromised the national interests of the host country (however these are defined), the examples are sparse. One frequently suggested example of an investor that is often perceived as "potentially threatening" is Gazprom. But Gazprom, of course, is not a sovereign wealth fund — it is a Russian, state-owned enterprise. The discussion of possible concerns about sovereign wealth funds is frequently conducted around the issue of governance. In very broad terms, the presumption is that if any public pools of capital are managed in a *transparent* way, according to a set of principles that are consistent with international best practice, then it would be more likely that sovereign wealth funds and state-owned enterprises could invest more freely in host country markets, except for investments which are reviewed and found to be inconsistent with a country's national security reservations.[1]

6.2. Differentiating Capital Pools

There are, in fact, five capital pools with meaningful distinctions where government ownership plays a role:

(a) Social security reserve funds — set up as part of the overall social security system, where the inflows are mainly surpluses of employee and/or employer contributions over current payouts, as well as government top-ups.
(b) Foreign exchange reserves — accumulated typically as a result of intervening in the foreign exchange market in the face of foreign capital inflow (typically invested in US treasuries or sub-managed by sovereign wealth funds or sovereign pension reserve funds).
(c) Sovereign pension reserve funds — established by government separately from the social security system to fund pensions at a specified future date.
(d) Sovereign wealth funds — which are pools of assets owned by governments to achieve broader national objectives (which are to diversify and improve the return on exchange reserves or oil revenue, to shield the domestic economy from commodity price fluctuations, or other unspecified objectives).

---

[1] Internationally accepted standards are the OECD Principles of Corporate Governance (OECD 2004), and "reservations" refers to previously negotiated exceptions to the free movements of capital allowed in the OECD Code of Liberalisation of Capital Movements (1961) and the OECD Declaration on International Investment and Multinational Enterprises (1976; 2000); see more generally Truman (2007) and Kimmitt (2008).

(e) State-owned enterprises — entities (separate from public administration) that have a commercial activity where the government has a controlling interest (full, majority, or significant minority) whether listed or not on the stock exchange. The rationale is often industrial/regional policy and/or the supply of public goods (often in utilities and infrastructure such as energy, transport, and telecommunications).

The social security reserve funds are shown in Table 6.1, but will not be discussed very much in this chapter. This is because fiduciary/prudential rules apply — a requirement of matching assets and liabilities over long-term horizons and investing according to pre-specified benchmarks (often in domestic government bonds). Nor will any reference be made to the very large funds run by governments but where the assets are actually owned by the beneficiaries (e.g. CalPERS). Similarly, the investment of a country's foreign exchange reserves will not be pursued in this paper. As noted above, these can create financial instability issues on a significant scale.[2] However, that issue is not the concern of this chapter. If reserves are not held in US Treasuries, and are sub-managed by sovereign wealth funds or sovereign pension reserve funds, then the governance and foreign investment issues are taken up in that context.

The major sovereign wealth funds, social security reserve funds, and sovereign pension reserve funds are shown in Table 6.1. At the time of writing, sovereign wealth funds had passed the $2.7 trillion mark, and pension funds in total (social security reserve funds and sovereign pension reserve funds) had grown to over $4.5 trillion. However, the sovereign pension reserve fund part of this (most comparable to sovereign wealth funds) is relatively small in comparison, at around only $431 billion — though growing quickly. If Norway's Government Pension Fund Global were included on the pension fund side this estimate would almost double.[3] We have chosen not to do this as this Norway fund, notwithstanding the word "pension" in its new formal name, may be used for purposes other than funding pensions liabilities. The founding act states that the fund "shall support central government saving to finance the National Insurance Scheme's expenditure on pensions and long-term considerations in the application of petroleum revenues."

State-owned enterprises are not pools of investable capital as such, but they may finance investments via their earnings, fiscal appropriations from the government, or from debt markets at a (possibly) distorted low cost of capital. In some sense

---

[2]See, for example, Blundell-Wignall and Atkinson (2008).
[3]Note that we include Norway's domestically oriented Government Pension Fund Norway in the sovereign pension reserve fund category.

Table 6.1   Sovereign Wealth and Pension Funds: Estimated Fund Size in US$ Billion, End of 2008 (or latest available, as of end-March 2009).

Sovereign Wealth Funds		Social Security & Sovereign Pension Reserve Funds		
Country & Name	US$bn	Country	Name of the fund/institution	US$bn
UAE (Abu Dhabi Investment Authority)	627.0	OECD: SSRF Canada	Canada Pension Plan	116.4
Saudi Arabian Monetary Authority	431.0	Denmark	Social Security Fund	0.7
Norway (Government Pension Fund-Global)	326.0	Japan	National Reserve Funds	1,217.6
Singapore (GIC)	247.5	Korea	National Pension Fund	152.2
Kuwait Investment Authority	202.8	Mexico	IMSS Reserve	7.4
China Investment Corporation	190.0	Spain	Fondo de reserva de la seguridad social	79.9
Russian Federation Oil Stabilisation Fund	137.1	USA	Social Security Trust Fund	2,418.7
Singapore (Temasek)	85.0			
UAE (Investment Corporation of Dubai)	82.0	OECD: SPRF Australia	Future Fund	42.2
Libyan Investment Authority	65.0	France	Fonds de réserve pour les retraites (FRR)	38.7
Qatar Investment Authority	62.0	Ireland	National Pensions Reserve Fund	22.8
Algeria Revenue Regulation Fund	47.0	New Zealand	New Zealand Superannuation Fund	6.9
Kazakhstan National Oil Fund	38.0	Norway	Government Pension Fund - Norway	12.5
Brunei Investment Agency	30.0	Poland	Demographic Reserve Fund (DRF)	1.2

(Continued)

Table 6.1 (Continued)

Sovereign Wealth Funds		Social Security & Sovereign Pension Reserve Funds		
Country & Name	US$bn	Country	Name of the fund/institution	US$bn
Korea Investment Corporation	27.0	Portugal	Social Security Financial Stabilisation Fund	8.3
USA Alaska Permanent Fund	26.7	Sweden	National Pension Funds (AP1-AP4 and AP6)	137.0
Malaysia Khazanah Nasional Berhad	23.1	OECD:Total		4,262.4
Chinese Taipei National Stabilisation Fund	15.2	Non-OECD: SSRF China	National reserve funds	94.6
Bahrain Mumtalakat Holding Company	14.0	Jordan	Social Security Corporation	5.3
Iran Oil Stabilisation Fund	13.0	Pakistan	Employees' Old-Age Benefits	2.4
Canada Alberta's Heritage Fund	11.9	Saudi Arabia	General Organisation for Social Insurance	8.6
USA New Mexico State Investm. Office Trust	11.7	Non-OECD: SPRF Thailand	Social Security Office	11.6
Azerbaijan State Oil Fund	11.2	China	National Social Security Fund	77.9
Other	40.0	Russia	National Welfare Fund	83.6
		Non-OECD:Total		284.0
Total Sovereign Wealth Funds	2,764.2	Total Social Security & Sovereign Pension Reserve Funds		4,546.4

Source: Sovereign Wealth Fund Institute (http://www.swfinstitute.org); Bortolotti et al. (2007); OECD; and national sources.

there is greater scope for financially less-constrained investment, and with strategic objectives very much in mind.

6.3.   Governance Issues

The G7 Finance Ministers have asked the IMF to prepare voluntary best practices for sovereign wealth funds in terms of governance, and the OECD (2008a) to prepare guidance for recipient country attitudes to investment from sovereign wealth funds. Some OECD work has drawn a distinction between sovereign wealth funds and sovereign pension reserve funds. They have many characteristics in common: both are large pools of capital that can be invested with return and other objectives in mind; and government ownership is a factor in both cases. The reason for the distinction is that while a sovereign pension reserve fund is not currently paying out pension liabilities, it has been earmarked to do so, bringing with it the transparency required where fiduciary responsibilities are present (future pensions) and where peer comparisons with private pension funds are made. As a result, some sovereign pension reserve funds have specific investment return targets and concomitant investment strategies that have been designed on purely financial grounds. It is relatively easy to find annual reports with objectives, benchmarks, returns, risk controls, etc. (see Blundell-Wignall *et al.* 2008). In contrast, most sovereign wealth funds have diffuse investment objectives, which can leave open the possibility of pursuing political objectives.

6.3.1.   OECD Pension Fund Guidelines

The OECD Guidelines on Pension Fund Governance (2005; 2008b) aim to ensure an appropriate division of operational and oversight responsibilities as well as the suitable accountability of those with such responsibility. The main elements of the pension guidelines are:

(a) A governing body with clearly set out fiduciary duties, a specific measurable mandate, and members who must possess the relevant expertise to carry out their functions. Where the members do not possess sufficient knowledge to discharge their duties they should seek external advice. Segregation from government is preferred to avoid political interference.

(b) Ring-fencing legislation to ensure that the assets of the fund are to be used exclusively for the payment of pensions.

(c) An investment committee which advises the board on investment strategy and an executive body that is in charge of operational management including asset management — the latter may be delegated externally, but in this case the governing body should retain fiduciary responsibility for the fund.

(d) Full public disclosure, normally through an independent audited annual report while also meeting all requirements to report to government. Accountability relies on this as the assets are owned by the government and therefore the governing body (unlike a private pension fund) is not independent of it. Disclosure is a particularly sensitive topic for both sovereign wealth funds and sovereign pension reserve funds. Commercial considerations argue against detailed disclosure of investments by both sovereign wealth funds and sovereign pension reserve funds. At the same time, there is a need to promote the transparency of the funds' investment policy. Public disclosure of asset allocation and investment performance at sufficiently long intervals (e.g. one year) and with prudent delays (a few months) can help meeting the goal of transparency without jeopardizing the fund's confidentiality regarding some aspects of its investment management.

(e) Appointment of a custodian.

(f) A code of conduct.

(g) Mechanisms to address conflict of interest situations and complaints from the public.

Most sovereign pension reserve funds are set up with these principles in mind. Good examples include the independent committee structure of the National Pensions Reserve Fund Commission in Ireland, the independent legal entity of the Board of the Guardians of the New Zealand Superannuation Fund (one of the strictest eligibility requirements for board members is in place in New Zealand, where all board members must have experience and expertise in investment management, and at least four must be qualified as investment professionals), and the Australian Future Fund, operated by a board of professionals independent of government (the board approves investment policies and makes critical operational decisions, such as the hiring of the president and chief executive officer and the setting of executive compensation). Such governance structures ensure a high degree of protection against political interference in the management of the reserve fund.

6.3.2. OECD Guidelines for State-Owned Enterprises

State-owned enterprises are very active in international investment, and their activities can give rise to concern. One reason for this is that while sovereign pension reserve funds and sovereign wealth funds often (though not always) invest in financial assets to meet a return objective (frequently with concentration limits), state-owned enterprises often attempt to obtain strategic commercial positions such as broader distribution, better returns by applying better management expertise, secure supply often via vertical integration (for example, to shore up resource inputs). Governance issues are, therefore, just as pressing as they are for sovereign wealth funds, if not more so. The OECD Steering Group on Corporate Governance has agreed to a set of guidelines for running state-owned enterprises, developed by the Working Group on Privatization and Corporate Governance of State-Owned Assets upon the Steering Group's request (see OECD 2005). The main over-arching components of these guidelines are:

(a) Ensuring an effective legal and regulatory framework for state-owned enterprises: The legal and regulatory framework for state-owned enterprises should ensure a level playing field in markets where state-owned enterprises and private sector companies compete in order to avoid market distortions. The framework should build on, and be fully compatible with, the OECD Principles of Corporate Governance.

(b) The state acting as an owner: The state should act as an informed and active owner and establish a clear and consistent ownership policy, ensuring that the governance of state-owned enterprises is carried out in a transparent and accountable manner, with the necessary degree of professionalism and effectiveness.

(c) Equitable treatment of shareholders: The state and state-owned enterprises should recognize the rights of all shareholders and in accordance with the OECD Principles of Corporate Governance ensure their equitable treatment and equal access to corporate information.

(d) Relations with stakeholders: The state ownership policy should fully recognize the state-owned enterprises' responsibilities towards stakeholders and request that they report on their relations with stakeholders.

(e) Transparency and disclosure: State-owned enterprises should observe high standards of transparency in accordance with the OECD Principles of Corporate Governance.

(f) The responsibilities of the boards of state-owned enterprises: The boards of state-owned enterprises should have the necessary authority, competencies, and objectivity to carry out their function of strategic guidance and monitoring of management. They should act with integrity and be held accountable for their actions.

Drawing out guidelines I.C, I.D and I.F:

"Any obligations and responsibilities that a state-owned enterprise is required to undertake in terms of public services [...] should be clearly mandated by laws or regulations. Such obligations and responsibilities should also be disclosed to the general public."

"State-owned enterprises should not be exempt from the application of general laws and regulations. Stakeholders, including competitors, should have access to efficient redress and an even-handed ruling when they consider that their rights have been violated."

"State-owned enterprises should face competitive conditions regarding the access to finance."

These "framework conditions" are at the heart of some of the main regulatory concerns that have been raised against state owned enterprises operating outside their home jurisdictions.

6.4. Sovereign Wealth Funds, Sovereign Pension Reserve Funds, and State-Owned Enterprise Investments in Host Countries

The International Working Group of Sovereign Wealth Funds, being managed by the IMF, has developed Generally Agreed Principles and Practices for sovereign wealth funds (Santiago Principles) that should be of great value as a benchmark. Some issues could of course remain, due to the less precise nature of the sovereign wealth fund investment mandate, which does not constrain the use of assets for specific purposes (and thereby leaves open the possibility of political objectives). But even if governance issues can be solved and full transparency achieved, the issue remains on the table as to what legitimate objections there might still be to the free flow of investment from these pools of capital (and/or state funding and debt). That is: even if "the window is cleaned" and full transparency is achieved, and even if governance practices move into line with appropriate guidelines, would there still be some legitimate objections to the free flow of capital left on the windowsill? The answer in practice for most OECD countries is "yes," and these objections most often take the form of concerns about "national security" and essential security interests.

6.4.1. OECD Investment Instruments and Principles

The OECD Investment Committee report, "Sovereign Wealth Funds and Recipient Country Policies," which represents the consensus view among OECD countries and also reflects inputs from emerging economies, was published in April 2008 (see OECD 2008a). Based on this report, ministers endorsed the following policy principles for countries receiving sovereign wealth fund investments. These principles reflect long-standing OECD commitments that promote an open global investment environment applying to all investments: private, state-owned enterprise, sovereign wealth fund, and sovereign pension reserve fund. They are consistent with OECD countries' rights and obligations under the OECD investment instruments. These are the OECD Code of Liberalisation of Capital Movements, adopted in 1961 (see OECD 1961), and the OECD Declaration on International Investment and Multinational Enterprises of 1976, as revised in 2000 (see OECD 1976; 2000). There are broad procedures for notification and multilateral surveillance under the oversight of the OECD Council (to ensure observance). The instruments embody the following principles:

(a) Non-discrimination: Foreign investors are to be treated not less favorably than domestic investors in like situations. While the OECD instruments protect directly the investment freedoms of those sovereign wealth funds established in OECD member countries, they also commit members to extend benefits of liberalization to all members of the IMF. Experience has shown that, in practice, OECD governments nearly always adopt liberalization measures without discriminating against non-OECD countries — investors from non-member countries reap the same benefits of free market access as OECD residents. Outright discrimination against non-OECD-based investors would be a major departure from OECD tradition. The important point here is that recipient countries should not discriminate among investors in like circumstances.

(b) Transparency: Information on restrictions on foreign investment should be comprehensive and accessible to everyone. In other words, it is important they be consistent and predictable.

(c) Progressive liberalization: Members commit to the gradual elimination of restrictions on capital movements across their countries.

(d) Standstill: Members commit to not introducing new restrictions (other than for national security and public order).

(e) Unilateral liberalization: Members also commit to allowing all other members to benefit from the liberalization measures they take and not to condition them on liberalization measures taken by other countries. Avoidance of reciprocity is an important OECD policy tradition. The OECD instruments are based on the philosophy that liberalization is beneficial to all, especially the country which undertakes the liberalization.

6.4.2. *National Security*

The OECD Investment Committee's project on "Freedom of Investment, National Security and 'Strategic Industries'" has, since early 2006, provided a forum for intergovernmental dialogue on how governments can reconcile the need to preserve and expand an open international investment environment with their duty to safeguard the essential security interests of their people. Dialogue has taken place in a series of discussions involving the 30 OECD members, the 10 non-member adherents to the declaration, and other major non-member countries. The "Freedom of Investment" project carries on a tradition of OECD dialogue on investment issues that has been framed by the OECD investment instruments.

The Freedom of Investment discussions have confirmed the continuing relevance of the basic principles underpinning these instruments: transparency, liberalization, and non-discrimination. They have focused on clarifying, in the current security context, the one exception to open investment policies provided for in these instruments: that governments may take measures they "consider necessary to protect essential interests." The Freedom of Investment discussions include peer-monitoring sessions through *tours d'horizon* of national developments, in-depth policy discussions of selected national security topics, and identification of good investment policy practices. The OECD Investment Committee has issued a report summarizing these discussions. A key finding of these discussions is that any restrictions designed to protect national security should be transparent, subject to accountability and proportional to the objective pursued. To the extent possible, other policy remedies to the problem should be used before considering new restrictions. In other words, any additional investment restrictions in recipient countries should only be considered when policies of general application to both foreign and domestic investors (e.g. competition policy, licensing, taxation, royalties, and financial regulation) are inadequate to address legitimate national security concerns.

A considerable amount of analytical work has been done on national security under the Freedom of Investment project over the past few years. The review of critical infrastructure policies, for example, shows that countries (a) are using broad definitions of critical infrastructure within their national security strategies, often including the financial sector, health care, etc.; (b) use a wide array of policy tools to protect critical infrastructure (e.g. law enforcement, defense, domestic and international intelligence, sector-specific policies); and (c) assign varying places to discriminatory investment policy in protecting critical infrastructure.

Here the concern that sometimes arises is that if foreign governments control the distribution of essential products and services they might be able to use them to achieve foreign policy aims. Other issues include foreign government control and/or access to defense-related technology. Such investments could provide a channel for the acquisition of dual-use technologies (civilian or military) by the acquiring country; could be used to deny access of such assets to the host country; or could be used for military intelligence purposes against the host country. But peer review of restrictive investment measures and transparency of those measures is absolutely necessary to ensure that this does not become a mechanism to pander to nationalism and domestic rent-seeking behavior in the sectors concerned.

OECD member countries have agreed that the national security clause of the OECD investment instruments should not be used as a general escape clause from their commitments to open investment policies. However, much more work needs to be done to achieve better consistency in practice; and the OECD Investment Committee is in the midst of work to achieve better consistency. There is particular interest in government-controlled investors in this work.

6.4.3. *Competition*

Foreign investment (including sometimes from governments) is generally regarded as a powerful competitive mechanism for host countries — it can contribute to lower and more stable prices and to the stability of supply. On the other hand, government-related investment may at times undermine economic efficiency if it directly interferes with the ability of a country to achieve a level playing field. This is a particular concern where state-owned enterprise investments are involved. For example, a state-owned enterprise may obtain state funding at a cost of capital unavailable to other players — both at the takeover phase and at the subsequent operating level.

In general, the sense of the OECD investment principles is that restrictions on particular investments should be a last resort in cases where general competition policy (and other policy) cannot be used adequately to address the issue. If investment review or sector bans on foreign and of sector-specific contracting and restriction is required then the above principles should apply where relevant. OECD countries should not impose standards on foreign state-owned enterprises that are greater than those they apply or expect from their own state-owned enterprises. In principle, if a foreign country follows the OECD guidelines for state-owned enterprises in their corporate governance and competition laws and guidelines, then this can go a long way in allaying fears over the investment strategies of its state-owned enterprises.

Allowing a foreign government-controlled entity to take over a private domestic company needs particular scrutiny — it is a form of nationalization (where a controlling interest is obtained), or worse, of re-nationalization if the private domestic company has previously been privatized by the domestic government. The whole reason for the OECD guidelines on state-owned enterprises is to try to obtain outcomes as close as possible to what they would be under private ownership — but in practice it is difficult to achieve.

6.4.4. *Natural Resources Policy*

Most countries have a variety of objectives in relation to exhaustible resources. Consuming nations want a reasonable (preferably lower) price trajectory and reasonable price and supply stability. Producing nations will generally want to adopt a strategy that maximizes the net present value of their natural resource assets and will wish to manage economic shocks relating to variability of resource revenues. They pursue these objectives with a variety of policy tools, of which investment policy is only a small part (tax policy, state-owned enterprises, property law, foreign policy, etc.). This section looks at the issue of resource rents, assuming the broad policy framework is well designed around market principles. Much public policy in globally traded exhaustible resources reflects a face-off between consuming and producing nations as they try to meet price and supply stability (and foreign policy) goals while also attempting to siphon off as much rent from one another as possible. Among other things, this implies that producing nations that are successful in this game share an interest in both generating and accruing natural resource rents.

Australia, for example, does have the legislation in place to use investment restrictions as a tool in this and other areas. The Foreign Acquisitions and Takeovers Act 1975 (FATA) states that non-residents need prior approval for: investments in Australian companies that exceed certain thresholds (AU$100 million gross assets — but AU$105 million for US investors in sensitive sectors only); portfolio investments in media of 5% or more, and all non-portfolio investment (for the US the thresholds for sensitive sectors and government entities apply); takeovers of offshore companies whose Australian subsidiaries' gross assets exceed AU$200 million (AU$913 million for US investors except in sensitive sectors where AU$210 million threshold applies); direct investments by foreign governments and their agencies irrespective of size; and all urban land. "Sensitive sectors" include: urban land, banking, civil aviation, airports, shipping, media, and telecommunications. The mechanism has been used occasionally to block significant takeovers of energy/resource companies (e.g. Shell's takeover of Woodside in 2001 was not in the "national interest").

As noted earlier, energy supply and distribution can be regarded as a national security issue. Nuclear non-proliferation is a good example, and Australia has used sector-specific bans in this area. But its use of FATA to restrict resource investment has been relatively infrequent. The question addressed here is whether there is a case for using investment powers in the process of appropriating economic rent — looking at the concept of "national interest" as opposed to "national security" in this context, but from the prior that openness is first-best policy in most circumstances.

6.4.5. *The Exhaustible Resource Rent Issue and the Hotelling Rule*

The world economy can be thought of as being made up of "produced" and "scarce" commodities, where the latter are comprised of exhaustible resources with differential costs of extraction depending on the location. A fundamental economic distinction arises between these two groups: for exhaustible resources a form of economic (or Ricardian) rent applies arising from differential costs of extraction and the overall scarcity factor, whereas this is not the case for produce commodities, like manufactures, where in competitive markets super profits can only arise out of market failures of some form. If a few simplifying assumptions are made, the concept of rent for exhaustible resources can be expressed simply in a diagram at a point in time (see Figure 6.1).[4]

Assets such as natural gas, oil, coal, iron ore, and base metals are not reproducible in the ground, and have no marginal product return, nor depreciation, so the return on a unit of the resource is its flow price when extracted. This entails costs, and a low-cost producer of a resource — for example, Australia in iron

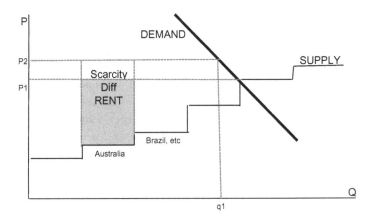

Fig. 6.1   Economic (Ricardian) Rent.

Source: OECD.

---

[4]Each country has constant returns to scale and a different (accessibility-determined) cost structure.

ore — will earn a rent (that cannot be competed away) shown in the shaded area (see Figure 6.1) extracted as shown, at a price set by the marginal producer of the resource. If the few major producers can restrict output in the face of strong inelastic demand (think of Chinese demand currently) a further scarcity rent can be extracted as shown. Over time the country should run down its exhaustible resource according to the Hotelling Rule (Hotelling 1931):

$$d\pi(t)/\pi(t) = r$$

where π is the net price (unit price less cost) and r is the long-term equilibrium rate of interest.

It states that the net price in asset market equilibrium should grow at the rate of interest. Costs may vary according to technical progress (declining prices) and the rate of extraction (rising prices). Prices will be determined by global demand and supply conditions, and by the nature of market structure (monopoly or oligopoly). In iron ore the structure is something like a cartel with a fringe of smaller players. Depending on the interaction of supply, demand, and market structure factors, the flow-net-price of the resource may fall for extended periods and then rise with the possibility of strong rents being earned in both cases (for low-cost producers). But the important point is that restricting output to take advantage of scarcity is not at all a bad thing in terms of maximizing total returns from the asset by achieving Hotelling optimality. Restricting output today (e.g. not expanding at a rate and price that a China-type economy might prefer) may be essential to take advantage of the Hotelling condition, and hence may be in the national interest of a country like Australia, Canada, Brazil, or South Africa.

Figure 6.2 shows the percentage change in the ASX200 Resources Earnings versus the Australian ten-year bond yield. The Resource Earnings percentage change is also shown as a ten-year average to smooth out volatility. As this is an EBIT (earnings before interest and tax) concept, it should sit well above the bond yield.

There have been extended periods in the past when the annual return on resources has been less than the bond yield. Currently, the EBIT return is in line with the bond yield, while the ten-year average return has, over the past eight years, been sitting well above the risk-free bond return. That is to say, investing in resource extraction has allowed sales at a profit well over the alternative use of investing in a risk-free bond allowing for taxation and rent sharing.

Economic rent accrues to a country due to its natural endowments, and because they will be depleted over time, the endowments and the rents will eventually disappear. A country's economic welfare therefore depends on capturing those rents for its citizens. Companies involved in exploration and development of natural resource

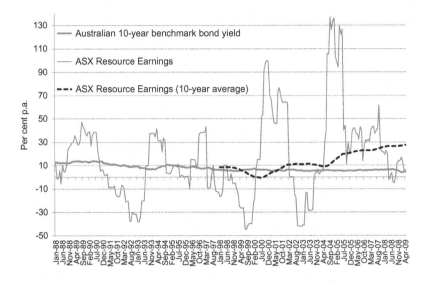

Fig. 6.2 Hotelling's Rule, Australia ASX 200 Resources.
Source: Thomson Financial Datastream, OECD.

projects often require tax incentives to undertake the heavy capital expenditure involved, given the significant risks with upstream exploration and development.[5] In principle, this should later be followed by increasing government involvement with the rising share of economic rent. Sharing in the economic rent can often take the form of royalty/production taxes, resource rent taxes, and production sharing/ equity participation. In principle, such approaches are to be favored over investment policies.

6.4.6. *Appropriating and Investing Resource Rents*

The basic problem for a country rich in natural but exhaustible resources is that living standards of all future generations will fall as the resource runs out, unless the rents can be appropriated and invested (in infrastructure, human capital, and knowledge) to maintain a sustainable consumption path indefinitely into the future (see Solow 1974; Hartwick 1977). This very process has led to the creation of sovereign wealth funds. It is the reason why there will be clear policy differences between these countries and others. Countries with sovereign wealth funds want

---

[5]For example, in Australia there is a 150% uplift of cost deductions for offshore natural gas exploration.

open markets to invest the rents in global markets, but before they can do this they must be able to appropriate the rents.

The question arises as to whether this can be done efficiently and independently of who owns the resources: the government, a private company, a foreign company, or a foreign government-related entity. If ownership by a foreign entity, including sovereign wealth funds and state-owned enterprises, reduces the rent obtainable under Hotelling, then a paradox would emerge where natural resource countries would have concerns about foreign investment in their resources, but would want open markets for their own investments. This paradox would constitute a difficult issue in the context of international negotiations.

The appropriation of rents from exhaustible resources in principle can involve four broadly different types of policies:

(a) State ownership and development of the resources locally.
(b) Private (domestic or foreign) ownership and a taxation regime to capture the rents.
(c) Foreign government-related ownership and a domestic tax regime.
(d) Selling the assets at a market price, which correctly discounts all future rent-income streams to any buyer and investing it in global assets.

In each case the potential relevance of investment restrictions will be touched on, with emphasis on whether there is anything specific to foreign government as opposed to generic issues relevant to all potential owners.

6.4.6.1. *State ownership production sharing and equity participation*

State ownership has been most common in oil and gas. In Norway, Statoil is over 70% owned by the government. In Saudi Arabia, ARAMCO is owned by the government; and this is common throughout the Middle East. In Russia, Gazprom is a state-owned enterprise, and so forth. Russia has moved further toward this approach in recent years, for example, with the nationalization of Yukos. Nationalization leaves little to chance — the rents accrue directly to the government. It avoids the issue of OECD investment instrument issues being breached quite neatly — there are no foreign takeover issues that can lead to concerns about to whom the economic rent accrues: the government owns the companies developing the resources. This is less common in OECD countries (other than Norway). Production sharing and equity participation is less common in hard-rock mining, where all of the same issues apply. This illustrates that nationalization is not necessary to capture exhaustible resource rents. The current Australian government has a proposal for a resource rent tax in the hard-rock mining sector under discussion with the states.

6.4.6.2. *Resource rent taxation and private owners*

In Australia, a resource rent tax applies to liquid natural gas development by private companies (where the offshore nature of the resource falls in the Commonwealth domain except in the North West Shelf where licensing areas are subject to excise and royalties). State government licensing and royalties are more common for onshore mining. For the liquid natural gas resource rent tax, a cost plus calculation is made for the natural gas production process, including capital expenditure. This defines the minimum price for the upstream producer. Then a netback price can be calculated for the downstream (integrated) producer where all upstream and downstream costs are deducted from the revenue achieved by selling at the liquid natural gas price. The rent to be shared comes from the difference in these two prices — some of the rent accrues to the company and some to the country, the proportions being determined as a part of the normal political process.

The main attraction of a resource rent tax is that it applies only to the rent necessary to keep the factor in its current production — the rent is shared between the producer and the government. Investors require a certain rate of return to undertake a project, and any return above that threshold results in investors receiving rent, so the tax applies after all costs associated with exploration, development, and production have been deducted, i.e. tying it to the profitability of the project. Given that the payback period of the non-production factors can be quite long, the tax may be back-loaded. This can be quite long in the case of developing countries, where infrastructure (ports, rail, expensive pipelines, etc.) are more limited.

Three potential disadvantages of private ownership combined with a resource rent tax are:

(a) That rent appropriation could be undermined by aggressive tax accounting.
(b) The netback price calculation becomes difficult to administer in the case of complex natural resource projects. For iron ore, for example, the cost side would involve: prospecting, remote area development (towns, schools, shops) and quarrying, housing and labor facilities, skilled-labor shortages (engineers), specialized equipment and explosives (ammonium nitrate demand and supply factor), crushing and screening hematite in remote areas, disposing of tailings, meeting environmental and land rights issues, road transport from remote areas, giant tipper trucks tire shortages with four-year waiting lists, rail and port infrastructure requirements, shipping delays and penalties, highly variable shipping freight rates (availability of cape-size vessels), etc.

(c) Most importantly, unlike liquid natural gas price taking, a producer country may have monopoly power in the global price setting process. Bulk commodities (e.g. iron ore) are frequently characterized as having cartel-versus-fringe structures where the few big players settle a price, and take into account the impact (price taking and production decisions) that it will have on the fringe — like a Stackelberg leader. The stronger the cartel, the higher the price that can be set for downstream users (e.g. steel mills). This is the case for iron ore in Australia. The annual iron ore price settlement is not independent of the ownership of the main suppliers. The net-back price could be a crucial factor in a direct conflict of interest with downstream producers (e.g. the steel mills for upstream iron ore). It is difficult to see how this input into a resource rent tax could be handled by tax policy, because ownership and the incentives of the owner are the critical variables.

Vertical integration with some influence on oligopoly price setting could impact the size and share of the rent unfavorably for the host country — a foreign steel company would buy a stake in exhaustible resources where scarcity rents apply to ensure better pricing for itself (that scarcity rents are not extracted against them), and use transfer pricing to impact the taxation take. The host country objective is to achieve the Hotelling condition, and the exercise of market power to achieve this condition is not a necessarily a bad thing where exhaustible resources are concerned. The question arises as to how the host country government can reconcile competing interests without resorting to investment restrictions. Investment restrictions may lead to reciprocity measures in other countries and adverse consequences for its sovereign wealth fund investments.

Foreign investment review rejections of takeovers have occurred where a government believes that the acquirer will not develop the license for the resource project concerned. The theoretical case arises when multi-national companies buy exhaustible resource companies when differential rents are present. Differential economic rent arises out of accessibility and extraction costs in different locations. Costs therefore vary with the rate of exploitation — typically as the rate of extraction advances at a particular site the resource becomes less easily accessible. If Figure 6.1 referred to a single site, one would move up the cost curve, exploiting cheapest deposits first, but causing all future costs to rise as the low-hanging fruit is taken away.

Hotelling's Rule can be rewritten (see Gaudet 2007) as:

$$d\pi(t)/\pi(t) - c[t, X(t)] = r$$

where c[t, X(t)] is a cost function dependent on technical progress over time t and the rate at which the stock of known reserves X(t) is being depleted. Exploitation with rising endogenous cost should be driven to the point where the Hotelling condition is achieved.

However, most major resource companies (BHP, RIO, Shell, Xstrata, etc.) operate globally at multiple locations at the same time, and conduct exploration and mergers and acquisitions to shore up future production possibilities. Economic efficiency requires that the lowest cost deposits are exploited before higher cost ones. So a multinational may invest in exploration rights or in another company in a national jurisdiction and hold onto it until its low-cost deposits elsewhere are exploited first. If the host country is looking to develop the resources, this may be dealt with through financial penalties or via foreign investment review and restriction — in this case, financial penalties would have the same effect as a restriction where other investors were not present. This case applies to all foreign investors (private, state-owned enterprise, and sovereign wealth funds).

6.4.6.3. Foreign government SWF and state-owned enterprise investment

If a foreign government-related entity attempts to buy a domestic exhaustible resource (in the ground or a company) where economic, differential, and scarcity rents are present, do any new issues arise in addition to the above generic ones? This is a very difficult area to discuss because OECD countries are committed to openness, as discussed above, and national security does not encompass resource rent (economic) issues. The above economic issues would better be described as falling within the domain of "national interest," rather than "national security." However, the purpose of this section is to raise issues that affect policy in practice, rather than to ignore them. If we consider nationalization, for example, many countries with a private enterprise culture have gone through a fairly systematic privatization process for good reason (efficiency, level playing fields, competition). Such governments may find it odd to allow foreign governments to reverse the process in general, and to do so in industries with rents that cannot be competed away in particular.

In the general case it is difficult to accept that aggressive tax accounting or complexity is sufficient reason to justify foreign investment restrictions to better capture rent. Taxation can be an efficient instrument where the project concerned is a price taker in global markets and self assessment on costs is policed and enforced. However, in the case of a sovereign wealth fund or a state-owned enterprise the problem of aggressive tax accounting has the added dimension that "property rights" are not even between countries, and were disputes to arise with state-owned enterprises and sovereign wealth funds they would be very difficult to pursue in the courts (sovereign immunity issues). If there were concerns with respect to ultimate owners within specific country jurisdictions, the case for investment restrictions would be increased — or at least the threat of such restrictions could be used to achieve a more effective sharing of the rent.

The exercise of market power, where it exists, is one potential reason why governments in a resource-rich country may opt for the investment restrictions approach. Does the case become stronger where owned enterprise/sovereign wealth fund investments occur? Consider the following cases:

(a) A foreign private resource extraction company like Xstrata buys a small resource company, like Oz Minerals or a fringe iron ore producer, with no global pricing power. No investment restriction issue should arise.

(b) A foreign private resource extraction company like Vale Inco buys a large Australian resource company with market power (like RIO), still no issues should arise as the company will use its market power to maximize price for shareholders and will be subject to taxation, which can be invested for the host country via a sovereign wealth fund.

(c) A foreign downstream company (e.g. a private steel mill) buys a small resource extraction company in a vertically integrated structure. Aggressive tax accounting issues may arise, but should be handled via tax policy. If the company is a state-owned enterprise/sovereign wealth fund this issue may be compounded by sovereign immunity issues. It is possible that the threat (but not use) of foreign investment policy may help achieve better outcomes.

(d) A foreign company buys a share of an exhaustible resource company that has market power. If the use of that market power is in the national interest, then some governments may be unwise to allow downstream companies or government-related entities to buy blocking stakes that might adversely impact the use of that market power. If this is a state-owned enterprise or a sovereign wealth fund, national strategic objectives come more directly into play — there may be divergent national interest issues when deciding on global pricing strategy and how the economic and scarcity rent is shared. The national interest issue here certainly deserves further study. If governments carry out policies in the national interest (a concept that has not been analyzed in OECD committee meetings) as opposed to national security, then a host of new economic (as opposed to security) issues arise.

6.4.6.4. *Selling the asset in a global auction*

Pricing a company (public or private) that owns a natural resource asset or license is different than pricing the natural resource product itself (the question that Hotelling deals with). In an efficient asset market, the original owner of a natural resource would accrue all available resource rents generated by future production because the seller would include the present value of these future rents in the minimum price he would accept for the asset. Subsequent owners would operate to ensure that product prices are set to make enough money on the operation to ensure that they cover the rent-related price premium they paid when they bought the natural resource asset from its original owners. The proceeds would be invested via a sovereign wealth fund to ensure that the Solow–Hartwick condition was met.

The oil price stayed between $2.57–3 per barrel from 1950 until 1967. After 1973, the OPEC oil cartel began to share the rent in a different way. If Saudi Arabia had sold all of its oil reserves in 1950 using $2.57 as the long-run price in its net present value, it would undoubtedly have under-priced the asset in a global auction.

Looked at another way, Figure 6.3 shows $100 invested in oil production in 1950, and that $100 dollars from a sale of the oil reserve to a company invested in bonds. Aside from the great disinflation bond rally from 1991 to 2002, it was better

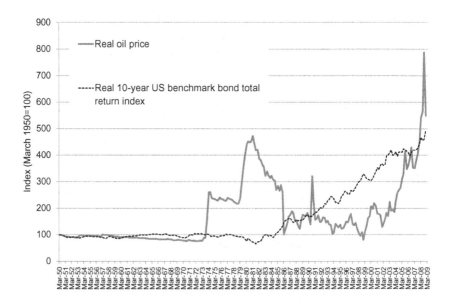

Fig. 6.3   Real Oil Price and Real 10-year US Bond Total Return Index.

Source: Thomson Financial Datasteam, OECD.

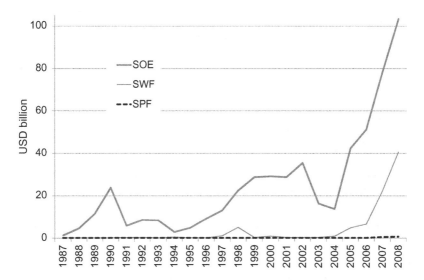

Fig. 6.4 State-owned Enterprise, Sovereign Wealth Fund, and Sovereign Pension Reserve Fund Global Cross-border Deal Flow.

Source: Thomson One Banker, OECD.

to invest in oil by 2008. A sale in 1950 would not have discounted the eight times increase in real oil prices. It would have made more sense to lease the resource, tax it with a resource rent tax, and invest the proceeds and adjust policy as required over the depletion period of the resource.

6.5. Foreign Investment Deal Flow

A time series of global cross-border deal flow from state owned enterprises, sovereign wealth funds and sovereign pension reserve funds is shown in Figure 6.4. The numbers refer to all deals involving foreign direct investment by the entities concerned.

Three observations stand out. First, the concern about sovereign wealth fund investment during the course of 2007, when international consulting firm studies and some policymakers raised the level of alarm, was not uncorrelated with the sudden pick-up in the deal flow in this sector. Second, state-owned enterprises, which have not been the subject of inquiry and reports by the OECD and the IMF in 2007 and 2008, have traditionally been much stronger foreign direct investors for a longer period of time than sovereign wealth funds. It is intriguing that the sovereign wealth funds have had more attention than state-owned enterprise investments over the period. Third, sovereign pension reserve funds are miniscule in the area of foreign investment — reflecting their preference for a portfolio approach to investment (mostly in exchange-traded instruments and with portfolio diversification limits in place) and with a strong home-country bias (sometimes mandated at 100% in domestic bonds).

6.5.1. *Changing Deal Flow Patterns*

The 50 biggest state-owned enterprise foreign investment deals since 1990 to date (mid April 2009) are shown in Table 6.2, and those for sovereign wealth funds are shown in Table 6.3. Both OECD and non-OECD countries are strongly involved in state-owned enterprise foreign investment. This may help explain why it has been very difficult for OECD countries to raise concern about state-owned enterprise foreign investment issues in contrast with sovereign wealth fund concerns. Of the 50 largest sovereign wealth fund deals since 1990, no OECD country (except South Korea in February 2008) figures in the list. It is consequently understandable that individual OECD countries would feel more comfortable raising issues about sovereign wealth fund investment when it began to pick up in 2006 and particularly in 2007.

Insofar as concerns about national security and the national interest are concerned, the main sectors with an *a priori* claim to potential issues in terms of the above discussion would be: (a) energy and power: security of infrastructure, rent/exhaustible resources; (b) telecommunications: security of infrastructure and military; (c) materials: rent/exhaustible resources; and (d) high technology, which has potential military use.

More than 63% of the target firms for state-owned enterprise deals are in these four national interest sectors. 23 of the top 50 deals shown took place prior to 2006, and 18 of these 23 acquisitions (over 78%) involved OECD country ultimate owners. 19 (almost 83%) of the targeted firms of these 23 deals were also in OECD countries. That is to say, prior to 2006, it was more or less an intra-OECD activity to buy into such industries. From 2006 onwards, however, the pattern has changed quite noticeably. 18 (over 70%) of the 27 top deals shown that took place from 2006 onwards were by non-OECD acquiring countries, and 17 (63%) of the target nations were OECD countries. All but one[6] sovereign wealth fund acquirers in the

---

[6]South Korea's Investment Corporation buying into Merrill Lynch in February 2008 being the exception.

Table 6.2   State-owned Enterprise Foreign Investment Deal Flow: 50 Largest Deals in Terms of Rank Value of Deal (incl. net value of debt of target) since 1990 until Mid-April 2009, in Descending Chronological Order.

Date Effective	Acquiror name	Acquiror nation	Acquiror macro description	Acquiror ultimate parent nation	Target name	Target nation	Target TF macro description	Deal transaction value (mio USD)	Deal value/ enterprise value
09/03/2009	Jarpeno Ltd	Cyprus	Financials	India	Imperial Energy Corp PLC	United Kingdom	Energy and Power	2,608.1	127.9%
03/02/2009	Lake Acquisitions Ltd	United Kingdom	Financials	France	British Energy Group PLC	United Kingdom	Energy and Power	16,938.4	127.2%
25/11/2008	StatoilHydro ASA	Norway	Energy and Power	Norway	Chesapeake Energy-Marcellus	United States	Energy and Power	3,375.0	32.5%
22/10/2008	Qatari Diar RE Invest Co QSC	Qatar	Real Estate	Qatar	Cegelec SA	France	Industrials	2,963.7	—
15/10/2008	China Unicom Ltd	Hong Kong, China	Telecommuni-cations	China	China Netcom Grp(HK)Corp Ltd	Hong Kong, China	Telecommuni-cations	25,416.1	83.5%
03/10/2008	CDC	France	Government and Agencies	France	Dexia SA	Belgium	Financials	2,824.5	0.3%
25/09/2008	Lake Acquisitions Ltd	United Kingdom	Financials	France	British Energy Group PLC	United Kingdom	Energy and Power	6,086.0	46.0%
23/09/2008	COSL Norwegian AS	Norway	Energy and Power	China	Awilco Offshore ASA	Norway	Energy and Power	2,500.9	—

(Continued)

Table 6.2 (*Continued*)

Date Effective	Acquiror name	Acquiror nation	Acquiror macro description	Acquiror ultimate parent nation	Target name	Target nation	Target TF macro description	Deal transaction value (mio USD)	Deal value/ enterprise value
23/07/2008	PETRONAS	Malaysia	Energy and Power	Malaysia	Santos Ltd-Gladstone Liquefied	Australia	Energy and Power	2,489.2	40.0%
22/07/2008	Qatar Holding LLC	Qatar	Financials	Qatar	Barclays PLC	United Kingdom	Financials	3,482.8	0.2%
21/07/2008	Saudi Telecommunications Co	Saudi Arabia	Telecommunications	Saudi Arabia	Oger Telecom	Utd Arab Emirates	Telecommunications	2,850.0	35.0%
24/03/2008	SinoSing Power Pte Ltd	Singapore	Energy and Power	China	Tuas Power Ltd	Singapore	Energy and Power	3,072.2	100.0%
14/03/2008	Fortum Oyj	Finland	Energy and Power	Finland	TGC-10	Russian Federation	Energy and Power	3,188.1	76.0%
16/01/2008	TAQA	Utd Arab Emirates	Energy and Power	Utd Arab Em	PrimeWest Energy Trust	Canada	Energy and Power	3,963.8	128.4%
15/11/2007	Infinity World Investments	Utd Arab Emirates	Financials	Utd Arab Em	CityCenter Holdings LLC	United States	Media and Entertainment	2,700.0	50.0%
09/10/2007	BayernLB Holding AG	Germany	Financials	Germany	Hypo Alpe-Adria-Bank	Austria	Financials	2,185.9	50.0%
01/09/2007	Saudi Telecommunications Co	Saudi Arabia	Telecommunications	Saudi Arabia	Binariang GSM Sdn Bhd	Malaysia	Telecommunications	3,050.0	25.0%

(*Continued*)

Table 6.2 (*Continued*)

Date Effective	Acquiror name	Acquiror nation	Acquiror macro description	Acquiror ultimate parent nation	Target name	Target nation	Target TF macro description	Deal transaction value (mio USD)	Deal value/ enterprise value
31/08/2007	SABIC	Saudi Arabia	Energy and Power	Saudi Arabia	GE Plastics	United States	Materials	11,600.0	—
14/08/2007	China Development Bank	China	Financials	China	Barclays PLC	United Kingdom	Financials	2,980.1	0.2%
30/05/2007	OAO Gazprom	Russian Federation	Energy and Power	Russian Fed	Beltransgaz	Belarus	Energy and Power	2,500.0	50.0%
15/05/2007	Swisscom AG	Switzerland	Telecommunications	Switzerland	FASTWEB SpA	Italy	High Technology	5,483.5	86.7%
18/04/2007	JTI (UK) Management Ltd	United Kingdom	Financials	Japan	Gallaher Group PLC	United Kingdom	Consumer Staples	14,683.6	78.2%
10/08/2006	Sinopec Corp Qingdao Br, China	China	Energy and Power	China	OAO Udmurtneft	Russian Federation	Energy and Power	3,500.0	93.2%
01/05/2006	PSA Corp Ltd	Singapore	Industrials	Singapore	Hutchison Port Holdings Ltd	Hong Kong, China	Industrials	4,388.0	20.0%
19/04/2006	CNOOC Ltd	China	Energy and Power	China	NNPC-OML130	Nigeria	Energy and Power	2,692.0	45.0%
12/03/2006	ETISALAT	Utd Arab Em	Telecommunications	Utd Arab Em	Pakistan Telecom Co Ltd	Pakistan	Telecommunications	2,599.0	26.5%

(*Continued*)

Table 6.2 (Continued)

Date Effective	Acquiror name	Acquiror nation	Acquiror macro description	Acquiror ultimate parent nation	Target name	Target nation	Target TF macro description	Deal transaction value (mio USD)	Deal value/ enterprise value
09/03/2006	Thunder FZE	Utd Arab Emirates	Industrials	Utd Arab Em	Peninsular & Oriental Steam	United Kingdom	Industrials	6,899.3	78.7%
26/10/2005	CNPC International Ltd	China	Energy and Power	China	PetroKazakhstan Inc	United Kingdom	Energy and Power	4,141.2	104.7%
26/10/2005	Transalpina di Energia SpA	Italy	Energy and Power	France	Edison SpA	Italy	Energy and Power	4,503.7	27.9%
16/09/2005	Transalpina di Energia SpA	Italy	Energy and Power	France	Edison SpA	Italy	Energy and Power	4,925.3	32.9%
22/06/2005	IPIC	Utd Arab Emirates	Financials	Utd Arab Em	Kuokwang Petro chemical Co Ltd	Chinese Taipei	Energy and Power	2,359.3	20.0%
30/07/2004	Singapore Power Ltd	Singapore	Energy and Power	Singapore	TXU Australia Ltd	Australia	Energy and Power	3,720.0	—
09/12/2002	Telia AB	Sweden	Telecommuni- cations	Sweden	Sonera Oyj	Finland	Telecommuni- cations	6,329.9	—
15/03/2002	Norsk Hydro ASA	Norway	Energy and Power	Norway	VAW Aluminium AG	Germany	Materials	2,764.8	—
27/02/2002	Fortum Oyj	Finland	Energy and Power	Finland	NYA Birka Energi	Sweden	Energy and Power	3,052.2	69.4%

(Continued)

Table 6.2 (*Continued*)

Date Effective	Acquiror name	Acquiror nation	Acquiror macro description	Acquiror ultimate parent nation	Target name	Target nation	Target TF macro description	Deal transaction value (mio USD)	Deal value/ enterprise value
17/09/2001	SingTel	Singapore	Telecommunications	Singapore	Cable & Wireless Optus Lt	Australia	Telecommunications	8,491.1	89.3%
07/02/2001	EDF	France	Energy and Power	France	EnBW Energie Baden-	Germany	Energy and Power	2,480.4	24.9%
30/10/2000	CDC Asset Management Europe	France	Financials	France	NVEST LP	United States	Financials	2,185.8	630.8%
06/12/1999	Tabacalera SA	Spain	Consumer Staples	Spain	Seita	France	Consumer Staples	3,029.4	121.2%
01/11/1999	ALITALIA-Passenger and Cargo	Italy	Consumer Products and Services	Italy	KLM Royal Dutch-Passenger	Netherlands	Consumer Products and Services	4,547.3	100.0%
12/05/1999	Japan Tobacco Inc	Japan	Consumer Staples	Japan	RJ Reynolds International	Netherlands	Consumer Staples	7,831.8	—
04/12/1998	EDF	France	Energy and Power	France	London Electricity (Entergy)	United Kingdom	Energy and Power	3,204.8	100.0%
01/04/1998	Nordbanken (Venantius/Sweden)	Sweden	Financials	Sweden	Merita Oy	Finland	Real Estate	4,292.0	8.8%

(*Continued*)

Table 6.2 (Continued)

Date Effective	Acquiror name	Acquiror nation	Acquiror macro description	Acquiror ultimate parent nation	Target name	Target nation	Target TF macro description	Deal transaction value (mio USD)	Deal value/enterprise value
07/03/1997	CITIC Pacific Ltd	Hong Kong, China	Financials	China	China Light & Power Co Ltd	Hong Kong, China	Financials	2,099.9	20.5%
31/12/1993	UAP	France	Financials	France	Vinci BV	Netherlands	Financials	2,553.1	73.8%
03/03/1992	Altus Finance SA	France	Financials	France	Executive Life Ins-Junk Bond	United States	Financials	3,250.0	—
08/11/1990	Nortel Inversora SA	Argentina	Financials	Italy	Telecom Argentina STET-France	Argentina	Telecommunications	2,578.0	93.3%
08/11/1990	Cointel	Argentina	Telecommunications	Spain	Telefonica de Argentina SA	Argentina	Telecommunications	3,016.0	60.0%
27/09/1990	Renault SA	France	Industrials	France	Volvo AB	Sweden	Industrials	2,661.7	9.8%
31/07/1990	Rhone-Poulenc SA	France	Materials	France	Rorer Group Inc	United States	Healthcare	3,476.0	60.3%

Source: Thomson One Banker, OECD.

Table 6.3 Sovereign Wealth Fund Foreign Investment Deal Flow: 50 Largest Deals in Terms of Rank Value of Deal (incl. net value of debt of target) since 1990 until Mid-April 2009, in Descending Chronological Order.

Date Effective	Acquiror name	Acquiror nation (ult.)	Target name	Target nation	Target TF macro description	Deal transaction value (mio USD)	Deal value/ enterprise value
02/03/2009	Advanced Technology Investment	Utd Arab Emirates	Advanced Micro-Mnfg Facilities	United States	High Technology	3,600.0	65.8%
09/02/2009	GIC Real Estate Pte Ltd	Singapore	ProLogis-China Operations	China	Real Estate	1,300.0	—
06/06/2008	Abu Dhabi Investment Authority	Utd Arab Emirates	Citigroup Inc	United States	Financials	7,500.0	4.9%
22/05/2008	Mubadala Development Co	Utd Arab Emirates	Pearl Energy Ltd	Singapore	Energy and Power	877.5	100.0%
14/05/2008	Khazanah Nasional Bhd	Malaysia	Parkway Holdings Ltd	Singapore	Healthcare	391.9	13.2%
05/03/2008	GIC	Singapore	UBS AG	Switzerland	Financials	9,760.4	0.6%
29/02/2008	DIFC	Utd Arab Emirates	OMX AB	Sweden	Financials	3,396.8	66.9%
26/02/2008	GIC Real Estate Pte Ltd	Singapore	Westin Tokyo	Japan	Media and Entertainment	721.8	100.0%
14/02/2008	DIFC	Utd Arab Emirates	OMX AB	Sweden	Financials	1,182.8	23.3%
05/02/2008	Temasek Holdings(Pte)Ltd	Singapore	Merrill Lynch & Co Inc	United States	Financials	600.0	0.1%
01/02/2008	Korea Investment Corp	South Korea	Merrill Lynch & Co Inc	United States	Financials	2,000.0	0.4%
31/01/2008	KIA	Kuwait	Merrill Lynch & Co Inc	United States	Financials	2,000.0	—

(Continued)

Table 6.3 (continued)

Date Effective	Acquiror name	Acquiror nation (ult.)	Target name	Target nation	Target TF macro description	Deal transaction value (mio USD)	Deal value/ enterprise value
28/01/2008	GIC	Singapore	Citigroup Inc	United States	Financials	6,880.0	0.4%
11/01/2008	Temasek Holdings(Pte)Ltd	Singapore	Merrill Lynch & Co Inc	United States	Financials	4,400.0	0.7%
31/12/2007	Dubai International Capital	Utd Arab Emirates	Alliance Medical Ltd	United Kingdom	Healthcare	1,248.7	—
28/12/2007	China Investment Corp	China	Morgan Stanley	United States	Financials	5,000.0	1.3%
30/11/2007	Dubai International Capital	Utd Arab Emirates	Och-Ziff Cap Mgmt Grp LLC	United States	Financials	1,258.6	9.5%
16/11/2007	Mubadala Development Co	Utd Arab Emirates	Advanced Micro Devices Inc	United States	High Technology	622.3	5.7%
23/09/2007	Mubadala Development Co	Utd Arab Emirates	Carlyle Group LLC	United States	Financials	1,350.0	7.5%
20/09/2007	DIFC	Utd Arab Emirates	London Stock Exchange PLC	United Kingdom	Financials	1,648.0	23.3%
07/09/2007	Istithmar PJSC	Utd Arab Emirates	Barneys New York Inc	United States	Retail	942.3	100.0%
31/08/2007	GIC Real Estate Pte Ltd	Singapore	InterContinental Chicago	United States	Media and Entertainment	450.0	49.0%
17/07/2007	GIC Real Estate Pte Ltd	Singapore	WestQuay Shopping Center	United Kingdom	Real Estate	612.0	50.0%
06/07/2007	Temasek Holdings(Pte)Ltd	Singapore	ABC Learning Centres Ltd	Australia	Consumer Products and Services	329.0	13.5%
27/06/2007	China Investment Corp	China	Blackstone Group LP	United States	Financials	3,000.0	9.9%

(Continued)

Table 6.3   (*continued*)

Date Effective	Acquiror name	Acquiror nation (ult.)	Target name	Target nation	Target TF macro description	Deal transaction value (mio USD)	Deal value/ enterprise value
20/06/2007	GIC Real Estate Pte Ltd	Singapore	Chapterhouse Holdings Ltd	United Kingdom	Real Estate	954.2	—
01/06/2007	Dubai International Capital	Utd Arab Emirates	Mauser AG	Germany	Materials	1,159.8	—
16/05/2007	GIC Real Estate Pte Ltd	Singapore	CSC-MetroCentre	United Kingdom	Real Estate	821.5	40.0%
30/04/2007	GIC Real Estate Pte Ltd	Singapore	Westfield Parramatta	Australia	Real Estate	595.6	50.0%
08/03/2007	GIC	Singapore	Hawks Town Corp	Japan	Retail	862.2	100.0%
08/03/2007	Istithmar PJSC	Utd Arab Emirates	Undisclosed Business Parks(2)	United Kingdom	Real Estate	386.3	—
01/12/2006	Istithmar PJSC	Utd Arab Emirates	Adelphi	United Kingdom	Real Estate	594.1	—
11/10/2006	Istithmar PJSC	Utd Arab Emirates	W Hotel Union Square, NY	United States	Media and Entertainment	285.0	—
07/09/2006	Dubai International Capital	Utd Arab Emirates	Travelodge Hotels Ltd	United Kingdom	Media and Entertainment	1,270.0	—
02/08/2006	GIC Real Estate Pte Ltd	Singapore	Hines-Office Properties(2)	Germany	Real Estate	383.7	—
17/07/2006	Istithmar PJSC	Utd Arab Emirates	Loehmanns Holdings Inc	United States	Retail	300.0	103.0%
06/06/2006	Istithmar PJSC	Utd Arab Emirates	280 Park Ave, New York, NY	United States	Real Estate	1,200.0	—
17/03/2006	Temasek Holdings(Pte)Ltd	Singapore	E Sun Financial Holding Co Ltd	Chinese Taipei	Financials	400.0	2.0%

(*Continued*)

Table 6.3 (Continued)

Date Effective	Acquiror name	Acquiror nation (ult.)	Target name	Target nation	Target TF macro description	Deal transaction value (mio USD)	Deal value/ enterprise value
24/01/2006	Istithmar PJSC	Utd Arab Emirates	Inchcape Shipping Services	United Kingdom	Industrials	289.4	—
03/01/2006	Dubai International Capital	Utd Arab Emirates	Doncasters PLC	United Kingdom	Industrials	1,240.6	—
06/10/2005	Khazanah Nasional Bhd	Malaysia	Lippo Bank Tbk PT	Indonesia	Financials	336.6	11.0%
05/10/2005	Istithmar PJSC	Utd Arab Emirates	One Trafalgar Square	United Kingdom	Real Estate	273.1	—
08/09/2005	Temasek Holdings(Pte)Ltd	Singapore	China Construction Bank Corp	China	Financials	1,400.0	5.1%
19/07/2005	Dubai International Capital	Utd Arab Emirates	Tussauds Group Ltd	United Kingdom	Media and Entertainment	1,495.2	—
27/04/2005	GIC Real Estate Pte Ltd	Singapore	30 Gresham Street	United Kingdom	Real Estate	524.6	—
24/03/2005	GIC Real Estate Pte Ltd	Singapore	Bluewater Shopping Centre	United Kingdom	Real Estate	594.3	17.5%
02/03/2004	Temasek Holdings(Pte)Ltd	Singapore	Telekom Malaysia Bhd	Malaysia	Telecommunications	421.6	1.4%
23/06/2000	GIC Real Estate Pte Ltd	Singapore	Seoul Finance Centre	South Korea	Real Estate	400.0	—
03/09/1998	Hong Kong Monetary Authority	Hong Kong, China	HSBC Holdings PLC{HSBC}	United Kingdom	Financials	4,688.9	1.1%
20/08/1997	Temasek Holdings(Pte)Ltd	Singapore	Shanghai Investment and Trust	China	Financials	762.1	32.5%

Source: Thomson One Banker, OECD.

top 50 deals are from non-OECD countries and target firms are almost always from the OECD (42 firms, 84%; see Table 6.3). Only five of the top 50 deals (10.9%) were in the areas most associated with strategic concerns (the four 'national interest' sectors as mentioned). Sovereign pension reserve funds (as defined in this chapter) have been little engaged in foreign investments and seem to have North American ultimate owners with interests in mixed sectors (see Table 6.4).

6.5.2. *Sovereign Wealth Funds as Risk-Taking Investors in the GFC*

Since 2007, sovereign wealth funds have invested more than $38 billion into the troubled sub-prime crisis firms Citi, Merrill Lynch, UBS, and Morgan Stanley (see Table 6.3). The global financial system is desperately short of capital and few domestic investors have been willing to take a long view and invest in the institutions to enable them to recapitalize and to avoid de-leveraging (with its potentially devastating implications on growth through credit crunch mechanisms). These beneficial risk-taking investments in 2007 and 2008 constitute almost to 58% of the $65.9 billion in large deals shown for this period (see Table 6.3).

6.5.2.1. *Australia as a target nation*

Australia's 50 large foreign government-related investment inflows are shown in Table 6.5. Since 1990 most (42 or 84%) of the 50 largest acquisitions have been from non-OECD government-related investors. The four most frequent investors have been Singapore (18 deals of the 50 shown), China (15), UAE (5), and New Zealand (4). Of the target industries, almost 48% have been in the areas where economic rent is an issue (materials, and energy and power), and over 60% in strategic industries (energy and power, telecommunications, materials, and high technology).

6.6. Conclusion

Governance regimes are of critical importance in terms of how government-related investors are perceived in host countries, and the OECD Guidelines for Pension Fund Governance, as well as the OECD Guidelines on Corporate Governance of State-Owned Enterprises, are a good example of what is expected for most players. Closeness to government in both governance and investments is not a good model for existing and newly emerging pools of capital. OECD investment guidelines are very important for maintaining an open global investment regime to enhance productivity and growth. Country reservations in the OECD codes relate to national security. Other economic rationale sometimes mentioned in the context of restrictions on other grounds include competition and level playing field

Table 6.4 Sovereign Pension Reserve Fund Foreign Investment Deal Flow: All Deals since 1990 until mid-April 2009, in Descending Chronological Order.

Date Effective	Acquiror name	Acquiror nation (ult.)	Target name	Target nation	Target TF macro description	Deal transaction value (mio USD)	Deal value/ enterprise value
31/03/2008	New York Common Retirement	United States	Shurgard Self Storage Europe	Belgium	Industrials	604.1	29.4%
22/06/2007	Caisse de Depot et Placement	Canada	Interconnector (UK) Ltd	United Kingdom	Energy and Power	329.9	18.6%
25/04/2006	Caisse de Depot et Placement	Canada	Aviza Technology Inc	United States	High Technology	15.0	12.5%
25/01/2006	Caisse de Depot et Placement	Canada	Shanghai Forte Land Co Ltd-For	China	Real Estate	–	–
02/12/2005	Caisse de Depot et Placement	Canada	Airport Partners Hungary	Hungary	Industrials	–	–
23/03/2005	Caisse de Depot et Placement	Canada	Travelpro International Inc	United States	Consumer Staples	–	–
03/11/2004	Caisse de Depot et Placement	Canada	Constellation Copper Corp	United States	Materials	3.2	–
28/06/2000	Caisse de Depot et Placement	Canada	Putnam Lovell Group Inc	United States	Financials	25.0	25.0%
08/01/1998	Caisse de Depot et Placement	Canada	Cie Generale des Eaux-Office	France	Real Estate	–	–
21/11/1997	Caisse de Depot et Placement	Canada	Walbro Corp	United States	Industrials	3.0	0.6%
12/01/1994	Caisse de Depot et Placement	Canada	Schroder Buy-Out Fund II	United Kingdom	Financials	–	–
14/09/1993	Caisse de Depot et Placement	Canada	Total Petroleum (North Amer) Ltd	United States	Energy and Power	3.1	–

Source: Thomson One Banker, OECD.

Table 6.5 Foreign Government-related Investment Flow into Australian Companies: 50 Largest Deals in Terms of Rank Value of Deal (incl. net value of debt of target) since 1990 until Mid-April 2009, in Descending Chronological Order.

Date Effective	Acquiror name	Acquiror nation (ult.)	Acquiror TF macro description	Target name	Target TF macro description	Deal transaction value (mio USD)	Deal value/ enterprise value
05/03/2009	IPIC	Utd Arab Em	Financials	Oil Search Ltd	Energy and Power	1,098.0	18.4%
24/02/2009	Hunan Hualing Iron & Steel Grp	China	Materials	Fortescue Metals Group Ltd	Materials	409.2	5.0%
12/02/2009	PTTEP Australia Browne Basin	Thailand	Energy and Power	Coogee Resources Ltd	Energy and Power	413.0	100.0%
20/11/2008	China Shenhua Energy Co Ltd	China	Materials	New South Wales-Coal Expl	Materials	260.9	—
24/10/2008	GIC Real Estate Pte Ltd	Singapore	Financials	GPT Group	Real Estate	269.7	6.4%
19/09/2008	Hunan Nonferrous Metals Corp	China	Materials	Abra Mining Ltd	Materials	62.2	98.9%
15/09/2008	Sinosteel Corp	China	Materials	Midwest Corp Ltd	Materials	1,376.9	—
06/08/2008	China Metallurgical Constr	China	Industrials	Cape Lambert Iron Ore-Project	Materials	373.4	—
23/07/2008	PETRONAS	Malaysia	Energy and Power	Santos Ltd-Gladstone Liquefied	Energy and Power	2,489.2	40.0%
18/07/2008	Cristal Australia Pty Ltd	Saudi Arabia	Materials	Bemax Resources Ltd	Materials	189.8	48.0%
18/06/2008	Sinopec Intl Petro Expl, Prodn	China	Energy and Power	AED Oil-Expl Permits (3)	Energy and Power	556.0	60.0%
21/04/2008	SINOCHEM Petro Expl & Prodn	China	Energy and Power	SOCO Yemen Pty Ltd	Energy and Power	465.0	100.0%
28/03/2008	Upper Horn Investments Ltd	China	Financials	Whitehaven Coal-Narrabri Coal	Materials	63.5	7.5%

(*Continued*)

Table 6.5 (Continued)

Date Effective	Acquiror name	Acquiror nation (ult.)	Acquiror TF macro description	Target name	Target TF macro description	Deal transaction value (mio USD)	Deal value/ enterprise value
24/01/2008	Nakheel Co PJSC	Utd Arab Em	Real Estate	Mirvac Group Ltd	Real Estate	300.0	3.8%
24/12/2007	Nakheel Co PJSC	Utd Arab Em	Real Estate	Mirvac Group Ltd	Real Estate	348.6	4.6%
04/09/2007	Angang Group Hong Kong Co Ltd	China	Financials	Gindalbie Metals Ltd	Materials	32.5	14.5%
06/07/2007	Temasek Holdings(Pte)Ltd	Singapore	Financials	ABC Learning Centres Ltd	Consumer Products and Services	329.0	13.5%
02/07/2007	CITIC Australia Coal Pty Ltd	China	Materials	Macarthur Coal Ltd	Materials	95.9	9.3%
30/04/2007	GIC Real Estate Pte Ltd	Singapore	Financials	Westfield Parramatta	Real Estate	595.6	50.0%
26/04/2007	AREVA SA	France	Energy and Power	Summit Resources Ltd	Materials	115.9	12.1%
16/01/2007	Real IS AG	Germany	Real Estate	Motor Trades-Geoscience	Real Estate	183.4	—
06/07/2006	ACN 118 927 914 Pty Ltd	China	Materials	Balmoral Iron Pty Ltd	Materials	200.0	100.0%
	ACN 118 791 772 Pty Ltd	China	Materials	Sino-Iron Pty Ltd	Materials	215.0	100.0%
31/01/2006	OMX AB	Utd Arab Em	Financials	Computershare-Markets Tech Bus	High Technology	30.8	—
01/10/2005	Real IS AG	Germany	Real Estate	Commonwealth Ppty Fund-11-13	Real Estate	103.5	—
31/03/2005	Optus Networks Pty Ltd	Singapore	Telecommunications	Reef Networks Pty Ltd	High Technology	71.7	100.0%

(Continued)

Table 6.5 *(Continued)*

Date Effective	Acquiror name	Acquiror nation (ult.)	Acquiror TF macro description	Target name	Target TF macro description	Deal transaction value (mio USD)	Deal value/ enterprise value
18/12/2004	CNOOC Ltd	China	Energy and Power	North West Shelf Gas Pty Ltd	Energy and Power	537.3	5.3%
03/08/2004	Optus Networks Pty Ltd	Singapore	Telecommunications	Uecomm Ltd	Telecommunications	49.6	27.6%
30/07/2004	Singapore Power Ltd	Singapore	Energy and Power	TXU Australia Ltd	Energy and Power	3,720.0	—
07/07/2004	Optus Networks Pty Ltd	Singapore	Telecommunications	Uecomm Ltd	Telecommunications	78.2	51.2%
10/08/2003	GIC Real Estate Pte Ltd	Singapore	Financials	Park Hyatt Melbourne	Media and Entertainment	82.0	—
27/06/2003	Reco Bay NSW Pty Ltd	Singapore	Real Estate	Ipoh Ltd	Real Estate	35.7	11.7%
30/04/2003	Meridian Energy Ltd	New Zealand	Energy and Power	Southern Hydro Ltd	Energy and Power	350.0	—
08/04/2003	Ascendas Land Invest Pte Ltd	Singapore	Real Estate	Colonial First State	Real Estate	75.2	25.0%
04/09/2002	GIC Real Estate Pte Ltd	Singapore	Financials	ANA Harbour Grand Hotel	Media and Entertainment	109.4	—
10/08/2002	GIC Real Estate Pte Ltd	Singapore	Financials	Westin Sydney Hotel	Media and Entertainment	89.0	—
19/11/2001	GIC Real Estate Pte Ltd	Singapore	Financials	Ipoh Ltd	Real Estate	97.9	39.2%
17/09/2001	SingTel	Singapore	Telecommunications	Cable & Wireless Optus Ltd	Telecommunications	8,491.1	89.3%
23/05/2001	Meridian Energy Ltd	New Zealand	Energy and Power	Power Facilities Pty Ltd-Hydro	Energy and Power	42.7	—

(Continued)

Table 6.5 (Continued)

Date Effective	Acquiror name	Acquiror nation (ult.)	Acquiror TF macro description	Target name	Target TF macro description	Deal transaction value (mio USD)	Deal value/ enterprise value
08/05/2001	New Zealand Dairy Board	New Zealand	Consumer Staples	Bonlac Foods Ltd	Consumer Staples	151.8	25.0%
19/12/2000	New Zealand Dairy Group	New Zealand	Consumer Staples	National Foods Ltd	Consumer Staples	41.6	10.7%
30/06/2000	Singapore Power Ltd	Singapore	Energy and Power	GPU Power Net Pty Ltd	Energy and Power	1,264.2	—
19/11/1999	GIC	Singapore	Financials	214 Adelaide Street, Brisbane	Real Estate	54.9	—
25/11/1996	Brunei Investment(Brunei)	Brunei	Financials	Macquarie Bank Ltd	Financials	122.8	3.1%
24/01/1996	GIC	Singapore	Financials	Thakral Holdings Group	Real Estate	28.3	9.3%
29/06/1995	Singapore Telecom Intl Pte Ltd	Singapore	Financials	AAPT Ltd	Telecommunications	39.7	24.5%
31/12/1994	Abu Dhabi Investment Authority	Utd Arab Em	Financials	No 1 OConnell Street, Sydney	Real Estate	219.0	—
31/12/1993	CITIC Australia Pty Ltd	China	Materials	Undisclosed Queensland Coking	Materials	66.2	—
30/11/1993	CITIC Australia Pty Ltd	China	Materials	Metro Meat-Remaining Divisions	Consumer Staples	66.2	—
19/03/1992	GD Net(Deutsche Bundespost, Ot)	Germany	Consumer Products and Services	TNT Express Worldwide(TNT Ltd)	Consumer Products and Services	292.7	—

Source: Thomson One Banker, OECD.

issues—but these are best handled by competition policy, not foreign investment restrictions. A second area of concern centers on natural resource policy, including exhaustible resource rent issues required to achieve the Hotelling condition where national interests may diverge. While there are practical difficulties on the supply side in measuring costs for rent sharing via resource rent taxation, this approach is to be preferred to foreign investment restrictions where possible.

The case for foreign investment restriction becomes stronger where a foreign downstream producer may buy the upstream producer with aim to block the use of market power in price negotiations, or where a purchase by another producer results in resource development delays because differential rent is present in the context of multinational enterprises. However, in both cases this would only apply in the case of relatively large investment deals (certainly not for small fringe companies). Particular problems associated with foreign state-owned enterprises and sovereign wealth funds include sovereign immunity and the difficulty of pursuing foreign governments in the courts. Secondly, state-owned enterprise and sovereign wealth fund investments where the ultimate government owner is likely to pursue objectives in its own national interest at the expense of the host country are problematic. The best example here is where the foreign government stake in a domestic exhaustible resource company is intended to block the use of market power in international price negotiations. At a broader level countries that have adopted a market-based development route may not wish to see industries nationalized by foreign governments for a variety of reasons. Most major government-related investment deals in areas of strategic concern during the past ten years have been from state-owned enterprises rather than sovereign wealth funds, suggesting the need for the debate to move into this area for both OECD and non-OECD countries.

References

Blundell-Wignall, A, & Atkinson, P, 2008, "The Subprime Crisis: Causal Distortions and Regulatory Reform", in Kent, C (ed.), *Lessons From the Financial Turmoil of 2007 and 2008*, Sydney: Reserve Bank of Australia.

Blundell-Wignall, A, Hu, Y, & Yermo, J, 2008, "Sovereign Wealth and Pension Fund Issues", *Financial Market Trends*, vol. 2008, no. 1.

Bortolotti, B, Fotak, V, Megginson, W, & Miracky, W, 2009, Sovereign Wealth Fund Investment Patterns and Performance. FEEM Working Paper No. 22.2009, available at http://papers.ssrn.com/sol3/papers.cfm?abstract_id=1364926, accessed 25 January 2011.

Foreign Acquisitions and Takeovers Act, 1975, available at http://www.comlaw.gov.au/Details/C2005C00050, accessed 25 January 2011.

Gaudet, G, 2007, "Natural Resource Economics under Hotelling", *Canadian Journal of Economics*, vol. 40, no. 4, November.

Hartwick, JM, 1977, "Intergenerational Equity and the Investment Rents from Exhaustible Resources", *American Economic Review*, vol. 67, no. 5.

Hotelling, H, 1931, "The Economics of Exhaustible Resources", *Journal of Political Economy*, vol. 39, no. 2.

Kimmitt, RM, 2008, "Public Footprints in Private Markets: Sovereign Wealth Funds and the World Economy", *Foreign Affairs*, Jan/Feb.

OECD, 1961, *The OECD Codes of Liberalisation of Capital Movements*, Paris: OECD.

OECD, 2000 [1976], *The OECD Declaration on International Investment and Multinational Enterprises*, Paris: OECD.

OECD, 2004, *OECD Principles of Corporate Governance*, Paris: OECD.

OECD, 2005, *OECD Guidelines on Corporate Governance of State-Owned Enterprises*, Paris: OECD.

OECD, 2008a, *Sovereign Wealth Funds and Recipient Country Policies*, OECD Investment, Report by the OECD Investment Committee, 7 April.

OECD, 2008b, *Draft OECD Guidelines for Pension Fund Governance*, consultative document, available at http://www.oecd.org/dataoecd/29/36/41087452.pdf, accessed 25 January 2011.

Solow, RM, 1974, "Intergenerational Equity and Exhaustible Resources", *Review of Economic Studies*, Symposium, pp. 29–46.

Truman, E, 2007, "Sovereign Wealth Funds: The Need for Greater Transparency and Accountability", Peterson Institute for International Economics Policy Brief PB07–06, August.

Chapter 7

Negotiating a Voluntary Code

David Murray

7.1. Introduction: The Setting

During 2007, public debate about sovereign wealth funds grew rapidly, fuelled by investment bankers' estimates of the size, growth rate and future value of the funds and by the politics of foreign acquisitions, particularly in the United States. This culminated in the IMF, whose membership included all the relevant countries, bringing the sovereign wealth funds together in October 2007 to discuss concerns raised by the IMF's International Monetary and Financial Committee (IMFC).[1] Representative Ministers, through the IMFC, wanted the development of "best practices" for sovereign wealth funds to condition their behavior and to give confidence that they acted from a commercial rather than strategic imperatives. Who would have believed that, within five months, the sovereign wealth funds would complete their "code" and the global financial crises would result in their being asked to intervene on less than normal commercial terms?

7.2. Organization

The introduction to the Santiago Principles sets out the process by which the work was done. The International Working Group of Sovereign Wealth Funds (IWG) was established at a meeting of countries with sovereign wealth funds on

---

[1]The IMFC is a committee of the Board of Governors of the International Monetary Fund (IMF), comprising representatives — typically ministers of finance and central bank governors — of all 185 IMF member countries.

April 30–May 1, 2008 in Washington, D.C.[2] In the meeting, it was agreed that the IWG would initiate the process, facilitated and coordinated by the IMF. Hamad Al Hurr Al Suwaidi, Undersecretary of the Abu Dhabi Finance Department, and Jaime Caruana, Director of the Monetary and Capital Markets Department of the IMF, were selected to co-chair the IWG.

The IWG met on three occasions — in Washington, D.C., Singapore, and Santiago (Chile) — to identify and draft a set of generally accepted principles and practices (GAPP) that properly reflects their investment practices and objectives. The Santiago Principles were agreed at the last meeting. A subgroup of the IWG — chaired by David Murray, Chairman of the Australian Future Fund Board of Guardians — was also formed to carry forward the technical drafting work. The drafting group met on three occasions, in Oslo, Singapore, and Santiago. In carrying out its work, the IWG used the findings of the IMF-commissioned voluntary sovereign wealth fund survey on current structures and practices (IWG 2008). It also drew from international principles and practices that have already gained wide acceptance in related areas. The IWG also benefited from input from a number of recipient countries — Australia, Brazil, Canada, France, Germany, India, Italy, Japan, Spain, South Africa, the United Kingdom, and the United States — as well as from the European Commission,[3] the OECD, and the World Bank.

7.3. Objectives

For the IWG to respond to the IMFC's request they needed to formulate an agreed set of objectives and develop an organizational approach. These things required a general level of comfort with the whole idea at the Washington meeting — but the mood in the room was distinctly uncomfortable. Sovereign wealth funds had been operating for up to 55 years without controversy. No evidence had been tabled to justify any of the public criticisms. The only points of agreement were that they had been "called in" by the IMF and that an open investment environment was in their own interests and the interests of recipient countries. Further, sovereign

---

[2]IWG member countries are Australia, Azerbaijan, Bahrain, Botswana, Canada, Chile, China, Equatorial Guinea, Islamic Republic of Iran, Ireland, Korea, Kuwait, Libya, Mexico, New Zealand, Norway, Qatar, Russia, Singapore, Timor-Leste, Trinidad and Tobago, the United Arab Emirates, and the United States. Permanent observers of the IWG are Oman, Saudi Arabia, Vietnam, the OECD, and the World Bank. For a complete set of countries and associated representatives, see Appendix II of Santiago Principles.

[3]At the IWG, the European Commission is acting on behalf of the European Union, as agreed by the European Council on 14 March 2008.

wealth funds felt that no serious effort was being made to free investment markets from the myriad of constraints already in place in recipient countries. The March 21 Joint Release of Policy Principles for Sovereign Wealth Funds and Countries Receiving Sovereign Wealth Funds by the United States, Abu Dhabi, and Singapore provided some comfort that a suitable set of objectives could be agreed. However, the IMFC's notion of "best practices" suggested there would only be one (best) practice whereas the funds were heterogeneous in nature. Hence our decision to adopt "generally accepted principles and practices" (GAPP). Underlying the discussion was the principle that sovereign funds had sovereign immunity and sovereign tax status. No government can either direct or tax another. No sovereign wealth fund was willing or able to concede that status. In the end the feeling that sovereign wealth funds needed open markets to invest wisely led to a consensus around the formation of the IWG and adoption of four objectives, namely:

(a) To help maintain a stable global financial system and free flow of capital and investment.
(b) To comply with all applicable regulatory and disclosure requirements in the countries in which they invest.
(c) To invest on the basis of economic and financial risk and return-related considerations.
(d) To have in place a transparent and sound governance structure that provides for adequate operational controls, risk management and accountability.

7.4. Getting Started

The IMF's role was important. It was a body already known to the people doing the work and had the technical know-how to help frame the principles. Its people are highly skilled and, importantly, they did not want to be the owner of the principles. Hence they became the facilitator for the IWG. The GAPP is a voluntary set of principles and practices that the members of the IWG support and either have implemented or aspire to implement. The GAPP denotes general practices and principles, which are potentially achievable by countries at all levels of economic development. The GAPP is subject to provisions of intergovernmental agreements, and legal and regulatory requirements. Thus, the implementation of each principle of the GAPP is subject to applicable home country laws. Library work by the IMF produced a framework of principles, which were divided into three parts: the legal framework, objectives, and coordination with macroeconomic policies; institutional framework and governance structure; and investment and risk management framework.

Sound practices and principles in the first area underpin a robust institutional framework and governance structure of the sovereign wealth fund, and facilitate formulation of appropriate investment strategies consistent with the sovereign wealth fund's stated policy objectives. A sound governance structure that separates the functions of the owner, governing body, and management facilitates operational independence in the management of the sovereign wealth fund to pursue investment decisions and investment operations free of political influence. A clear investment policy shows a sovereign wealth fund's commitment to a disciplined investment plan and practices. In addition, a reliable risk management framework promotes the soundness of its investment operations and accountability.

Teams from the IWG with a lead anchor for each part volunteered to draft the principles. In international negotiations of this type consensus is required on every point. Although by commercial standards this creates a near impossible negotiating environment, the mutual recognition of "concerns" at the outset ultimately helped get the job done. Functioning as a secretariat, the IMF followed a process of informing every member of everything (with the odd skirmish over an honest omission). The skill of the group made the result. Despite language differences, newly formed funds, varying levels of experience, and the intensity of the work, the participants all had a capacity to argue principles and learn from one another. In addition to forming the three sub-groups, a program of meetings and locations was established together with a preference to complete the work in time for release at the October IMF/World Bank meetings that year.

7.5. Issues

International Working Group members were confident that within their own countries their funds were guided by a risk and return mission. To understand this one needs to look to the definition and purpose of sovereign wealth funds. Much effort went into a robust definition of sovereign wealth funds to ensure commonality of interest in the IWG's work. Three criteria underpin the definition:

(a) A shared economic interest in the assets they hold on behalf of their community.
(b) A fund of the general government.
(c) A special purpose distinct from the normal annual budgetary process and reserve asset management role of the central bank.

About 80% of sovereign wealth fund assets are estimated to be associated with managing resource depletion and inter-generational wealth objective. The remainder, broadly speaking, is associated with the use of surplus reserves from rapid early stage growth being used to bolster long-term economic development. Regardless of any outside interest in the motivation of the sovereign wealth funds, their own communities and governments are vitally concerned with the rate of return on the funds. This is what drives both a commercial focus and accountability framework in each country and fund.

Disclosure was the main focus of outside interest from various researchers and the media. Within the group, however, it was apparent that significant differences existed in structures and home country policy approaches. The view was that disclosure of absolute size was not a key issue in demonstrating commercial intent. A more relevant factor was the scope of the principles themselves. For this reason the group worked hard on a comprehensive framework that created a "closed loop" from purpose through to reporting. To comply with the Santiago Principles a sovereign wealth fund must disclose sufficient information for the reader to be able to infer either a commercial or non-commercial intent.

7.6. Outcome

In the end the Santiago Principles were completed with full consensus within five months — a very quick period for an international code. They were presented at the IMF Annual Meeting as planned. Both the timely delivery and the comprehensive nature of the document resulted in a very positive reception from critics of sovereign wealth funds. It was a coincidence that the weekend on which this happened in October 2008 was the same weekend of the G20 emergency meeting during the financial crisis at which the US president proposed globally coordinated decisive action. In our press conference that weekend we were asked if the sovereign wealth funds would fund bail-outs of insolvent banks to help ameliorate the crisis. To take on this role, in light of the size of the task in an uncertain environment where other assets would have to be sold, would have been non-commercial. Hence the critics who supported us being "called in" were asking us to do what they originally regarded as needing regulation and constraint.

Reference

IWG, 2008, Sovereign Wealth Funds: Current Institutional and Operational Practices. Available at http://www.iwg-swf.org/pubs/eng/swfsurvey.pdf, accessed 21 December 2009.

Section 3: Legal Implications

Mapping the Trajectory of the Regulatory Debate: Securing the National Interest or Justifying Protectionism?

Justin O'Brien

8.1. Introduction

The sovereign wealth fund sector has traditionally shunned the media spotlight. There is unmistakable bristling, however, at demands that the sector be governed by higher standards of transparency and accountability than those expected of other critical institutional groups, particularly hedge funds and private equity, which, arguably, operate shorter-term and potentially more destabilizing investment strategies for both individual listed corporations and their stakeholders and for the wider financial architecture. Notwithstanding the recent rise in the authority of the G20, the demand for greater regulation of state-backed pools of capital can be seen, therefore, as a partial and self-serving rewriting of the rules governing the global financial order. This is particularly marked in the shifting geopolitical strategic implications of China's desire to ensure security of supply over essential commodities in countries as diverse as Australia, Bolivia, Venezuela, Nigeria, Angola, and Guinea. Uncertainty over China's strategic intentions, combined with investment in financial services in Europe and the United States, sparked an increasingly acrimonious debate over the consequences of the rise of state-backed capitalism.

Established funds were incredulous at the demands for greater regulation. This was most notable in the case of the Abu Dhabi Investment Authority. It stated that the Abu Dhabi "government has never and will never use its investment organizations or individual investments as a foreign policy tool" (Otaiba 2008). The Abu Dhabi Investment Authority emphasized that financial experts manage 80% of its investments. Moreover, the fund claimed that it has "operated predominantly as a passive investor, with the overwhelming share of its portfolio consisting of minority stakes in companies that have included no control rights, no board seats and no involvement in the management or direction of the receiving companies" (Otaiba 2008).[1] It further cautioned, however, that "in a world thirsty for liquidity, receiving nations should be mindful of the signals sent through protectionist rhetoric and rash regulation" (Otaiba 2008). Similar sentiment was evident in Beijing. The vice president of the China Investment Corporation, Jesse Wang, expressed irritation at the calls for the sector to draw up a code of conduct, saying it was "unfair" and that "the claims that sovereign wealth funds are causing threats to state security and economic security are groundless" (Ruan 2008; Wong 2008; see more generally Schwartzman 2008, 13). This unease is directly related to accusations that the debate on what constitutes the national interest in many recipient countries lacks internal coherence or international consistency.

Despite or because of the suspicion, the major funds established an International Working Group (IWG) to address systematically the causes of concern — inappropriate exercise of soft power, deficient accountability mechanisms, and systemic threat — in conjunction with the International Monetary Fund (IMF). In a series of meetings, beginning in April 2008, the IWG negotiated an overarching code of conduct, which was agreed in the Chilean capital in September 2008 and formally launched the following month in Washington. Remarkably, given the tenor of the initial debate, the publication of the sovereign wealth funds Generally Accepted Principles and Practices (the "Santiago Principles") attracted little media attention (see Murray, Chapter 7). The release of the Santiago Principles coincided with the fallout from the collapse of Lehman Brothers and the concomitant intensification of the Global Financial Crisis. The lack of analysis reflects more than an inability to influence an overcrowded media agenda in Washington and other Western capitals. It also exposes the partial nature of the solution outlined in Chile. The Santiago Principles do not and were not designed on their own to resolve either the broader strategic geopolitical questions or indeed the narrower question of how the governance of state-backed asset pools impact on recipient countries perception

---

[1]The phrasing is instructive in its ambiguity. The passivity is predominant but not exclusive. It is unclear whether the portfolio balance is based on size or value. Furthermore, the lack of control, board representation, and directional guidance may not necessarily be used in all cases. More generally, it is mistaken to believe that the absence of voting rights precludes the exertion of influence. No entrenched management team is likely to ignore the voice or (perceived) interests of significant shareholders.

of what constitutes the national interest. While providing a cohesive and coherent framework to address the alleged transparency and accountability deficit that had animated the earlier debate, the progress in Santiago demonstrated, conclusively, that the intricate policy conundrum facing recipient countries in relation to the governance of foreign direct investment remained and remains unresolved. The failure to address the lack of transparency and accountability in the management of these processes raises profound questions about recipient countries commitment to principles of equity of treatment, the cornerstone of globalization.

The very fact that the principles were negotiated and agreed within a five-month time frame represents a tactical triumph for the International Monetary Fund and the participating funds. They also point to an erosion of the authority and legitimacy of the OECD, precisely because of its failure to secure demonstrable commitment of its member states to reduce artificial barriers to entry. This chapter maps the trajectory of the global debate on state-backed asset pools, with particular reference to the sovereign wealth fund sector, which is governed by the Santiago Principles. First, the principles themselves are explored and evaluated. Second, the rationale for restricting market access on grounds of national security and the more nebulous concept of national interest are explored, with particular reference to the United States and Australia. Finally, the impact of the Santiago Principles on those conceptions is evaluated.

8.2. The Santiago Process

The negotiations leading to Santiago began in earnest with a meeting in Washington on 30 April 2008 at which an International Working Group of countries with sovereign wealth funds agreed to a process facilitated and coordinated by the Monetary and Capital Markets Department of the International Monetary Fund.[2] Over the course of five months the formal group met three times while a drafting sub-committee was established, chaired by David Murray, Chairman of the Australian Future Fund Board of Guardians. This sub-group also met three times, with a preparatory meeting in Oslo, a not surprising development given the fact that the governance arrangements followed by the Norwegian Government Pension Fund Global is widely regarded as a benchmark. At a press conference in Santiago, David Murray argued that the "governance and accountability arrangements give considerable comfort especially in the area of the separation of operations of

---

[2]The Director of the Monetary and Capital Markets Department of the IMF, Jamie Caruana, served as co-chair of the International Working Group alongside the Undersecretary of the Abu Dhabi Finance Department.

the sovereign wealth funds from its owner, and the investment policies and risk management together with the other things that are intended to make it clear that sovereign wealth funds act from a commercial motive and not other motives" (Murray 2008). Moreover, the metastasizing Global Financial Crisis provided the funds with a tailor-made opportunity to demonstrate caution, prudence, and responsibility. Notwithstanding the paper losses on many investments in financial service firms, in the text accompanying the publication of the principles, the IWG note the sector's "ability in many circumstances to take a long-term view in their investments and ride out business cycles brings important diversity to the global financial markets, which can be extremely beneficial, particularly during periods of financial turmoil or macroeconomic stress" (IWG 2008, 3).

The principles set out the legal, institutional, and macro-economic strategies to be adopted by each subscribing fund. They are underpinned by four multi-faceted objectives, which delimit the freedom of the sector. They pledge: (i) to help maintain a stable global financial system and free flow of capital and investment; (ii) to comply with all applicable regulatory and disclosure requirements in the countries in which they invest; (iii) to invest on the basis of economic and financial risk and return-related considerations; and (iv) to have in place a transparent and sound governance structure that provides for adequate operational controls, risk management, and accountability (Santiago Principles 2008, 4). The emphasis on stability transcends obligations placed on other institutional actors. It simultaneously differentiates the sector from purely profit-driven entities. The IWG suggests, however, that this curtailment of strategic options, although designed to safeguard broader stability, comes at a price. The adoption of the principles is based on the explicit requirement for "a constructive and collaborative response from recipient countries [...] Increased transparency — both by the sovereign wealth funds on their structure and operations, and by recipient countries on their investment screening processes and equal treatment of investors — is one of the key factors in achieving this shared goal" (IWG 2008, 4).

The principles are voluntary. Implementation is contingent on the maturity of particular funds, with the principles providing guidance on the minimum levels of transparency and disclosure required. In total, 24 guiding themes are enunciated. The first requires disclosure of the legal foundation while the second highlights the importance of clearly defining and disclosing the policy purpose. The third envisages mechanisms for the integration of particular funds with other aspects of the domestic financial architecture. The policies, rules, and procedures relating to the general approach to funding, withdrawal, and spending operations should be publicly disclosed (Principle 4), with statistical data provided on a timely basis to the ultimate owner (Principle 5), although the need for confidentiality trumps granular public disclosure. The overarching governance structure of the fund should also be disclosed, with particular reference to the division of roles and responsibilities, irrespective of whether the fund is established as an independent entity or operates under the auspices of a relevant government department (Principle 6). Moreover, these arrangements must be consistent with the OECD Principles of Corporate Governance. Mechanisms for appointing (Principle 7) or removing (Principle 8) senior management are to be disclosed and the mandate provided to responsible officers (Principle 8 and Principle 9) clearly specified to minimize either the perception or the reality of external political interference.

The wider accountability framework for evaluating ongoing performance should be clearly defined in the relevant legislation, charter, other constitutive documents, or management agreement (Principle 10), with risk management systems developed and monitored to ensure compliance (Principle 22). These should be disclosed in an annual report compiled in accordance with recognized international or national accounting standards (Principle 11). Accompanying financial statements should be compliant with recognized auditing standards and subject to external review (Principle 12). More significantly, the professional and ethical standards followed by the fund should be defined and embedded throughout the organization (Principle 13).[3] Relations with third parties should also be governed by disclosed clear rules and procedures (Principle 14). A commitment to follow applicable regulatory and disclosure obligations within recipient countries is stated (Principle 15) along with the need to provide information to the wider market. The principles do not suggest, however, that all of the information must be made available through an annual report. "Relevant financial information to demonstrate its economic and financial orientation, so as to contribute to stability in international financial markets and enhance trust in recipient countries" (Principle 17) can be disseminated through corporate websites or freedom of information procedures. Relevant information includes asset allocation and risk appetite, while the extent to which investment policy is guided internally or through external contractors and use of leverage should be specified (Principle 18).

Although a central goal is the need to maximize "risk-adjusted financial returns" (Principle 19), there is recognition that religious, cultural or ethical factors may preclude certain investments. These factors are not regarded with suspicion as

---

[3] "To the extent applicable, the governing body(ies) should require establishment of a code of conduct for all members of the governing body(ies), management, and staff, including compliance programs. Furthermore, members of the governing body(ies), managers, and staff should be subject to conflicts of interest guidelines, and rules. These codes, guidelines, and rules are critical in ensuring a high level of integrity and professionalism" (IWG 2008, 18).

long as the framework is itself disclosed. More problematically, the need to curtail trading based on asymmetrical possession of trading is recognized (Principle 20) although the mechanisms that could be used to ensure this are not specified. Conversely, Principle 21 states that "if a sovereign wealth fund chooses to exercise its ownership rights, it should do so in a manner that is consistent with its investment policy and protects the financial value of its investments. The sovereign wealth fund should publicly disclose its general approach to voting securities of listed entities, including the key factors guiding its exercise of ownership rights".[4] Investment performance is to be monitored (Principle 23) along with commitment to and implementation of the Santiago Principles themselves (Principle 24).

There are many caveats in the proposals making it difficult to readily rank compliance. It will take some time to develop the integrated benchmarking frameworks envisaged by the principles. The most recent comprehensive study on the sector (Risk Metrics 2009) reports that a year after the enactment of the Santiago Principles, public disclosure levels remain patchy. Equally, however, the rationale for invasive regulation is also absent. As such, it also confirms many of the findings in this volume: the size of the sector and its concomitant potential threat to stability has been exaggerated (e.g. Balding, Chapter 3); there is an absence of any identified practice that could reduce confidence in the probity of any actual fund (e.g. Fernandez, Chapter 4); profound methodological difficulties exist in generating generalizations of intent because the heterogeneity of investment form and purpose means that attributing motive can be inaccurate and misleading (e.g. Grenville, Chapter 1), with political rather than economic factors driving the trajectory of reform (e.g. Persaud, Chapter 5). The Risk Metrics study notes that with the partial exception of Temesek Holdings and the Government Investment Corporation of Singapore, which both take board seats in portfolio companies in which they have either a controlling or significant minority interest, formal passivity tends to be the norm. The extent to which and how individual funds actually engage with management is, however, difficult to ascertain. With the exception of the Norwegian Government Pension Fund Global, no fund has published proxy

---

[4]"To dispel concerns about potential non-economic or non-financial objectives, sovereign wealth funds should disclose *ex ante* whether and how they exercise their voting rights. This could include, for example, a public statement that their voting is guided by the objective to protect the financial interests of the sovereign wealth fund. In addition, sovereign wealth funds should disclose their general approach to board representation. When sovereign wealth funds have board representation, their directors will perform the applicable fiduciary duties of directors, including representation of the collective interest of all shareholders. To demonstrate that their voting decisions continue to be based on economic and financial criteria, sovereign wealth funds could also make appropriate *ex post* disclosures" (IWG 2008, 23).

records. This, however, is a problem that extends far beyond the sovereign wealth fund sector, a fact acknowledged by Risk Metrics (2009, 23). More problematically, perhaps, the Risk Metrics study found evidence of a tick-the-box approach to compliance. The detail of how the governance structures actually work is not sufficiently granulated to allow for evaluation of soundness and effectiveness of the legal frameworks adopted by many funds within its survey group. While the policy imperative was in all cases disclosed, the paucity of information released on risk management and accountability mechanisms meant that it was impossible to rate performance in relation to ongoing sources of concern, such as minimizing the risk that the funds may take advantage of asymmetrical information advantages. These hypothetical concerns continue to provide a useful cover for the failure of recipient countries to enhance the level of accountability and transparency in the arrangements governing foreign direct investment.

8.3.   Defining the National Interest

Many countries impose restrictions on foreign direct investment in dual-use technologies or protect core communication portals and transport providers from undue external influence (e.g. GAO 2008). The restrictions can be complete, partial, or entail a review process, which, in turn, may or may not privilege broader security concerns. Unless the process is governed by clearly enunciated and applied guidelines, however, there is a danger that policy is susceptible to political and economic populism. The implications of that populism on the integrity of investment review processes are now examined in relation to the United States and Australia.

8.3.1.   *The United States*

The current legal framework in the United States dates from the 1988 "Exon-Florio" amendment to the Defense Production Act. The amendment authorized presidential right of veto if a foreign investment risked the integrity of national defense. Investigative authority was delegated to the Committee on Foreign Investment in the United States (CFiUS), an inter-agency agency established 13 years earlier to further inward investment. From the start, two competing philosophical worldviews were in conflict (see GAO 2002; 2005). The problems are exacerbated by a failure to define what constitutes national security in either the underpinning legislation or regulatory procedures. There are of course sound policy reasons for such an approach. Most notably, it gives policymakers exceptional flexibility. Nevertheless, the failure to disentangle the national interest and how to order potentially incommensurable commercial and military imperatives severely compromised the integrity of the system.

The abortive investment by state-owned Dubai Ports World in P&O's stevedore operations on the US eastern seaboard in 2005 demonstrates the potential unintended consequences (Graham and Marchick 2006). The controversy centered on the interpretation of an Executive Order (13010), which held that "certain national infrastructures are so vital that their incapacity or destruction would have a debilitating impact on the defense or economic security of the United States." Despite having the support of the Bush administration, political contestation in Congress convinced Dubai that it had, in reality, little choice but to divest. This political pressure demonstrates that the voluntary system of review could be short-circuited by policy entrepreneurs.

The Foreign Investment and National Security Act (2007) was designed to address this defect by codifying the entire foreign investment review process. Significantly, the financial services industry was omitted from the list of controlled sectors in the primary legislation. Individual agencies have, however, maintained the sector as a component of critical infrastructure. As such, the Committee on Foreign Investment in the United States remains a politically charged arena. Moreover, the underpinning legislation specifically calls on the Committee to take into consideration "the relationship of the acquiring country with the United States, specifically on its record of cooperating in counter-terrorism efforts" (GAO 2008, 34). This ambiguity is particularly problematic for Chinese-domiciled investors. The scale of distrust was already evidenced in the blocking of the sale of a Californian-based oil company to the Chinese National Oil Corporation in 2006. This unease re-emerged in the machinations surrounding the recent attempted takeover of 3Com, a leading telecommunications firm. The deal was structured to give the Chinese conglomerate Huawei just 16.5% of the stock; the remainder was held by a US private equity group, Bain Capital. It was derailed, in part, because of fears — expressed outside the committee process — about the integrity of network security protocols. The alleged links between Huawei and the Chinese People's Liberation Army presented an even more nebulous concern. Recognition that these concerns could not be readily dismissed — at least in the court of public opinion — led to the withdrawal of the $2.2 billion offer (Kirchgaessner: 2008a, 30; 2008b, 30).

There are important structural and policy differences between 3Com and those recently consummated within the financial sector. The latter have been scoped to remain below mandatory government review thresholds. Under US law, if there are no accompanying voting rights (or the portfolio investment is below 10%), then it is automatically deemed passive and therefore not subject to formal review.

Secondly, as noted above, the passage of the Foreign Investment and National Security Act explicitly deleted financial services from the list of prescribed sectors. This does not mean, however, that monetary policymakers lacked the capacity to block financial investments. The Bank Holding Company Act requires Federal Reserve approval before direct or indirect investment of more than 25% of voting shares can be authorized. In addition, a controlling interest, which is defined as having 10% of voting shares, can trigger a formal review. The critical question is whether the Committee on Financial Investment can or should have the capacity to second-guess the Federal Reserve. Reinstating the financial sector gives rise to understandable ire on the part of sovereign wealth funds who see in the current debate geo-political gamesmanship devoid of policy cohesion. Be this as it may, it is questionable, however, absent a fundamental overarching agreement on how to deal with expanded state reach in the United States, whether Chinese-controlled investment vehicles, in particular, can gain ongoing political support in Washington (see Bayh 2008).

Within the academy, this emasculating imperative has gone even further. Two leading US legal academics (Gilson and Milhaupt 2008) proposed what they termed a minimalist solution, with the suggestion that sovereign wealth funds should be automatically stripped of ownership rights. They argue that the political problem of how to "ensure that market-based capitalist regimes are protected against incursion by new mercantilist regimes" can be resolved by "a simple corporate governance fix" whereby "the equity of a US firm acquired by a foreign government-controlled entity would lose its voting rights, but would regain them when transferred to non-state ownership" (Gilson and Milhaupt 2008, 10). Forcing sovereign wealth funds to disengage from ownership responsibility is unlikely to solve one key dimension of the crisis. Indeed, it is likely to exacerbate it. A defining feature of the contemporary crisis facing the financial services sector was the failure of institutional investors to take their ownership responsibilities seriously enough. In this regard it is significant that the Santiago Principles explicitly reject any attempt to restrict sovereign wealth funds from exercising ownership rights.

8.3.2. *Australia*

The global demand for resources has been central to Australia's relative insulation from the effects of the credit crisis. The country has globally significant supplies of alumina, zircon, and tantalum as well as liquid natural gas, nickel, and iron ore, much of it in Western Australia. The state is the world's leading producer of bauxite, rutile, and zircon. Moreover, there is significant room for further growth. Western Australia has the largest reserves of nickel and the second largest supply of iron ore, gold, bauxite, and diamonds. The reserves raise significant policy questions about how to develop the infrastructure, ensuring sustainable development and competition while safeguarding national interest.

Chinese concerns have become some of the most significant competitors to the dominant domestic holdings, BHP Billiton and Rio Tinto (both of which are dual-listed on the London market) and the increasingly important Fortescue Metals Group. China has become Western Australia's most significant trading partner. While the investments to date have generally been facilitative joint ventures, major Chinese corporations have begun placing hostile bids for control of medium-sized Australian operations. There are clear commercial grounds for such an approach. It reduces reliance on the major Australian exporters. Facilitation of inward capital flows from China may also, however, have the longer-term effect of depressing prices, thus benefiting disproportionately the customers of Australian resources.

The policy implications have sharpened because of a (failed) strategic raid by Chinalco and its (junior) American partner, Alcoa, on the Rio Tinto share register in London; itself the target of BHP Billiton's attempt to consummate the largest takeover in history. As the raid was on the London share register there was no formal requirement under either law or policy to notify or seek prior approval from the federal government in Canberra (although the failure to do so soured relations between the Australian bureaucracy and the negotiators representing Chinalco). Two weeks after the raid the Australian federal government attempted to reconcile competing objectives by refining the principles used to evaluate potentially controversial commercial deals. The effect, however, has been to introduce further uncertainty in the marketplace.

Under Australian law, foreign investment is evaluated under the Foreign Acquisitions and Takeovers Act (1975). The legislation delegates the evaluative function to a Foreign Investment Review Board. The enunciated principles make clear that the Foreign Investment Review Board retains an advisory role. Ultimate decision-making authority remains with the Treasurer, who suggested that six core principles underpinned the investment review process (Swan 2008a). The principles do little to provide clarity. They are simultaneously nebulous and — in the case of the first two — easily transacted around. The first principle covers the investor's independence from the relevant government (designed to monitor for actual foreign government control). It is unclear what degree of independence is deemed appropriate. Moreover, it is uncertain whether this provision could be enforced against a publicly listed entity in which a state or regional government held a minority interest. Second, the Foreign Investment Review Board will review the investor's litigation record and "common standards of business behavior" (i.e. the extent to which the investor has clearly expressed commercial objectives and the quality of its corporate governance). It is uncertain whether this could apply to a newly listed corporation or one with no previous litigation history. Third, the Foreign Investment Review Board will assess the impact of the investment on competition (to be determined in consultation with the Australian Consumer and Competition Commission). Such an approach may have value in the case of major mergers or acquisitions, such as the proposed (and aborted) link between the iron-ore operations in the Pilbara involving BHP Billiton and Rio Tinto, which effectively torpedoed a further attempt by Chinalco to strengthen its link with Rio Tinto through access to Chinese domestic markets and credit facilities (see Golding and Basil, Chapter 9). It is questionable what impact the transfer of a mid-tier company could have on competition policy, making the provision largely irrelevant. Fourth, the Foreign Investment Review Board will evaluate the impact of the proposed investment on government revenue or other policies, including tax and environmental protection. It is hard to see how this could be utilized only against state-owned investment vehicles without compromising equity of treatment principles. Fifth, the Foreign Investment Review Board will evaluate national security considerations, which includes undefined "strategic interests." Sixth, the board will determine the impact of the proposed investment on the operation and direction of an Australian business, "as well as its contribution to the Australian economy and broader community," which includes taking into consideration "the interests of employees, creditors and other stakeholders."

The proposals have generated considerable ire in Western Australia. Those involved in facilitating inward investment complain that it is important "to differentiate between stock market and real miners" (Interview with author, Perth 23 August 2008). They also suggest that linking the national interest to the need to separate supply and demand misunderstands the dynamics of the mining industry. This is precisely the message the Federal Treasurer promulgated in a speech in Melbourne (Swan 2008b). Wayne Swan argued that the government had approved a Chinese investment once every nine days since coming to office. He also intimated, however, that Chinese investment proved exceptionally complex and often required a more detailed examination, which in turn allowed for an expansion of the time frame for approval beyond 30 days. The rationale for such an interventionist approach was explicitly justified by reference to the international debate on the regulation of sovereign wealth funds.

Relations between Canberra and Beijing have become increasingly strained. The arrest and subsequent conviction of Rio Tinto's chief negotiator in Shanghai has further complicated matters as has the claim by one of Australia's most successful mining executives that the Foreign Investment Review Board practices, as applied to Chinese firms, has a racist tint (Hayward 2010). The racism row followed a rare public admission by the director of the Foreign Investment Review Board, Patrick Colmer, that the clear policy preference was for Chinese investments to be limited to 15 percent within existing entities or less than 50 percent of new projects. Colmer expressed irritation that deals were announced and presented to the Foreign Investment Review Board for adjudication, thereby foreclosing the opportunity of private discussions. He suggested a better approach would be for representatives of Chinese firms to engage in ongoing dialogue with the agency so that potential obstacles could be identified (and resolved) at an early stage (Kirchner 2010). While such an approach adds significantly to flexibility (and minimizes adverse publicity) it does little to advance the cause of transparency, a key imperative of the Santiago process.

It is entirely appropriate for national governments to protect legitimate national interests. If the process is opaque, however, there may be a concomitant undermining of legitimacy. Authority requires clearly defined parameters. In addition, the rationale must be explained and the rules applied in a proportionate impartial manner. To do otherwise obviates longstanding principles of equity in international investment. As the OECD has commented in its "Transparency and Predictability for Investment Policies Addressing National Security Concerns: A Survey of Practices" report (2008b, 2), transparency, "involves offering concerned parties the opportunity to comment on new laws and regulations, communicating the policy objectives of proposed changes, allowing time for public review and providing a means to communicate with relevant authorities." Moreover, the OECD maintains the need for international cooperation. This is necessary "to ensure policy transparency by defining common standards [procedural fairness] and providing support for multilateral peer review and capacity building" (OECD 2008b, 2). Such lofty aspiration is not matched by realities on the ground. The OECD's table of procedural transparency and predictability speaks volumes about serious wider deficiencies in the accountability regime at national recipient level. The lack of formal requirements to publicly announce outcomes, table reports to legislative bodies or publish an annual report with sufficient information to ascertain review patterns is the norm in all countries surveyed, with the exception of the United States and (partially) Australia (OECD 2008a, 9). Introducing policy changes in an incremental manner through bilateral agreements, as in the United States, runs counter to OECD principles. In Australia, the articulation of Foreign Investment Review Board principles was not subject to external debate or validation. Rather, the initiative was presented as a bureaucratic clarification. As such, it did not require prior notification to or consultation with interested parties. In both cases, the introduction of new criteria to adjudication state-owned or -controlled investment entities reflect discriminatory impulses.

8.4. Conclusion

There are sound policy reasons for calls for greater transparency within the sovereign wealth fund sector. Greater disclosure could provide an early warning system of volatile build-ups of capital within particular sectors. Greater oversight reduces the potential of sudden capital withdrawals causing or amplifying financial crises. Thirdly, it serves broader development aims, including a hoped-for increase in the transparency of overarching domestic fiscal policy in emerging markets. Sovereign wealth funds already have an obligation to follow requisite rules and regulations in the recipient jurisdiction. Greater exposure and commitment to the substance of these rules and the regulatory framework can act as a reverse transmission belt. As a result, it has the potential to improve the quality of the corporate governance regime in the donor country. This is particularly the case for countries in which the wider accountability regime is either undeveloped or untested. Fourthly, requiring sovereign wealth funds to render explicit their investment strategies reduces perception that foreign policy objectives trump commercial ones. This, however, is ultimately a subjective judgment, which, if misapplied, could intensify rather than ameliorate tension. The critical unresolved policy question remains, therefore, how to ensure compliance to a substantive code that has the potential to deliver meaningful transparency and accountability. Success in this endeavor can only be vouchsafed if clarification extends to foreign investment review processes thereby guaranteeing commitment to long-standing principles governing equity of treatment. There is, however, an unacceptable degree of ambiguity in the proposals emanating from Brussels, Washington, and Canberra. Each maintains political discretion over ill-defined "strategic interests." The search for accountability is a symbiotic process. It requires careful sequencing. Sovereign wealth funds need and have begun to address deficiencies in their own governance. Recipient countries have, to date, succeeded only in erecting artificial barriers to entry that lack consistency. If demands to regulate sovereign wealth funds continue to be used merely as a cover for a nascent protectionism, the cause of financial liberalization is set back. In such a scenario, both lender and recipient are egregiously impoverished.

References

Associated Press, 2008, "Lawmakers Want CFIUS Rules Clarified", *Wall Street Journal*, 14 March.
Bayh, E, 2008, "Time for Sovereign Wealth Fund Rules", *Wall Street Journal*, 13 February.
Executive Order 13010, 1996, "Critical Infrastructure Protection", *US Federal Register*, available at http://frwebgate.access.gpo.gov/cgi-bin/getdoc.cgi?dbname=1996_register&docid=fr17jy96-92.pdf, accessed on 25 January 2011.

Gilson, R, & Milhaupt, C, 2008, "Sovereign Wealth Funds and Corporate Governance: A Minimalist Response to the New Mercantilism", available at http://www.ssrn.com/abstract=1095023, accessed on 25 January 2011.

Government Accountability Office (GAO), 2002, *Defense Trade: Mitigating National Security Concerns under Exon-Florio Could be Improved* (GAO-02-736), Government Accountability Office, Washington DC.

Government Accountability Office (GAO), 2005, Defense Trade: Enhancements to the Implementation of Exon-Florio Could Strengthen the Law's Effectiveness (GAO-05-686), Government Accountability Office, Washington DC.

Government Accountability Office (GAO), 2008, *Foreign Investment: Laws and Policies Regulating Foreign Investment in 10 Countries,* Government Accountability Office, Washington DC.

Graham, E, & Marchick, D, 2006, *US National Security and Foreign Direct Investment,* Institute for International Economics, Washington DC.

Hayward, A, 2010, "Policy on Chinese Investment Not Balanced", *The Australian,* 10 February, available at http://www.theaustralian.com.au/business/news/policy-on-chinese-investment-not-balanced/story-e6frg90f-1225828865494, accessed on 09 December 2010.

International Working Group on Sovereign Wealth Funds (IWG), 2008, Sovereign Wealth Funds: Generally Accepted Principles and Practices (The Santiago Principles), available at http://www.iwg-swf.org/pubs/eng/santiagoprinciples.pdf, accessed on 08 December 2010.

Kirchgaessner, S, 2008a, "US Insiders Point to Bain Errors over 3Com", *Financial Times,* 4 March.

Kirchgaessner, S, 2008b, "Washington Obstacle Course Sees Chinese Companies Re-Examine Their US Ambitions", *Financial Times,* 4 March.

Kirchner, S, 2010, "More Inscrutable than the Chinese", *The Australian,* 19 February, available at http://www.theaustralian.com.au/news/opinion/more-inscrutable-than-the-chinese/story-e6frg6zo-1225831954203, accessed on 09 December 2010.

Murray, D, 2008, Press conference to launch the Santiago Principles, Santiago, 2 September, available at http://iwg-swf.org/tr/swftr0802.htm#Readmore, accessed on 08 December 2010.

OECD, 2005, *OECD Guidelines on Corporate Governance of State-Owned Enterprises,* OECD, Paris.

OECD, 2008a, *Sovereign Wealth Funds and Recipient Country Policies,* OECD Investment, Report by the OECD Investment Committee, 7 April.

OECD, 2008b, *Transparency and Predictability for Investment Policies Addressing National Security Concerns: A Survey of Practices,* Organization for Economic Co-operation and Development, Paris.

Otaiba, Y, 2008, "Our Sovereign Wealth Plans", *Wall Street Journal,* 19 March.

Risk Metrics, 2009, *An Analysis of Proxy Voting and Engagement Policies and Practices of Sovereign Wealth Funds,* available at http://www.riskmetrics.com/docs/2009sovereign_wealth_funds_report, accessed on 08 December 2010.

Ruan, V, 2008, "China's Investment Fund Pushes Back", *Wall Street Journal,* 7 March.

Rudd, K, 2008, Speech delivered at Sydney Institute, 16 April, Sydney.

Schwartzman, S, 2008, "Reject Sovereign Wealth Funds at Your Peril", *Financial Times*, 20 June.

Swan, W, 2008a, "Government Improves Transparency of Foreign Investment Screening Process", Media Release 009, available at http://www.treasurer.gov.au/DisplayDocs. aspx?doc=pressreleases/2008/009.htm&pageID=003&min=wms&DocType=0, accessed on 25 January 2011.

Swan, W, 2008b, Australia, China and this Asian Century, Speech delivered at Australia-China Business Council, 4 July, Melbourne.

Wong, E, 2008, "An Emboldened China Scolds US over Economy", *International Herald Tribune*, 17 June.

Chapter 9

Australian Regulation of Investments by Sovereign Wealth Funds and State-Owned Enterprises

Greg Golding and Rachael Bassil

9.1. Introduction

Investments by sovereign wealth funds are said to raise concerns for recipient countries because of their size, the lack of transparency, their potential to disrupt financial markets, and the risk of them being used to progress political objectives (Truman 2007). The policy issues that arise for recipient countries include financial stability, political motives, and national security. The debate on financial stability centers on the fact that sovereign wealth funds and their operations are largely unregulated and may lack transparency. Due to their size and financial capacity there are concerns that a lack of transparency of sovereign wealth funds will mean that certain investment decisions could have destabilizing effects on the financial system.

Some commentators suggest that sovereign wealth funds in fact have a stabilizing effect on the financial system by virtue of their long-term investment horizon, mainly un-leveraged positions, and capacity to be able to enhance the depth and breadth of markets (see IMF 2008). The issue of transparency is one that is currently being considered and addressed by the International Working Group for Sovereign Wealth Funds (IWG), which was responsible for developing a voluntary code of conduct for sovereign wealth funds, known as the Santiago Principles (see Murray, Chapter 7; O'Brien, Chapter 8).

Due to the influence the sovereign power may have over the operations and investment decisions of the sovereign wealth fund there is also the concern already highlighted throughout this volume that sovereign wealth funds may exercise their control over recipient companies for political rather than commercial purposes. There is also concern that foreign governments may get access to information or technology that jeopardizes the recipient country's national security. The public interest in investments by sovereign wealth funds is also a significant issue for recipient governments to grapple with and is particularly the case where local "icons" are involved.

There is a need to distinguish between sovereign wealth funds and state-owned enterprises. Sovereign wealth funds and state-owned enterprises are different in function as well as purpose. As already noted, a sovereign wealth fund can take the form of a fund set up from foreign exchange reserves or commodity revenues that is designed to shield the economy from fluctuations in commodity prices (generally referred to as a stabilization fund such as the Abu Dhabi Investment Authority and the Norway Government Pension Fund).

The term sovereign wealth fund can also refer to a fund set up by a government from the proceeds of sales of public assets to meet the needs of future deficits of the social security system or to contribute to intergenerational savings (such as Australia's Future Fund) or funds set up out of employee contributions to fund pension plans (such as the Denmark Social Security Fund).

State-owned entities on the other hand are commercial entities that are owned by the government. Sovereign wealth funds tend to make portfolio investments or indirect investments through private equity funds whereas state-owned entities tend to make more commercially strategic investments so as to gain synergies, economies of scale, or otherwise supplement or support their commercial operations.

9.2. Overview of Australia's Foreign Investment Regime

Foreign investment in Australia is regulated principally under the Foreign Acquisitions and Takeovers Act 1975 ("Act"), and by the Australian Government's Foreign Investment Policy ("Policy"). The Federal Treasurer is ultimately responsible for all decisions relating to foreign investment and for administration of the Policy. The Treasurer is advised and assisted by the Foreign Investment Review Board, which administers the Act in accordance with the Policy. The Foreign Investment Review Board is an administrative body with no statutory existence, and the Act makes no reference to it. However, the Policy confirms its role. All decisions by the Treasurer relating to a foreign investment proposal are underpinned by analysis and recommendations made by the Foreign Investment Review Board.

The purpose of the regime is to empower the Treasurer to make orders in respect of proposals that ultimately are considered by the Treasurer to be "contrary to the national interest". That is the test against which all proposals are assessed. There is no definition of the national interest and it is assessed on a case-by-case basis. In considering whether the national interest test is met, the Treasurer may impose conditions on the statement of no objection which the Treasurer considers necessary to protect the national interest. In the event that a condition is not complied with, this would be contrary to the national interest and would reactivate the Treasurer's powers.

There are three key areas of Australia's foreign investment regime. These are acquisitions that require prior notification and "approval"[1] under the Act, those that enliven the Treasurer's powers of divestiture under the Act, and those that require prior approval under the Policy. The requirements for prior approval for any investment by a sovereign wealth fund or state-owned enterprise where the investor acquires less than 15% voting power or interests in shares is under the Policy, not the Act. The Policy has no legislative force, but adherence to its requirements is achieved in practice by a number of means, including by refusal to grant necessary ministerial or other approvals under other Australian legislation and by the prospect of ongoing resistance from the Australian Government to the relevant investor, including the likelihood that future applications under the Act might be refused.

9.2.1. *Prior Approval Under the Act*

Under the Act, foreign persons must seek prior approval to acquire control of 15% or more of voting rights, or to acquire interests in 15% or more of the issued shares in an Australian company that has gross assets of AU$231 million or more (2010, indexed annually).[2] Under Section 26 of the Act it is a criminal offence to enter into such an acquisition without giving prior notification and obtaining a statement of no objections under the legislation. For the purposes of the requirement to seek prior approval an Australian corporation is one that is formed within the

---

[1] Strictly speaking, what is obtained under the Act is a "statement of no objections," however, we refer to it as an "approval" for the purposes of this paper.

[2] Section 26 of the Act sets out the requirement to give prior notification and section 13A(4)(b)(ii) of the Act and regulation 5(2) of the Foreign Acquisitions and Takeovers Regulations 1989 ("Regulations") provides an exemption where the corporation has gross assets of less than A$231m. For US investors a $1005 million threshold applies (calendar year 2010) except for prescribed sectors or an entity controlled by a US government — see Section 17E of the Act and Regulation 9 of the Regulations.

Commonwealth of Australia or an Australian Territory.[3] The Treasurer, Wayne Swan (2009a), announced on 12 February that the government would amend the Act to "ensure that any investment, including through instruments such as convertible notes, will be treated as equity for the purposes of the Act." Whether such investments will require mandatory prior approval or whether they will activate the Treasurer's additional powers under the Act will depend on whether the usual thresholds under the Act are otherwise met.

9.2.2. *Treasurer's Additional Powers Under the Act*

The Act also gives the Treasurer power in certain circumstances to make an order prohibiting a proposed transaction, directing that a foreign person must not be in a position to control votes or hold interests in shares and, where the transaction has already completed, to direct a foreign person to dispose of shares.

The Treasurer's powers apply to a broader range of acquisitions than is captured by the pre-approval requirement. However, the powers will only be activated where the result of the acquisition is contrary to Australia's national interest. The Treasurer's powers extend to investments in prescribed corporations that carry on an Australian business[4] and holding companies of such prescribed corporations (Section 18(1) of the Act).[5]

The Treasurer's powers are enlivened if the corporation becomes controlled by foreign persons or there is a change in foreign control. Control by a foreign person is control of 15% of the voting power or 15% of the issued shares by an individual foreign person or control of 40% of the voting power or 40% of the issued shares by foreign persons in aggregate (Section 9(1) of the Act). A change in foreign control occurs where a corporation is already at least 40% foreign controlled in aggregate and there is a change to the make-up of those foreign holders, unless the Treasurer is satisfied that, having regard to all the circumstances, those persons are not in a position to determine the policy of the corporation (Section 9(1)(b) and (2) of the Act).

A "prescribed corporation" includes offshore companies with certain Australian assets where the gross Australian assets of the company are valued at AU\$231 million (2010) or more and make up more than 50% of the company's

---

[3] Separately, the Act provides for a notification regime which is compulsory in respect to acquisitions of interests in Australian urban land for which there is no monetary threshold (Section 26A). This chapter, however, focuses on the regulations applying to investments in corporations.

[4] Section 7(1) of the Act provides that a reference in the Act to an Australian business is a business carried out wholly or partly in Australia in anticipation of profit or gain, either alone or together with another person.

[5] The concept of a prescribed corporation is much broader in scope than "Australian corporations" which is relevant to the prior approval test (Section 26 of the Act).

global assets[6] or an offshore company with certain Australian assets where the gross Australian assets of the company are valued at AU\$231 million or more (2010). The Treasurer's powers may therefore be activated in circumstances where prior approval was not required. The Treasurer's powers also extend to transactions that give a foreign person control of a corporation through an agreement or amendment to a constituent document that results in the directors of the corporation being under an obligation to act in accordance with the directions, instructions or wishes of a foreign person who has a substantial interest in the corporation and where the result of that arrangement would be contrary to the national interest (Section 20 of the Act).

Under the Act, the Treasurer also has powers to unwind certain transactions and arrangements that put foreign persons in a position to control an Australian business where the value of the businesses' total assets is AU\$231 million or more (2010) and the result of the acquisition is contrary to the national interest (Sections 19, 21 and 13A(4) of the Act and Regulation 5(3) and 5(4)). These powers are activated if a foreign person acquires assets from a business carried on solely by a prescribed corporation with the result that, in the case of a business not controlled by foreign persons, that business would be controlled by foreign persons, and the result of that acquisition would be contrary to the national interest such that the Treasurer would have the power to direct the foreign person to dispose of those assets (Section 19 of the Act).

The powers are also activated if a foreign person gains control of such a business by entering into an arrangement relating to the leasing or other rights to use assets of that business, or relating to the participation in the profits or management of that business and where the result is contrary to the national interest (Section 21 of the Act). The Treasurer is also empowered to make divestment orders in relation to acquisitions of urban land by a foreign person where the acquisition is contrary to the national interest (Section 21A of the Act).

9.2.3. *Applications Under the Act*

If a foreign person is required to obtain prior approval under the Act or if they wish to make an application under the Act so that the Treasurer's powers are de-activated, then the applicant must provide the Foreign Investment Review Board with certain information about the company and the target. Once notification of the proposed transaction has been lodged, the Treasurer has 30 days to make a decision and then 10 days to notify of that decision (Section 25 (1B) and 25(2) of the Act).

---

[6] Section 13(1)(g) of the Act provides that a foreign corporations whose Australian assets make up not less than one half of its gross assets is a prescribed corporation. Section 13A(4)(b)(ii) of the Act and regulation 5(2) of the Regulations provide an exemption for companies where the total assets does not exceed \$100m.

If the applicant has not proceeded with the transaction and no notification by the Treasurer is given in that time, the Treasurer ceases to have power in respect of that proposal. However, the Treasurer may make an interim order if more time is required to enable due consideration of the application (Section 22(1) of the Act). An interim order prohibits the applicant from proceeding with the proposal for a period of up to 90 days, after which the Treasurer has a period of 10 days in which to notify of his decision.

9.2.4. *Prior Approval Under Policy*

Australian government policy imposes additional restrictions on investments by foreign persons in sensitive sectors (such as banking, civil aviation, telecommunication, airports and airlines, shipping, and media) as well as in relation to investments by foreign governments and their agencies. Prior to 17 February 2008, the government's published policy in respect of investments by foreign governments was that any direct investment by foreign governments and their agencies would require prior approval and that such applications would be dealt with on a case-by-case basis. Guidance on the issue was exceedingly brief: "All direct investments by foreign governments or their agencies irrespective of size are required to be notified for prior approval. [...] This applies whether the investment is made directly or through a company that is owned 15% or more by a foreign government."

The Australian Treasurer released a set of Guidelines for Foreign Government Investment Proposals on 17 February 2008, which purported to "enhance the transparency of Australia's foreign investment screening regime." In a speech to the Australia-China Business Council in Melbourne on 4 July 2008, the Treasurer made the following comments in relation to the Guidelines: "These guidelines were those used by the previous government; they are what we use too. They are not new" (Swan 2008a). However, many commentators consider that the release of these guidelines indicated a shift in the government's approach. The Treasurer refuted that by saying:

> You will have heard, as I have, a couple of arguments about our approach to Chinese investment — broadly, that we have changed our policy to a more restrictive stance, and furthermore, are slowing down the processing of Chinese applications. I don't think either of these stand up when considered against the facts. I have approved a Chinese investment proposal on average once every nine days since coming into office. This is certainly not a slowing pace (Swan 2008a).

In the guidelines of 17 February 2008, the Treasurer said that proposed investments by foreign governments and their agencies are assessed on the same basis as private sector proposals and that national interest implications are determined on a case-by-case basis. The guidelines then set out a list of six issues to which the government will have regard when considering whether a proposal by a state-owned entity or sovereign wealth fund is contrary to the national interest. In understanding the potential reach of the pre-approval requirement for investments by sovereign wealth funds and state-owned entities it is necessary to consider what is meant by "direct investment" and which investors would be considered a "foreign government agency."

There is very little guidance as to what constitutes a "direct" investment.[7] It is clear that the size of the investment does not affect the requirement to seek prior approval (Australian Department of Treasury 2008). The government also considers the term "direct" to extend to offshore investments in companies or funds that have assets or operations or other economic links to Australia. Debt structures that are considered "quasi-equity" are also likely to be treated by the government as a direct investment.[8] The Treasurer's announcement in February 2008 regarding "irrespective of structuring" is also being applied to the Policy requirement further diluting the concept of "direct" investment.

For the purposes of the Act, a "foreign government investor" is an entity that is owned or controlled by a foreign government where the foreign government has an interest of 15% or more. However, the requirement that all investments by "foreign governments and their agencies" seek prior approval is under the Policy, not the Act. The guidelines of 17 February 2008 made it clear that foreign government agencies include sovereign wealth funds and state-owned enterprises.[9] Moreover, it indicated that the policy would apply to investors owned or controlled by a foreign government.[10] Our recent experience suggests that in the current political environment the Australian government would take a broad view of what constitutes a foreign

---

[7]The Foreign Investment Review Board website stated that a "direct investment" is a "non-portfolio investment," however, that is not reflective of the government's approach in relation to investments by foreign government agencies. This definition is however relevant to investments in the sensitive sector of media where different tests apply to direct (being non-portfolio) investments and portfolio investments.

[8]Funding arrangements that include debt instruments having quasi-equity characteristics will be treated as direct foreign investment (Australian Department of Treasury 2008).

[9]The *Guidelines* (Australian Department of Treasury 2008) state "Proposed investments by foreign governments and their agencies (e.g. state-owned enterprises and sovereign wealth funds) are assessed on the same basis as private sector proposals."

[10]The *Guidelines* (2008) state "National interest implications are determined on a case-by-case basis. However, the fact that these investors are owned or controlled by a foreign government raises additional factors that must also be examined."

government agency and would look at decision-making processes and other indicia of control rather than focusing only on the ownership of a particular entity.

The interpretation of the Policy is obviously fluid and is likely to be influenced by the sensitivity attaching to the sector in which the target company operates. As noted in the Summary of Australia's Foreign Investment Policy "The Government determines what is 'contrary to the national interest' by having regard to the widely held community concerns of Australians" (Australian Department of Treasury 2008). The guidelines of 17 February 2008 set out the six issues to which the government will typically have regard when assessing whether a proposal by a state-owned entity or sovereign wealth fund is contrary to the national interest. The six issues are the extent to which: (a) an investor's operations are independent from the relevant foreign government; (b) an investor is subject to and adheres to the law and observes common standards of business behavior; (c) an investment may hinder competition or lead to undue concentration or control in the industry or sectors concerned; (d) an investment may impact on Australian government revenue or other policies; (e) an investment may impact on Australia's national security; and (f) an investment may impact on the operations and directions of an Australian business, as well as its contribution to the Australian economy and broader community.

The key point to note in relation to these guidelines is that no guidance has been given by the government as to how their consideration of the national interest would be impacted by each of these factors and the extent to which each factor is or is not satisfied or to what level the government will need to be satisfied of each factor (see Clegg and Crowe 2009; Clegg et al. 2009). While the international debate on the policy issues surrounding investments by sovereign wealth funds tends to focus on economic risks raised by the participation of sovereign wealth funds and in particular the lack of transparency in their operations, the issues raised by the Australian government are more focused on non-economic issues.

9.3. Case Studies

In 2008 and 2009 there were a number of significant investment proposals by Chinese state owned enterprises in the Australian resources sector.

9.3.1. *Chinalco's Acquisition of Rio Tinto Shares — the "Dawn Raid"*

On 1 February 2008, Shining Prospect Pte Ltd, a company incorporated in Singapore and a wholly owned subsidiary of Aluminum Corporation of China, known as Chinalco, acquired a 12% interest through market purchases in Rio Tinto Plc. Chinalco is a Chinese state-owned entity. Rio Tinto Plc is a company incorporated in England and listed on the London Stock Exchange and is the English arm of the dual-listed Rio Tinto Group. The Australian arm of the Rio Tinto Group is Rio Tinto Limited, a company incorporated in Australia with its primary listing on the Australian Stock Exchange.

The two listed Rio Tinto entities are separate legal entities with separate assets, share listings, and share registers. The dual nature of the Rio Tinto Group is effected through a series of contracts and constitutional provisions which prescribe, among other things, joint voting arrangements, common board appointments, and restrictions on control transactions unless the transaction relates to both the UK and Australian listed entities. By virtue of the dual-listing arrangements, the two Rio Tinto listed entities are intended to operate and be managed as a single economic unit. In practice, this is primarily effected through the voting arrangements of the two companies. Decisions that affect both companies are put to a joint decision such that the public shareholders of each of Rio Tinto Plc and Rio Tinto Limited effectively vote in aggregate. Chinalco's 12% shareholding in Rio Tinto Plc equates to an approximate 9% economic interest in the group.

As has been widely reported, Chinalco had legal advice that it did not require prior approval for an investment in Rio Tinto Plc up to 14.9% because it was acquiring shares in a company incorporated in England and listed on the London Stock Exchange. As reported by Jennifer Hewitt:

> Chinalco insisted at the time that the company did not need approval from the Foreign Investment Review Board because the shares it had acquired were those of a London-listed company. Chinalco's chief executive, Xiao Yaqing, told *The Australian* newspaper that it submitted the proposal to the Foreign Investment Review Board as 'an expression of goodwill.' (The government has never accepted this interpretation of law or politics, *The Australian* 25 August 2008).

On 24 August 2008, the Australian Treasurer announced that he had decided not to raise any objections to Chinalco acquiring up to 14.99% of Rio Tinto Plc on the basis of two undertakings. In the words of the Treasurer:

> First, Chinalco has undertaken to me that it would not raise its shareholding above this level without notifying and receiving fresh approval from the government under Australia's foreign investment review arrangements. Second, Chinalco has also undertaken that it will not seek to appoint a director to Rio Tinto Plc or Rio Tinto Limited for as long as it holds a shareholding of below 15% (Swan 2008b).

Jennifer Hewitt commented that "the practical impact of getting Chinalco to formally agree not to repeat a raid is limited, because Chinalco has already said it would not do so — just as it has already said it would not seek board representation." (*The Australian* 25 August 2008)

9.3.2. Sinosteel and Murchison Metals

Sinosteel launched a hostile takeover bid for Midwest Corporation Limited, a Western Australian iron-ore mining company on 14 March 2008. This came following Sinosteel's acquisition of a strategic stake of 19.89% through on-market purchases beginning on 24 January 2008. It is understood that Sinosteel obtained Foreign Investment Review Board approval to make the takeover bid at the time of seeking clearance for its initial investment in January 2008.[11]

On 26 May 2008, Midwest announced that it had received a merger proposal from Murchison Metals Limited (a 9.2% shareholder in Midwest) to combine the two companies with Midwest being retained as the listed entity. Under the merger proposal Midwest shareholders would own 47.8% of the merged entity such that if Sinosteel was successful in gaining 100% of Midwest it would own less than 50% of the merged entity. Sinosteel (2008b) expressed concerns with the merger proposal. However, as the transaction was to be structured as a reverse merger with Midwest retaining its Australian Stock Exchange listing, only a 50.1% approval by Midwest shareholders was required. A few days later Sinosteel (2008c) increased its offer for Midwest and waived the defeating conditions. By 12 June 2008, Sinosteel's shareholding in Midwest had increased to 44%. On 7 July, Murchison (2008) and Midwest announced that they were unable to get the support of Sinosteel and consequently the merger proposal was terminated. The Sinosteel offer closed on 15 September by which stage it had a relevant interest in 98.52% of Midwest shares and therefore moved to compulsorily acquire the remaining shares (see Sinosteel 2008d).

Sinosteel also lodged an application with the Foreign Investment Review Board to acquire a substantial shareholding in Murchison Metals.[12] An interim stop order was issued on 25 June prohibiting that transaction for 90 days while the government considered the application further. This occurred at the same time as speculation was growing that the government was considering imposing a 49.9% limit on investments by sovereign corporations and sovereign wealth funds.

---

[11] "The Australian Treasurer has already confirmed through FIRB that there is no objection to the Offer and accordingly the Offer is not conditional on FIRB approval." (Sintosteel 2008a)

[12] Media reports suggest that the application had been formulated and resubmitted (see Frith 2008; Maiden 2008).

Shortly after the close of Sinosteel's takeover of Midwest, the Australian Treasurer approved Sinosteel's application to acquire up to 49.9% of Murchison Metals.[13] The Treasurer's comments indicate that an application for more than 49.9% was originally submitted but would not have been approved and that in determining the effect on Australia's national interest the government as concerned to ensure "diversity of ownership" of iron ore in the Midwest region:

> In approving Sinosteel's application, I have determined that a sharehold-ing of up to 49.9% in Murchison will maintain diversity of ownership within the Midwest region. The government considers the development of such potentially significant new resource areas should occur through arrangements that are open to multiple investors. This approach is con-sistent with the national interest principles we released in February and with the approach I have outlined previously, including in discussions with my Chinese counterparts (Swan 2008c).

Sinosteel's applications were both made pursuant to the Act (rather than the Policy) as they both involved acquisitions of more than 15% of Australian compa-nies. However, the national interest test is equally applicable to applications under the Policy.

9.3.3. *OZ Minerals and Minmetals*

On 16 February 2009, OZ Minerals Limited ("OZ Minerals"), an Australian listed company announced that it had entered into a Scheme Implementation Agreement with China Minmetals Non-ferrous Metals Company Limited ("Minmetals"), a Chinese state-owned enterprise, for the proposed acquisition of all outstanding shares in OZ Minerals by Minmetals at a cash price of 82.5 cents per share. OZ Minerals had been struggling financially following the collapse of commodity mar-kets in 2008 and had been unable to complete the sale of various assets which it had hoped would allow it to meet its $1.3 billion debt repayment due on 31 March 2009.

The Minmetals proposal provided for a full repayment of OZ Minerals' out-standing debt upon successful completion. The all-cash offer was unanimously recommended by the OZ Minerals Board, subject only to there being no superior proposal and an independent expert concluding that the scheme is in the best inter-ests of shareholders. Implementation of the scheme was subject to a number of conditions including, amongst others, OZ Minerals' financiers agreeing to extend

---

[13] The Treasurer's media release dated 21 September notes that Sinosteel's application to acquire up to 100% of Murchison had been withdrawn and that a revised application for up to 49.9% of Murchison was approved.

the repayment of OZ Minerals' debt facilities and the approval of Australian and Chinese regulatory authorities, including the Foreign Investment Review Board. On 23 March 2009, the Foreign Investment Review Board issued an interim order extending the period for evaluation of Minmetal's application by 90 days. Given the precarious financial position of OZ Minerals and the looming 31 March repayment deadline, the decision by the Foreign Investment Review Board to extend the consideration period was seen as a high-risk move. Analysts predicted that without the Minmetals deal, OZ Minerals would be forced into administration: "Southern Cross Equities director Charlie Aitken said that without the Chinese deal, OZ's only alternative was administration, the likely loss of 6000 jobs, and operating mines being placed on care and maintenance as the administrators conducted a fire sale." (Tasker 2009a) On 27 March 2009, the Treasurer released a statement advising that the government had determined that, on national security grounds, the scheme could not be approved if it included OZ Minerals' Prominent Hill mining operations but was willing to consider alternative proposals in relation to OZ Minerals' other assets and businesses. In the words of the Treasurer:

> Under the Foreign Acquisitions and Takeovers Act 1975, all foreign investment applications are examined against Australia's national interest. An important part of this assessment is whether proposals conform with Australia's national security interests, in line with the principles that apply to foreign government related investments. OZ Minerals Prominent Hill mining operations are situated in the Woomera Prohibited Area in South Australia. The Woomera Prohibited Area weapons testing range makes a unique and sensitive contribution to Australia's national defense. It is not unusual for governments to restrict access to sensitive areas on national security grounds. The Government has determined that Minmetals' proposal for OZ Minerals cannot be approved if it includes Prominent Hill. [...] Discussions between the Foreign Investment Review Board and Minmetals are continuing in relation to OZ Minerals' other businesses and assets, and the government is willing to consider alternative proposals relating to those other assets and businesses (Swan 2009b).

The decision came as a surprise to the market and left commentators wondering whether the national security issue was merely a convenient façade (*Australian Financial Review*, 'Decision came out of left field,' 28 March 2009; *The Australian*, 'Shock as OZ deal is shot down,' 28 March 2009). It also provided no guidance as to the government's thinking or policy position on the broader issue of investment by Chinese state-owned enterprises in Australia's resources sector:

> For those seeking clarity from Canberra about its views on Chinese investment in Australia, Treasurer Wayne Swan's announcement on

Friday on the OZ Minerals takeover will be very disappointing. The announcement does not address the government's broader attitude to Chinese investment in resources, and some may see the use of a defense argument as either a signal to the Chinese to back off or a technical excuse to fend off the day when the government has to make a broad-based policy decision (Vaughan 2009).

When asked about the decision in the context of OZ Mineral's financial position, the Treasurer responded that

> The government makes no apology for applying our national interest guidelines in this particular case. National security issues are serious, and it was on the grounds of national security issues that I said to the company that the Prominent Hill site could not be included in any application. There is a balance to be struck here — a balance between foreign investment which creates jobs, and our national interest principles as well. Here the balance was in favor of national security, and I make no apology for that whatsoever (Swan 2009c).

OZ Minerals announced on 1 April 2009 that it had renegotiated the transaction with Minmetals so as to exclude Prominent Hill. The revised proposal involved the sale to Minmetals for US$1,206 million of Sepon, Golden Grove, Century, Rosebery, Avebury, Dugald River, High Lake, Izok Late, and certain other exploration and development assets. This would mean that OZ Minerals would continue as a listed entity, retaining Prominent Hill and certain other assets. Subject to the approval of Australian and Chinese regulatory authorities and OZ Minerals' shareholders and other conditions, completion of the transaction was expected in June 2009. Barry Cusack, Chairman of OZ Minerals, commented that "while this is a structurally different proposal to the previous cash proposal from Minmetals [it] provides a complete solution to OZ Minerals' refinancing issues." (Cusack 2009)

9.3.4. Hunan Valin and Fortescue

On 25 February 2009, Fortescue Metals Group Ltd ("Fortescue"), an Australian listed iron ore mining company, announced that it had entered into a Cooperation Agreement and Share Subscription Agreement for a proposed AU$558 million investment by Hunan Valin Iron and Steel Group Company Ltd ("Hunan Valin"), a Chinese state-owned steel manufacturer.

Under the proposed transaction, Fortescue and Hunan Valin would establish a joint venture to develop lower grade resources from some of Fortescue's tenements and to give Hunan Valin the option to participate in any additional new projects Fortescue undertakes. Key components of the arrangements include the right for Hunan Valin to appoint one director to the Fortescue board (Fortescue 2009), iron ore off-take arrangements, raw ore processing, utilization of lower grade hematite ore, and the development of future new projects. In a separate transaction, Hunan Valin entered into a conditional agreement to purchase 275 million existing shares from Harbinger Capital Partners ("Harbinger"), an American hedge fund and Fortescue shareholder.

On 9 March 2009, Fortescue announced it agreed to a request from Hunan Valin to amend the size of the share issue taking the size of Hunan Valin's proposed investment in Fortescue to AU$644.8 million. When combined with the purchase of 275 million existing shares from Harbinger Hunan Valin's total proposed shareholding in Fortescue would be 17.4%. The Foreign Investment Review Board issued an interim order on 18 March 2009, extending the Foreign Investment Review Board review period of the proposed transaction for up to 30 days. On 31 March 2009, the Treasurer approved Hunan Valin's application under the Act on the basis of undertakings given by Hunan Valin and Fortescue. The undertakings were: (a) that any person nominated by Hunan Valin to Fortescue's Board will comply with the Director's Code of Conduct maintained by Fortescue; (b) any person nominated by Hunan Valin to Fortescue's Board will submit a standing notice under the Corporations Act 2001 (Cth) of their potential conflict of interest relating to Fortescue's marketing, sales, customer profiles, price setting, and cost structures for pricing and shipping; (c) Hunan Valin and any person nominated by it to Fortescue's Board will comply with the information segregation arrangements agreed between Fortescue and Hunan Valin; and (d) Hunan Valin must report to the Foreign Investment Review Board on its compliance with the undertakings with penalties payable for non-compliance. The Treasurer explained:

> These undertakings ensure consistency with Australia's national interest principles for investments by foreign government entities, which I set out in February 2008. They ensure the appropriate separation of Fortescue's commercial operations and customer interests, and support the market-based development of Australia's resources (Swan 2009d).

9.3.5. Chinalco and Rio Tinto — Strategic Partnership

On 12 February 2009, Rio Tinto announced that it had entered into a Cooperation and Implementation Agreement with Chinalco for a proposed US$19.5 billion strategic partnership. The proposed transaction involved the investment by Chinalco of US$7.2 billion through Convertible Bonds as well as a US$12.3 billion investment in certain Rio Tinto assets. The Convertible Bonds would be issued in two tranches with an average conversion price of US$52.5 per share and on conversion would give Chinalco a 19% interest in Rio Tinto plc (when combined with its existing 12% stake) and a 14.9% interest in Rio Tinto Limited. The Convertible Bonds do not carry voting rights prior to conversion. The asset investment comprises minority stakes in Rio Tinto's Hamersley Iron, Weipa, Yarwun, Boyne, Gladstone Power Station, Escondida, Kennecott, La Granja, and Grasberg assets. Pursuant to the proposed arrangements, Chinalco would be entitled to nominate two directors to the Rio Tinto boards, one of whom must be independent. On 13 March 2009, the Foreign Investment Review Board issued an Interim Order extending the period of consideration of the proposal by up to 90 days.

The proposal attracted extensive public comment and debate. Key features of the debate include what level of control or influence the Chinese state has over the operations of Chinalco, what access to information Chinalco will have from the multi-layer nature of the proposed investment, and whether Chinalco is likely to have access to or potential influence over pricing negotiations in respect of key assets such as iron ore. The transaction was ultimately terminated by Rio Tinto in June 2009. It is not clear whether or not it would have been approved by the Treasurer.

9.4. Conclusion

Drawing from the case studies we can identify some key messages coming from the Australian government in relation to foreign investment and in particular investments by state-owned enterprises in the resources sector. These are: (a) diversity of ownership of Australian resources should be maintained so that Australian resources continue to be a reliable supplier to all trading partners; (b) appropriate separation of commercial operation of resources and their customers interests should be maintained (for example, through the restriction of access to information); and (c) resources should continue to develop according to market-based principles.

These are messages that were also laid out by the Treasurer in his speech to the Australia China business council on 4 July 2008:

> The key is that investments are consistent with Australia's aim of maintaining a market-based system in which companies are responsive to shareholders and in which investment and sales decisions are driven by market forces rather than external strategic or political considerations. In particular, Australian governments — now as in the past — are particularly attentive when the proposed investor in an Australian resource is also the buyer of that resource or linked with the buyer of the resource … We usually welcome and encourage some participation by the buyer, because that offers the buyer some security of supply and the seller some stability in the market. But we need to ensure that investment

is consistent with Australia's aim of ensuring that decisions continue to be driven by commercial considerations and that Australia remains a reliable supplier in the future to all current and potential trading partners (Swan 2008a).

When asked subsequently how important the Treasurer considers it is for Australia to secure our energy resources, the Treasurer referred the journalist to that speech and said:

> There are very important issues involved here, which is why the government published its guidelines at the beginning of last year. We put them out in some detail in a way which has never been done before. And we acted then because we thought these issues were very important then and we still think they are very important.

As set out earlier, the statutory process established by the Act does not deal with applications under policy and therefore no time limits apply in respect of the government's response to such applications. Applications by foreign government entities were taking months to be considered in 2008 and 2009. This leads us to consider the question of whether the Australian government is being protectionist or cautious. Where a recipient country imposes restrictions on foreign investment for national security reasons, the OECD has determined guidelines that should guide governments in the design and implementation of such measures. These guidelines suggest that a recipient government's policy towards foreign investment should be transparent, predictable, proportionate, non-discriminatory, and accountable.

References

Australian Department of Treasury, 2008, Guidelines for Foreign Investment, available at http://www.firb.gov.au/content/_downloads/Australia's_Foreign_Investment_Policy_Jan_2011.pdf, accessed on 25 January 2011.

Clegg, B, & Crowe, D, 2009, "China Spree Puts Heat on Foreign Investment", *Australian Financial Review*, 17 March.

Clegg, B, Greg, E, & Vaughan, M, 2009, "Staying Open is Still in our Best Interests", *Australian Financial Review*, 18 March.

Commonwealth of Australia, Special Gazette, Tuesday 24 March 2009.

Cusack, B, 2009, "Proposed Transactions with Minmetals", Media Release, 1 April, available at http://www.ozminerals.com/Media/docs/ASX_20090401a_Minmetals_Alternative-79cb6b4c-fb57-4649-8d63-729f56a89224-0.pdf, accessed on 25 January 2011.

Fortescue, 2009, "Fortescue Strikes Share Subscription Agreement with Valin", Media Release, 25 February, available at http://www.fmgl.com.au/IRM/Company/ShowPage.aspx?CPID=1762&PageName=Fortescue%20signs%20Share%20Subscription%20Agreement%20with%20Valin, accessed on 25 January 2011.

Frith, B, 2008, "Mid West Ore Merger Hangs on Canberra", *The Australian*, 27 June.

Hewitt, J, 2008, "Just One Move in Bigger Game", *The Australian*, 25 August 2008.

International Monetary Fund, 2008, "Sovereign Wealth Funds — A Work Agenda", Monetary and Capital Markets & Policy Development and Review Departments, 29 February.

Maiden, M, 2008, "Swan and Co Tread a Fine Line in the China Shop of Progress", *The Sydney Morning Herald*, 27 June.

Sinosteel, 2008a, Sinosteel's Bidder's Statement, 14 March.

Sinosteel, 2008b, "Sinosteel says Offer Price for Midwest now Final. Murchison Proposal Unlikely to Succeed", Sinosteel announcement, 28 May.

Sinosteel, 2008c, "Sinosteel Increases Offer. Freed from Defeating Conditions", Sinosteel announcement, 30 May.

Sinosteel, 2008d, "Close of Sinosteel's Takeover Offer for Midwest Corporation Ltd", Sinosteel announcement, 17 September.

Swan, W, 2008a, Australia, China and This Asian Century. Speech delivered at Australia–China Business Council, Melbourne, 4 July.

Swan, W, 2008b, "Chinalco's Acquisition of Shares in Rio Tinto", Media Release 094, 24 August, available at http://www.treasurer.gov.au/DisplayDocs.aspx?doc=pressreleases/2008/094.htm&pageID=003&min=wms&Year=2008&DocType=0, accessed on 25 January 2011.

Swan, W, 2008c, "Foreign Investment Approval: Sinosteel's Interests in Murchison Metals Ltd", Media Release 100, 21 September, available at http://www.treasurer.gov.au/DisplayDocs.aspx?doc=pressreleases/2008/100.htm&pageID=&min=wms&Year=&DocType=0, accessed on 25 January 2011.

Swan, W, 2009a, "Amendments to Foreign Acquisitions and Takeovers Act", Media Release 017, 12 February, available at http:// www.treasurer.gov.au/DisplayDocs.aspx?doc=pressreleases/2009/017.htm&pageID=&min=wms& Year=&DocType=0, accessed on 25 January 2011.

Swan, W, 2009b, "Foreign Investment", Media Release 029, 27 March, available at http://www.treasurer.gov.au/DisplayDocs.aspx? doc=pressreleases/2009/029.htm& pageID=&min=wms&Year=&DocType=0, accessed on 25 January 2011.

Swan, W, 2009c, "Doorstop Interview, Vagelis Café and Bar, Brisbane", Transcript 046, 28 March, available at http://www.treasurer.gov.au/DisplayDocs.aspx?doc=transcripts/2009/046.htm&pageID=004&min=wms&Year=&DocType, accessed on 25 January 2011.

Swan, W, 2009d, "Foreign Investment Decision", Media Release 032, 31 March, available at http://www.treasurer.gov.au/DisplayDocs.aspx?doc=pressreleases/2009/032.htm&pageID=&min=wms&Year=&DocType=0, accessed on 25 January 2011.

Tasker, SJ, 2009a, "FIRB Dawdles on OZ Rescue", *The Australian*, 24 March.

Tasker, SJ, 2009b, "Shock as OZ Deal is Shot Down", *The Australian*, 28 March.

Truman, EM, 2007, "Sovereign Wealth Funds: The Need for Greater Transparency and Accountability", Peterson Institute for International Economics Policy Brief PB07-06, August.

Vaughan, M, "Decision Came Out of Left Field", *Australian Financial Review* (28 March 2009).

Conclusion

Sovereign Wealth Funds: What Have We Learned?

David Vines

1. Introduction

The build-up of current account surpluses in emerging market economies, and the resulting rise in the wealth holdings of the governments of these countries, has led to a rapid increase in the size of sovereign wealth funds. These funds invest internationally, and create large pools of internationally mobile capital, which are managed by governments, instead of by the private sector. It is widely believed that important policy issues arise as a result of this fact. The book emerged from a wish to understand these policy issues. The result is a book which provokes a number of thoughts. My aim in this short concluding chapter is to draw these thoughts together into just two strands.

My first aim is to show how this book helps us to understand, much better, what sovereign wealth funds are and what they do. It is important to do this because, as Stephen Grenville points out (in the first chapter in this volume) "different people have used the term [sovereign wealth funds] with different meanings, and, more importantly, with different intentions." He goes on to protest that without a clear agreement on what is meant by the term "sovereign wealth fund," one is likely to end up with "prescriptions which are so general, so motherhood and so mundane as to be largely content free." He is right. But the definition that Grenville wants is offered by Christopher Balding (Chapter 3), and it is supported by a number of the chapters in the volume. This definition defines a sovereign wealth fund as "a pool of capital controlled by a government, or government-related entity, that invests in assets seeing returns above the risk-free rate of return." This definition deliberately enables us to draw a dividing line between those activities which are those of a sovereign wealth fund, and those which are not, and this dividing line is one which excludes state-owned enterprises from the sovereign wealth fund category. Once we have drawn the dividing line in this way, we can then have a useful discussion about the policy concerns concerning sovereign wealth funds; the kind of discussion that Grenville wants.

My second aim is to summarize this policy discussion. There are, it seems, three sets of policy issues to do with sovereign wealth funds, the second and third of which are not immediately obvious. The first — and most obvious set of issues — concerns the need to ensure that sovereign wealth funds comply with regulatory requirements, including those of competition policy, in host countries; that they invest on the basis of sound principles; and that they have a transparent governance structure. The second set of issues arises from the need to ensure that sovereign wealth funds do not act as cover for any state-owned enterprises that they own in such a way as to enable the state-owned enterprises to pursue objectives not in the interest of a host country. The third set of issues is particular to the case of natural resources, and is explained in detail below.

2.   The Nature of Sovereign Wealth Funds

What is a sovereign wealth fund? The definition offered above includes in sovereign wealth funds pools of capital that are controlled by a government, rather than pools of capital which are owned by a government. Before reading this book, my starting point was, instead, the idea that a sovereign wealth fund is a fund which is owned by a government. I coupled this thought with the idea that the government comes to own the wealth which is held by such a fund by accumulating this wealth. A government accumulates wealth by receiving an income (in the form of taxes and interest receipts) which is in excess of its expenditure (be it current expenditure, capital expenditure, or expenditure on the payment of interest), i.e. by running a fiscal surplus.[1] I thus thought of a sovereign wealth fund as a fund of capital owned by a government, obtained by means of running fiscal surpluses. The Australian Future Fund is a fund of this kind. In Australia, policymakers observed that they lived in an economy in which tax revenues were growing rapidly, because the economy was growing rapidly. They also decided that the private sector was not saving enough in these circumstances, and so decided that the state should put aside some of the increase in taxes, in order to invest for the future. It would do

---

[1] In addition to this there is also asset appreciation and the accumulation of interest income.

this by diverting some of its tax receipts into a Future Fund, rather than using these receipts to finance an increase in government expenditure.

Before reading this book, I also thought that this was a good description of how sovereign wealth funds arose in emerging market economies. I imagined that these emerging market funds grew in the way that they did because the current account surpluses of these economies led to increases in tax receipts and so to increases in the wealth of governments. It was, I thought, this increase in the government ownership of wealth which led to the growth of the sovereign wealth funds.

But sovereign wealth funds have grown rapidly in size in emerging market economies largely as a result of the increase in governments' holdings of foreign exchange reserves. And, as Avanash Persaud (Chapter 5) points out, increases in foreign exchange reserve holdings are not increases in the net wealth of the government. They are increases in the gross wealth of the government, since such increases in foreign exchange reserves come with an offsetting liability.[2]

An increase in foreign exchange reserves is not something which occurs as a result of an increase in the wealth owned by the state. And yet it causes an increase in the pool of funds controlled by the state, at least some of which will come to end up in a sovereign wealth fund. Furthermore, some other forms of what is apparently net wealth of the state also turn out to have a corresponding liability attached. An obvious example of this is a pension fund, in which case the corresponding liability is the obligation to pay pensions in the future. And yet we would normally want to describe a sovereign pension fund as a sovereign wealth fund, and we would want to include all of the assets of such a fund in the value of the fund, even although the net value of the fund was much less than its gross value.[3]

This discussion explains why we should see a sovereign wealth fund as a pool of assets over which a sovereign government has control — rather than as a pool of assets which a government owns. But Balding's definition suggests that we should not label all of the pools of assets over which the government has control as belonging to a sovereign wealth fund, but only those assets which are "invested so as to seek a return above the risk-free rate of return." There are two aspects to this restriction.

First, this restriction obviously excludes from sovereign wealth funds those funds which are invested just so as to yield the risk-free rate of return. The case of

---

[2]"The investor who has given US dollars to the central bank in order to receive the equivalent in local currency [...] has only done so on condition that if and when he or she wishes [...] they can receive dollars [in exchange] for their [funds]." (Persaud)

[3]One could make a similar observation about the Australian Future Fund. That fund has an obligation to pay money to Australians for particular purposes in the future.

foreign exchange reserves shows why this restriction is important. Some of a state's holdings of foreign exchange reserves are normally held by the central bank in a highly liquid form, for example, in the form of short-term US government bonds. This is a form in which the value of the assets is easily realizable. But, as reserve-holdings by emerging market economies have become increasingly large over the past ten years, governments have come to hold additional reserve holdings not in such liquid assets. Instead, governments have placed their reserves in longer-term assets which, although less liquid, yield a higher rate of return. As Persaud says, the management of these assets requires "very different asset and risk management skills and approaches" from the management of funds which are held in a highly liquid form. It is funds managed in this rather different way, rather than the totality of foreign exchange reserves, which are included in the sovereign wealth fund category.

Second, Baldwin's restriction implies that state-owned enterprises are not sovereign wealth funds. This is because the assets of state-owned enterprises are not assets that are "invested so as to seek a return above the risk-free rate of return." They are, instead, assets which are held so as to enable the state-owned enterprise to do what it does, which is to generate electric power, or to provide water, or to provide gas, provide port services, or whatever. Thus Balding, in Box 3.1 in his chapter, suggests that we should not describe US Public Utilities as sovereign wealth funds, essentially for this reason.[4] The reasons for this separation are that, as we shall see below, the policy questions to do with state-owned enterprises are different from those to do with sovereign wealth funds. Adrian Blundell-Wignall and Gert Wehinger (Chapter 6) suggest some further restrictions on the types of funds controlled by governments which we should label as sovereign wealth funds. But I can see no good reason to make any further restrictions of this kind.

How have sovereign wealth funds emerged? David Murray (Chapter 7) writes that "about 80% of sovereign wealth fund assets are estimated to be associated with a resource depletion and intergenerational wealth objective. The remainder, broadly speaking, is associated with the use of surplus reserves from rapid early stage growth being used to bolster long-term economic development." David Fernandez (Chapter 4) goes into more detail as to how sovereign wealth funds have arisen. It is helpful to list the three reasons that he provides.

(a) Sovereign wealth funds have emerged as commodity income funds as a result of tax revenue received from the sale — especially the export — of commodities (including oil and gas and other minerals). Such commodity revenues

---

[4]Truman does, however, include such utilities in the sovereign wealth fund category, thus revealing the difficulty in reaching an agreement about the definition.

are normally net wealth, since they have no corresponding liability on the government's balance sheet.

(b) Sovereign wealth funds have emerged in countries where there is a fiscal source of funds, either from fiscal surpluses, "or from property sales and privatizations or transfers from the government's main budget to a special purpose vehicle." Many of these transfers involve increases in net wealth, although some have offsetting liabilities.

(c) Sovereign wealth funds have been set up in countries which have run current account and/or capital account surpluses and accumulated foreign exchange reserves. As noted above, the share of such reserves which are managed by sovereign wealth funds is typically that part of reserves which is over and above what is needed for short-term liquidity needs. As also noted above, such increases in reserves often represent "borrowed wealth," since the reserve build-up in many such cases stems from sterilized foreign exchange interventions, in which case the central bank issues interest-bearing liquidity notes to fund the interventions and mop up the excess liquidity.[5]

The reasons for which countries run current account and/or capital account surpluses — which lead to sovereign wealth funds of this third kind — have to do with the desire of countries to insure against financial crises, and/or the desire of countries to achieve export-led growth. The accumulation of foreign exchange reserves is the means by which these surpluses are brought about. Such countries have established sovereign wealth funds because they wish to invest their reserves in a wider range of assets than short-term US Treasury bills. The reason for the existence of this kind of sovereign wealth fund is thus rather different from the reason for the existence of the second kind of sovereign wealth fund — which comes from there being a fiscal source of funds.

What do sovereign wealth funds do? Fernandez identifies four rather different types of sovereign wealth fund, which I now also list.[6] The differences in type between these different kinds of sovereign wealth funds are only partly related to the three different sources of funds for sovereign wealth funds which we have just identified.

(a) Revenue stabilization funds are designed to cushion the impact of volatile commodity revenues on the government's fiscal balance and on the overall economy. Funds of this kind are made possible by tax regimes which fall heavily on

---

[5]However, part of the foreign reserves may represent net wealth, thanks to asset appreciation and the accumulation of interest income.

[6]Julie Kozack, Doug Laxton, and Krishna Srinivasan (Chapter 2) subdivide this list, arriving at six different types. Adrian Blundell-Wignall and Gert Wehinger, by contrast, suggest that some parts of this list be separated off from sovereign wealth funds.

the high revenues which are received when commodity prices are high, such as a resource rent tax.

(b) Future-generation or savings funds are meant to invest wealth over longer periods of time. In some cases these funds are earmarked for particular purposes such as to cover future public pension liabilities, in others not. The fiscal sources of these funds, which support funds of this kind, arise from a tax system which delivers surpluses, because of a concern by government about issues such as an ageing population and the need for retirement incomes.

(c) General purpose sovereign wealth funds are funds whose objectives can be described as optimizing the risk-return profile of wealth holdings. Foreign exchange reserves provide one of the sources of finance for such funds.

(d) There are also holding funds which manage governments' direct investments in companies, including domestic state-owned enterprises, private companies, and private companies abroad.

Each of the four types of sovereign wealth fund listed above requires an investment strategy. Sovereign wealth funds may have investment strategies which are just like those of large private sector fund managers; there may be no real difference between a sovereign wealth fund and a private equity fund or a hedge fund. But that may not be true.

Firstly, sovereign wealth funds may differ from such private-sector investors because they:

(i) have a longer-term time horizon and seek longer-term returns;
(ii) have a different attitude to risk as compared with private sector funds;
(iii) have less leverage, making them a less risky source of funds for those who are funded by them; and
(iv) provide, because of their low leverage, a source of funds for the purchase of distressed assets.

This last point might mean that sovereign wealth funds have a beneficial economic effect on recipient countries, and might also mean that sovereign wealth funds are helpful in stabilizing the international financial system. For example, as a number of the authors note, sovereign wealth funds purchased assets in distressed US banks at the beginning of the financial crisis, simply because they were sovereign wealth funds and so not collateral-constrained in the way that other financial institutions were constrained during the crisis.

Secondly, funds of type (d) identified above are likely to have their asset allocation constrained by the company assets which the state has decided to hold. As Fernandez notes, funds of this kind "typically support the government's overall development strategy."

Third, some sovereign wealth funds may turn out not to be really like normal investment funds — which balance risk and return — but instead vehicles for the pursuit of other interests of the government which controls them. These interests may include national economic objectives, foreign policy objectives, or political objectives more generally.

3. Policy Issues for Countries which Host Investment

Persaud discusses the need for a set of principles that govern how sovereign wealth funds should be run. David Murray (Chapter 7) describes how the Santiago Principles came to be developed for this purpose. These principles include the pursuit of the following three objectives:

(a) Sovereign wealth funds should comply with all regulatory and disclosure requirements in the countries in which they invest. This principle clearly implies that competition policy will need to form part of the oversight in relation to sovereign wealth fund investments. As Blundell-Wignall and Wehinger argue, "allowing a foreign government-controlled entity to take over a private domestic company needs particular scrutiny [in relation to competition policy] — it is a form of nationalization (where a controlling interest is obtained); or worse, renationalization if the private domestic company had previously been privatized by the domestic government."

(b) Sovereign wealth funds should invest on the basis of economic and financial risk and return-related considerations.

(c) Sovereign wealth funds should have in place a transparent and sound governance structure that provides for adequate operational controls, risk management, and accountability.

Having such a set of principles is important, especially given the point made at the end of the previous section. The definition of sovereign wealth funds which we have adopted includes pension funds. As Blundell-Wignall and Wehinger document, there are additional OECD guidelines in relation to the operation and governance of these funds. These principles seek to ensure similar sorts of objectives to those highlighted in points (a) to (c), particularly for pension funds.

3.1. *Sovereign Wealth Funds and State-Owned Enterprises*

The definition of sovereign wealth funds which we have adopted deliberately excludes state-owned enterprises. The reason for this is — as we have noted — that state-owned enterprises are engaged in productive activity, whilst sovereign wealth funds are investment organizations, which invest in assets so as to achieve some combination of risk and return, rather than actually managing the assets for productive purposes. This difference in the nature of the activity gives rise to different regulatory needs, and it is precisely because of these different regulatory needs that it is desirable to separate sovereign wealth funds from state-owned enterprises.

Nevertheless, it is important to be aware of the regulatory requirements in relation to state-owned enterprises, in thinking about the regulatory requirements for sovereign wealth funds. This is because there is a possibility that sovereign wealth funds may act as a "front" for state owned enterprises. In Box 3.1 of his chapter, Balding documents a revealing case which makes clear the nature of this difficulty. Baldwin would not include a state-owned airline as a sovereign wealth fund. This is because he follows the principle which we have identified above; a state-owned airline is a state-owned enterprise because it is primarily engaged in the activity of being an airline. But he does describe Singapore Airlines as a sovereign wealth fund. He does this because Singapore Airlines, although a state-owned enterprise, is owned by the Temasek Holdings, which is itself a sovereign wealth fund owned by the Singapore government.

The assets of Singapore Airlines are assets held by Temasek, in pursuit of its activity as a sovereign wealth fund, and so these assets count as the assets of a sovereign wealth fund. Of course, nobody would wish to argue that the policy issues raised below are of concern in relation to Singapore Airlines. But this Singapore Airlines example reveals clearly the need to be sure that state-owned enterprises do not hide behind sovereign wealth funds so as to be able to do things which policy towards state-owned enterprises would normally prevent. In considering policy issues in relation to sovereign wealth funds it is therefore important to be aware of the policy issues as they relate to state-owned enterprises, and to be sure that any difficulties are guarded against in relation to sovereign wealth funds. There are two things to guard against.

First, in pursuit of its productive activity, a state-owned enterprise will seek commercial advantage, and may do this in a way which is not in the interests of the host country. Consider the case in which a state-owned enterprise carries out inward investment into a country, in an upstream industry, so as to achieve vertical integration and secure its source of supply. The interests of the state-owned enterprise are then to obtain supply as cheaply as possible, which may well be at odds with the interests of the host country, which are to obtain the best possible return for its exports. There is clearly a risk to the host country that such inward investment by the state-owned enterprise in its upstream source of supply, will lead to an underpricing of the country's exports. This risk would not arise in the case of foreign direct investment by a sovereign wealth fund which was seeking a best combination of risk and return, because such a sovereign wealth fund would seek to maximize the return obtained by exporting from the host country. Blundell-Wignall and Wehinger (Chapter 6) describe a set of OECD guidelines for running state-owned enterprises, which are designed to guard against such difficulties. It is important that these guidelines be respected in relation to sovereign wealth fund investments, in cases like that of Temasek, where a sovereign wealth fund is in fact the owner of a state-owned enterprise.

Second, a state-owned enterprise may also act with the broader interests in mind of the government which owns it, beyond the commercial interests of its own productive activity. There may be an objective attached to the FDI done by a state-owned enterprise to acquire foreign technology and to use it not just within the state-owned enterprise in question, but more broadly within the country from which the investment originates. Or the government of the country from which FDI originates may be interested in acquiring skills through this investment which may then be used for defense purposes. The host country may have reasons to be concerned about both of these things. The set of OECD guidelines for running state-owned enterprises is designed to guard against such difficulties. It is important that these guidelines are followed in cases where a sovereign wealth fund is the owner of a state-owned enterprise.

3.2. The Exhaustible-Resource Rent Issue

As Adrian Blundell-Wignall and Gert Wehinger demonstrate in Chapter 6, countries which own exhaustible resources have additional policy concerns to do with foreign investment, including investment by sovereign wealth funds. These concerns arise out of the particular nature of exhaustible resources. They arise even if all of the issues discussed in Section 3.1 are dealt with. They mean that "even if the window is cleaned, and full transparency is achieved, and even if governance practices move into line with appropriate guidelines, [there may still be] some objections to the free flow of capital left on the windowsill." Blundell-Wignall and Wehinger discuss two such objections.

First, for any form of resource there is an economic rent (or Ricardian rent) which accrues to at least some of the supplying countries. This rent arises from the differential costs of extraction of the resource in different countries, and from the overall global scarcity of the resource. As Blundell-Wignall and Wehinger point out, this is not something which is normally the case for produced commodities, like manufactures, where in competitive markets super-normal profits can only arise out of market failures of some form. Figure 6.1 in their chapter illustrates the issue.

If the global market for resources is competitive, then there will be a rent accruing to the owners of low-cost facilities (e.g. in the case of Australia, as depicted in Figure 6.1). It is in the interest of the country in question (e.g. Australia) that the rent accrues to the nation, rather than to private owners of the facility, particularly if these owners are foreign.

In addition, a further rent — which Blundell-Wignall and Wehinger call a "scarcity rent" — can be extracted if global supply is restricted. This will be possible if the global market for the resource in question is monopolistic, so that a few major producers can restrict output in the face of strong inelastic demand. In this case a supply below the amount which would be made available if there were free competition amongst all of the global suppliers would benefit the suppliers taken as a group. It may well be in the interest of the country in question (e.g. Australia) that the global output be restricted in this way — relative to what would be produced if there were globally free competition in the supply of this resource — providing that some mechanism can be found for sharing the scarcity rent. But it will be in the interests of the supplying country that this happens only if all or some of this additional rent accrues to the nation, rather than to private owners of the facility, particularly if these owners are foreign. There are thus policy issues here.

Second, for exhaustible resources there is an additional issue of inter-temporal choice. If the expected rate of increase in the price of the exhaustible resource is greater than the (long-term) rate of interest, then the resource should be left in the ground rather than extracted and sold. This is the Hotelling Rule. Following this principle will enable the country to increase the rent obtainable from owning the resource, by selling it for a higher price in the future. As Blundell-Wignall and Wehinger make clear, restricting the output of resources may be in the interest of individual countries like Australia, Canada, Brazil, and South Africa, in order to earn this second, additional kind of rent, even though independent action by any one country may not influence the world price in an appreciable manner. It will be in the interest of the country supplying the resources to act in this way only if the rent resulting from restricting output accrues in full or in part to the nation rather than to private owners of the facility, particularly if these are owners are foreign. There are thus policy issues here for an additional reason.

How are these additional policy issues, to do with investment by sovereign wealth funds in exhaustible-resource projects, best dealt with? Consider a case in a country in which a resource comes to be owned, as a result of FDI, by a foreign sovereign wealth fund. In this case the host government would lease the resource to the foreign sovereign wealth fund, tax the rents with (say) a resource rent tax, and then invest the proceeds in its own sovereign wealth fund. Blundell-Wignall and Wehinger provide an extended general discussion of how to deal with the policy issues to do with exhaustible resource projects. From this we can extract the following three points which are relevant to this case.

The first kind of difficulty which may arise concerns whether the sovereign wealth fund to which the resource is sold chooses to deplete the resource at a rate which is line with the Hotelling Rule. It is not clear that a sovereign wealth fund will choose the same rate of depletion which would be chosen by the government of the host country. This problem will arise with all potential owners other than the government of the host country. But the implementation of a tax policy designed to influence the depletion rate may be harder in the case where the asset is owned by a foreign government controlled by a sovereign wealth fund than in the case where the owner is in the private sector. As Blundell-Wignall and Wehinger note, property rights are not well defined across national boundaries and, should disputes arise between the two governments, would be difficult to pursue in courts because of sovereign immunity issues.

A second kind of difficulty may arise due to difficulties to do with aggressive tax accounting in relation to the resource rent tax which is levied. As Blundell-Wignall and Wehinger note, aggressive tax accounting will create a problem in determining the level of costs, and so in calculating the residual value of the rent which is to be taxed. Disputes between two governments about this issue would also be difficult to pursue in courts because of sovereign immunity issues.

The third kind of difficulty may occur when the sovereign wealth fund is an owner of a state-owned enterprise. We have described above in Section 3.2 the case of a state-owned enterprise which carries out inward investment into a country, into an industry which is upstream of its own activity, so as to achieve vertical integration and thereby secure its source of supply. This difficulty is particularly likely to apply in the case of resources industries. The interests of the state-owned enterprise, which for example may be a steel producer, are to obtain supply as cheaply as possible. As discussed above, this may well be at odds with the interests of the host country in which the state-owned enterprise invests, which are to obtain the best possible return for its exports. It is particularly important that the OECD guidelines for running state-owned enterprises be respected in relation to sovereign wealth fund investments, in the resources sector, as and when a sovereign wealth fund is in fact the owner of a state-owned enterprise.

There is a valuable review of Australian policy in relation to these issues in the chapter by Golding and Russell (Chapter 9). The authors describe the Australian government's guidelines of February 2008 which detail the issues of concern that will guide the Australian government when assessing whether an investment by a state-owned enterprise is contrary to the national interest. But, as the authors say, the guidelines give no guidelines as to how, in each case, it will be determined whether the issue of concern has been dealt with. The exposition in this book, summarized above, clarifies the analytic questions which will need to be dealt with if these guidelines are to be made clearer and more transparent in the necessary way.

4. Conclusion: The Politics of Investment

This volume shows that there are indeed many questions of policy interest in relation to foreign investment by sovereign wealth funds. In Chapter 8 in the volume, Justin O'Brien provides a clear review of the difficulties which still stand in the way of finding clear principles for dealing with these policy questions. In the course of this review he describes the process which led to the Santiago Principles. And he also discusses the ways in which both Australia and the US have defined their national interest as they have dealt with these questions, so far. He shows very clearly how protectionist interests will continue to make it hard to resolve these difficulties.

Index